Michael M. Dediu

Corneliu Leu
Writer on the same wavelength as Mark Twain

An American viewpoint

DERC Publishing House
Tewksbury (Boston), Massachusetts, U. S. A.

Published and printed in the
United States of America

Library of Congress Control Number: 2015904110

Dediu, Michael M.

Corneliu Leu – writer on the same wavelength as Mark Twain
An American viewpoint

ISBN-13: 978-1-939757265

1-2226037281
05645D
25KC6A22
1-10T8PIA
1-10TFJPW

Preface

René Descartes (1596 – 1650) elucidated the idea of a separation between the objective reality and the subjective reality, or, in other words, between the exterior world and the interior world. The pre-Cartesian philosophy and literature did not show much interest in this separation between interior and exterior, or between subjective and objective.

For example, Aristotle (384 BC - 322 BC) gives the impression to see a harmony between the exterior objects (real forms), feelings and rational thinking (potential form). But before him Plato (circa 428 BC – 347 BC) does not see a harmony between interior and exterior, because the truth and reality can only be found in interior, through memory and rational thinking.

It seems that the oriental literature (Tsurayuki, Basho), as the pre-Cartesian literature, does not make a precise distinction between subjective and objective. On the other hand, writers and artists from Europe and America (Dickens, Twain, Hugo, Goethe, Solzhenitsyn, Cervantes, Manzoni, Eminescu) were trying to convince the public to see the world as they were seeing it.

Corneliu Leu, in the same Cartesian spirit, uncovers for us a fascinating world that appears live and vibrant in front of our eyes. His books clearly are on the same wavelength with those of Mark Twain, appearing from the depth of the European and American being, with grandeur which flabbergasts even the most refined reader. In this book we chronologically present happenings from Leu's and Twain's lives, as well as many other interesting facts, and conclude with samples of Leu's works.

The wealth of the events, personages and places from Corneliu Leu's books, the same like those of Mark Twain's books, represent a valorous contribution to the European and American history and cultural heritage, and will remain as an eloquent testimony for the future generations.

Michael M. Dediu, Ph. D.

Boston, U. S. A., 17 March 2015

Michael M. Dediu is also the author of these books (which can be found on Amazon.com):

1. Aphorisms and quotations – with examples and explanations
2. Axioms, aphorisms and quotations – with examples and explanations
3. 100 Great Personalities and their Quotations
4. Professor Petre P. Teodorescu – A Great Mathematician and Engineer
5. Professor Ioan Goia – A Dedicated Engineering Professor
6. Venice (Venezia) – a new perspective. A short presentation with photographs
7. La Serenissima (Venice) - a new photographic perspective. A short presentation with many photos
8. Grand Canal – Venice. A new photographic viewpoint. A short presentation with many photos
9. Piazza San Marco – Venice. A different photographic view. A short presentation with many photos
10. Roma (Rome) - La Città Eterna. A new photographic view. A short presentation with many photos
11. Why is Rome so Fascinating? A short presentation with many photos
12. Rome, Boston and Helsinki. A short photographic presentation
13. Rome and Tokyo – two captivating cities. A short photographic presentation
14. Beautiful Places on Earth – A new photographic presentation
15. From Niagara Falls to Mount Fuji via Rome - A novel photographic presentation
16. From the USA and Canada to Italy and Japan - A fresh photographic presentation
17. Paris – Why So Many Call This City Mon Amour - A lovely photographic presentation
18. The City of Light – Paris (La Ville-Lumière) - A kaleidoscopic photographic presentation
19. Paris (Lutetia Parisiorum) – the romance capital of the world - A kaleidoscopic photographic view
20. Paris and Tokyo – a joyful photographic presentation. With a preamble about the Universe

21. From USA to Japan via Canada – A cheerful photographic documentary
22. 200 Wonderful Places, In The Last 50 Years – A personal photographic documentary
23. Must see places in USA and Japan - A kaleidoscopic photographic documentary
24. Grandeurs of the World - A kaleidoscopic photographic documentary

Michael M. Dediu is the editor of these books (also on Amazon.com):

1. Sophia Dediu: The life and its torrents – Ana. In Europe around 1920
2. Proceedings of the 4th International Conference “Advanced Composite Materials Engineering” COMAT 2012
3. Adolf Shvedchikov: I am an eternal child of spring – poems in English, Italian, French, German, Spanish and Russian
4. Adolf Shvedchikov: Life’s Enigma – poems in English, Italian and Russian
5. Adolf Shvedchikov: Everyone wants to be HAPPY – poems in English, Spanish and Russian
6. Adolf Shvedchikov: My Life, My Love – poems in English, Italian and Russian
7. Adolf Shvedchikov: I am the gardener of love – poems in English and Russian
8. Adolf Shvedchikov: Amaretta di Saronno – poems in English and Russian
9. Adolf Shvedchikov: A Russian Rediscovers America
10. Adolf Shvedchikov: Parade of Life - poems in English and Russian
11. Adolf Shvedchikov: Overcoming Sorrow - poems in English and Russian
12. Sophia Dediu: Sophia meets Japan
13. Corneliu Leu: Roosevelt, Churchill, Stalin and Hitler: Their surprising role in Eastern Europe in 1944
14. Proceedings of the 5th International Conference “Computational Mechanics and Virtual Engineering” COMEC 2013
15. Georgeta Simion – Potanga: Beyond Imagination: A Thought-provoking novel inspired from mid-20th century events
16. Ana Dediu: The poetry of my life in Europe and The USA
17. Ana Dediu: The Four Graces
18. Proceedings of the 5th International Conference “Advanced Composite Materials Engineering” COMAT 2014”
19. Sophia Dediu: Chocolate Cook Book

Table of Contents

Chapter 1. The first 32 years – the very young Leu

It was a scorching Thursday, July 21st , **1932** (which was a leap year), when Belgium had its National holiday, and the Emergency Relief and Construction Act was enacted in the United States (as the first major-relief legislation to fund public works, hoping to put millions back to work, enabled under the 31st President (1929-1933) Herbert Clark Hoover (1874-1964)), just 9 days before the opening ceremony of the Games of the X Olympiad in Los Angeles (where United States, Italy, France, Sweden and Japan (out of 37 countries) will win the most medals), despite a world-wide economic depression, only 12 days before the positron (positive electron, the first known antiparticle of the electron) was discovered and photographed by the Nobel Laureate American Physicist Carl David Anderson (1905 – 1991), when the young Mrs. Valentina Leu (physician, leu means lion, and leu is also the Romanian currency: 1 leu = $0.26) gave birth to her baby boy Corneliu in Medgidia (the father came from Bessarabia), a small city in Romania, 30 km north-west of Constanta (former Tomis, where the Roman poet Publius Ovidius Naso (Ovid, 43 BC – 18 AD) was exiled by the founder of the Roman Empire Augustus (63 BC-14 AD) in 8 AD, wrote Tristia and Epistulae ex Ponto, and died at 61), 15 km north-west of Murfatlar (with very good wines), and 170 km east of Bucharest.

There is a strong connection between Romania and the Roman Empire: the birth of the Romanian people can be seen on Columna Traiani in Forum Traiani, in Rome. Rome exists for over 2,500 glorious years, and the ancient Romans built massive concrete structures that have withstood the elements for more than 2,000 years. Recently specialists analyzed samples from a Roman breakwater that has been submerged in the Bay of Napoli (Naples) for over two millennia, and they observed the technique of crystal chemistry that allowed Roman seawater concrete to resist chemical attack and wave action for all this time. It was noted that the manufacture of extremely durable Roman maritime concrete released much less carbon than most modern concrete does these days. Some Roman roads are still in use, and we also celebrated in 2013 the 1900 years anniversary of Columna Traiani (Trajan's Column), built in 113 AD.

Trajan's column (113, center-left), la Chiesa Santissimo Nome di Maria al Foro Traiano (center-right), both at the north-west end of Forum Traiani. The five fragments of columns (in front) were part of Basilica Ulpia, which was in the center of the Forum in 113 AD, south-est of the column. The East (Latin) Library was to the right (north-est) of the column, and the West (Greek) Library was to the left (south-est) of the column.

Leu's family burial sign from 1504.

The Leu family has a long history, and a great geographical distribution. Ion C. Leu, lawyer, he had a brother Grigorie Leu, Episcope of Husi (1881 – 1949, he had a son Vasile Leu), their father was Constantin Leu (priest, died 1925), mother Sultana Leu (died 1934), they had 8 children) and Mrs. Leu, the parents of Corneliu, were very happy to have this little baby boy. They liked to read, and had many literary books, including books on the themes of childhood and adolescence by Ionel Teodoreanu (1897 – 1954).

But many big events took place when Corneliu was a child.

Corneliu was just one month and one day old when British Broadcasting Corporation (BBC) begins experimental regular TV broadcasts, and on December 19th begins transmitting overseas. On October 3rd, 1932, Iraq gains full independence from Britain, and joins the League of Nations. Then on November 1st, Wernher von Braun (1912 – 1977), only 20 years old, was named the head of the German liquid-fuel rocket program. On November 8th, Franklin D. Roosevelt (1882 – 1945) was elected the 32nd President of the United States.

On November 30, 1932, many celebrated the 97th anniversary of the birthday (**1835**, in the city Florida, Missouri, USA) of Samuel Langhorne Clemens (later known by his pen name Mark Twain). His father was John Marshall Clemens (1798 – 1847), an attorney and judge, and his mother Jane (1803 – 1890). Twain was the sixth of seven children.

On December 11, 1932, Aleksandr Solzhenitsyn was 14 years old (born in 1918, in Kislovodsk, Russia (200 km east of the Black Sea, 300 km west of the Caspian Sea, 600 km southwest of Volgograd). His father died six months before his birth.

When Corneliu is a little over 4 months, Poland and USSR sign a non-aggression treaty, and when he is exactly 5 months old, Fred Astaire and Ginger Rogers appear together in their first joint movie "Flying Down to Rio".

The Christmas and New Year **1933** are celebrated by Mr. and Mrs. Leu together with their little baby Corneliu, and when the baby is a little over 6 months, the German president Paul von Hindenburg appoints Hitler (1889-1945) as chancellor, and 2 days later he dissolves the Parliament. On February 8th in the U.

S., the first flight of all-metal Boeing 247 takes place, and just one day before Corneliu is 7 months old, the Congress repeals the alcohol Prohibition law. On March 6th Poland occupies the free city Danzig (Gdansk). Corneliu is a little over 8 months old and very happy, but his parents hear very bad news: German Reichstag grants Hitler dictatorial powers, and soon after Japan leaves the League of Nations. On May 10th Paraguay declares war on Bolivia.

On July 21, 1933, Corneliu is 1 year old, began to talk and walk, his parents are very happy, and Haifa Harbor in Palestine opens. Four days later, Duke Ellington (1899-1974) appears in the first Dutch live radio concert. On August 30th Air France forms. On September 4th, the airplane JR Wendell establishes a new speed record of 483 km/h, in Glenview, IL, US. A little south, in Cuba, Batista (1901-1973) becomes dictator at 32. On October 2nd, Eugene O'Neill's (1888-1953, American playwright, Nobel laureate in Literature) comedy "Ah, Wilderness" premieres in New York City, USA. When the first detergent “Dreft”, by Procter & Gamble, goes on sale in the US? When Corneliu walks quite well, talks a few good words with his parents - on October 10th, 1933. On November 16, Brazilian President Getulio Vargas (1883-1954) declares himself dictator, and the United States recognizes the Soviet Union, establishes diplomatic relations and opens trade. To celebrate their recognition by the US, on November 25th the first Soviet liquid fuel rocket is launched and reaches the altitude of 80m. On December 2nd, Fred Astaire's (1899-1987, between the first five American stars, 31 musical films) first film, "Dancing Lady", is released in the US. December 9th was an important day for Corneliu’s parents and for many others: the Romanian government prohibits the fascist organization Iron Guard. Just one day before Corneliu is 1 year and 5 months, on December 20, Bolivia and Paraguay sign a cease fire agreement. And when Corneliu is 1 year and 5 months, on December 21, 1933, many events: dried human blood serum is for the first time prepared at the University of Pennsylvania in the US, Fox Films in the US signs Shirley Temple (1928-2014), 5 years and 8 months old, only 4 years and 3 months older than Corneliu, to a studio contract (less than 4 months later Shirley Temple appears in her first movie, "Stand Up & Cheer"), and, in Canada, the Dominion of Newfoundland reverts to being a crown colony of Great Britain.

At Christmas and New Year **1934** Corneliu is much more active, under the permanent care of his mother and father. Before Corneliu is 1.5 years, on January 18th, 1934, Eugene O'Neill's "Days Without End" premieres in New York City, and after, on January 26th, Germany and Poland sign a non-attack treaty for 10 years (until 1944). On February 9th, 1934, in Athens, Greece, the Pact of Balkan Entente alliance forms between Yugoslavia, Greece, Turkey and Romania, to defend themselves against territorial expansion, but the Soviet Union, Hungary, Bulgaria, Albania and Italy refused to sign the document. A day later Stalin (1878-1953) ends the 17th congress of the Communist Party of the Soviet Union. On March 1st, Henry Pu Yi is crowned emperor Kang Teh of Manchuria, by Japan. Rudolf Kuhnold presents the first radar in Kiel, Germany, on March 20th. Karlis Ulmanis names himself fascist dictator of Latvia on May 15th, 1934. Four days later there is a military coup, by Col Damian Veltsjev, in Bulgaria. On June 9th, the first Donald Duck cartoon, in Wise Little Hen, is released in the US. The next day, USSR and Romania re-establish diplomatic relations. On June 14th, Hitler and Benito Mussolini (1883-1945) meet in Vienna, Austria. The first x-ray photo of an entire body is taken in Rochester, NY, USA, on July 1st.

Corneliu has 2 years on July 21st, 1934, and the day is very hot: actually in the state of Ohio, in USA, near the small city of Gallipolis, a new state record of 45 degrees C is reached. Estonia, Latvia and Lithuania sign the Baltic Entente, against the USSR, on September 12th. Five days later, RCA Victor releases the first 33 1/3 rotations/minute recording, with Ludwig van Beethoven's (1770-1827) Symphony Number 5 in Mi minor (1808). Also the USSR joins the League of Nations, with the Netherlands, Switzerland and Portugal voting no. On October 1st, 1934, Hitler expands German army and navy, and creates an air force, violating the 15 years old Treaty of Versailles (June 28, 1919). On October 16th, Mao Zedong (1893-1976) and 25,000 troops begin the Long March (9000 km over 370 days) to retreat from the attacks of the troops of Chiang Kai-shek (1887-1975). On November 23rd, an Anglo-Ethiopian boundary commission in the Ogaden discovers an Italian garrison at Walwal, which lay well within Ethiopian territory. This leads to the Abyssinia Crisis. On December 29th 1934, Japan renounces the Washington Naval Treaty of 1922 (which limited naval construction) and the London Naval Treaty of 1930 (which regulated submarine warfare and limited naval shipbuilding).

Corneliu, 3 years and 5 months, is a pure joy at Christmas and New Year 1935! He was growing fast in 1935, and his parents were discussing some of the news, like the fact that the first US surgical operation for relief of angina pectoris was performed in Cleveland, and the inventor Edwin Armstrong gave the first public demonstration of FM broadcasting in the United States, at Alpine, New Jersey.

In **1936** Corneliu is 4 years old, and 97 years ago (1839), when Twain was 4, Twain's family moved to Hannibal, Missouri, a port town on the Mississippi River that inspired the fictional town of St. Petersburg in *The Adventures of Tom Sawyer* and *Adventures of Huckleberry Finn.*

What new events were discussing Corneliu's parents? Probably some of these: Edward VIII (1894 – 1972) succeeds, on January 20, 1936, British king George V (1865 – 1936), but King Edward VIII marries Mrs. Wallis Simpson, and abdicates throne on December 11, 1936. Italian troops occupy Addis Abeba, the capital city of Ethiopia. The 11th Olympic Games take place in Berlin, August 1 – 16, 1936. Germany and Japan sign the anti-Komintern pact. The Duke of York becomes, on December 11, 1936, King George VI (1895 – 1952). After many Japanese attacks, the Chinese leader Chiang Kai-shek declares war on Japan.

In **1937** Corneliu is 5 years old, plays all day long, while, in the world, the first Charlie Chaplin talkie, "Modern Times," is released in the US, the Japanese troops attack the Marco Polo Bridge to invade China, the first US congressional session takes place in air-conditioned chambers, Italy withdraws from the League of Nations, the Japanese troops conquer Nanjing (China), and Octavian Goga becomes Prime Minister of Romania.

Solzhenitsyn, 19, is a student of mathematics at Rostov University in Russia. Rostov is one of the oldest towns in Russia, located on the north shores of Lake Nero, 200 km northeast of Moscow.

Here comes **1938**, Corneliu is 6, talks a lot, runs around, and his parents are concerned about the events which take place: King Carol II (1893 – 1953) of Romania drives out dictator Octavian Goga; German troops invade Austria (Anschluss); trials of Soviet leaders begins in the Soviet Union; teflon is invented by Roy J. Plunkett in the US; Austria becomes a state of Germany; Japan declares war on China; a 500 ton meteorite lands near Pittsburgh, Pennsylvania, USA; instant coffee is invented in the US; archaeologists discover engraved gold and silver plates from King Darius (550 BC – 486 BC) in Persepolis (Iran); the Treaty of Munich is signed by Hitler, Mussolini, Daladier (1884 – 1970) and Chamberlain (1869 – 1940); Germany annexes Sudetenland (1/3 of Czechoslovakia); Japanese troops occupy Canton, Hankou and Wuhan in China; DuPont, in the US, announces its new synthetic fiber will be called "nylon"; a fascist coup in Romania fails; a French-German non-attack treaty is signed (Ribbentrop-Bonnet Pact).

In **1939** Corneliu is 7, begins to go to school, and his parents quietly discuss the many big events taking place in the world, which still have great impact to this day: the uranium atom first split takes place at Columbia University, USA; Eugenio Pacelli was chosen as Pope Pius XII (1876 – 1958); Germany occupies Czechoslovakia; Hungary annexes the republic of Karpato-Ukraine; the Sino-Japanese War (1937-1945) continues with the Battle of Nanchang; the Spanish Civil War ends and Madrid falls to Francisco Franco (1892 – 1975); Faisal II (1935 – 1958) ascends to the throne of Iraq at the age of 4, and is the last King of Iraq; Italy invades Albania; Hungary leaves the League of Nations; Stalin requests and then signs British-French-Soviet Union anti-nazi pact; Germany and Italy announce an alliance known as the Rome-Berlin Axis; the first king and queen of the UK to visit the USA, George VI and Elizabeth; the test flight of the first rocket plane, using liquid propellants, takes place in Germany; the Russian offensive, under General Zjoekov, against Japanese invasion in Mongolia, takes place; Molotov-Ribbentrop pact: East Europe will be divided between Hitler and Stalin - Poland will be divided in half, Bessarabia from Romania will be occupied by Stalin; formally Germany and USSR sign a 10-year non-aggression pact; Belgium, Netherland and Poland mobilize; Isoroku Yamamoto is appointed the supreme commander of the

Japanese fleet; the Japanese invasion army is driven out of Mongolia by the Russians; Switzerland proclaims neutrality.

Even the little Corneliu feels that something very bad happened in the fall of 1939: The World War II (WW II) starts, Germany invades Poland, and takes Danzig • Britain declares war on Germany • France follows 6 hours later, quickly joined by Australia, New Zeeland, South Africa and Canada • Netherlands and Belgium declare neutrality • the USA declare themselves neutral • Iraq and Saudi Arabia declare war on Germany • Poland's president Moscicki and Prime Minister Slawoj-Skladkowski flee to Romania • Soviet Union invades Eastern Poland and takes 217,000 prisoners • the Versailles Peace Treaty (June 28, 1919) forgot to include Andorra, so Andorra and Germany finally, after 20 years, sign an official treaty ending World War I • Estonia accepts Soviet military bases • the Soviet-German treaty agrees on the 4th partition of Poland and gives Lithuania to the USSR • last Polish troops surrender and Germany annexes Western Poland • Albert Einstein (1879 – 1955) informs the US President Roosevelt of the possibilities of an atomic bomb • LaGuardia Airport opens in New York City • nylon stockings go on sale for first time in Wilmington, Delaware, USA • the first air conditioned automobile (Packard) was exhibited in Chicago, USA • four soviet soldiers are killed on the Finnish-Russian border, then the Soviet government revokes the Russian-Finnish non-attack treaty, and USSR invades Finland and bombs Helsinki • the League of Nations excludes the Soviet Union • Pope Pius XII makes a Christmas Eve appeal for peace.

Corneliu Leu's house wall, 2013.

Now we enter **1940**, Corneliu is 8, goes to school, and feels the great concerns of his parents. Let's see some of the events in 1940: Sergei Prokofiev's (1891 – 1953) ballet Romeo and Juliet premieres in Leningrad • Soviets bomb cities in Finland • the Polish pianist and composer Ignacy Jan Paderewski (1860 – 1941), Knight Grand Cross of the Order of the British Empire, at 80 becomes premier of the Polish government in exile • Finnish troops vacate Koivisto island • Walt Disney's (1901 – 1966) animated movie "Pinocchio" is released in the US • the US population is 131,669,275 • Finland initiates the Winter War peace negotiations • the first opera telecast, in New York City, is "I Pagliacci" (written in 1892) by Ruggero Leoncavallo (1857 – 1919) • Finland surrenders to the USSR and gives Karelische Isthmus • Mussolini joins Hitler in Germany's war against France and Britain • Karelo-Finnish SSR becomes the 12th Soviet republic (until 1956) • Germany invades Norway and Denmark (Denmark surrenders) • Italy annexes Albania • British troops land at Narvik, Norway • the first electron microscope is presented by RCA in Philadelphia, USA • Rear Admiral Joseph Taussig testifies, before the US Senate Naval Affairs Committee, that war with Japan is inevitable •

Norwegian King Haakon VII (1872 – 1957, King for 52 years) and his government flee to England • the 1940 Olympics at Helsinki are cancelled • Winston Churchill (1874 – 1965) succeeds Neville Chamberlain as Prime Minister of Britain • German armies attack The Netherlands, Belgium and Luxembourg • Germany blitz conquest of France begins by crossing Muese River • Dutch Queen Wilhelmina (1880 – 1962, Queen for nearly 58 years, starting at age 10) flees to England • Germany bombs Rotterdam, The Netherlands, (600 dead) • The Netherlands surrender to Germany • McDonald's opens its first restaurant in San Bernardino, California • Germany occupies Brussels, Belgium • French tanks counter attack at Pronne, under General Charles de Gaulle (1890 – 1970) • the first successful helicopter flight takes place in the US, with Vought-Sikorsky US-300, designed by the Russian American aviation pioneer Igor Ivanovich Sikorsky (1889 – 1972, immigrated to the US in 1919) • Operation Dynamo begins, to evacuate defeated Allied troops from Dunkirk, France • Belgium surrenders to Germany and King Leopold III (1901 – 1983) gives himself up • British-French troops capture Narvik in Norway • Premier Winston Churchill flies to Paris to meet with the 84 years old Marshal Philippe Pétain (1856 – 1951) , who announced he is willing to make a separate peace with Germany • German forces enter Paris • the first synthetic rubber tire is exhibited in Akron, Ohio, USA • British and French troops evacuate Narvik in Norway • the discovery of the first chemical transuranic element with atomic number 93, neptunium (Np, a radioactive actinide metal, named after planet Neptune, itself named after Roman god of the sea Neptune), is announced in the US • General Charles de Gaulle's first meeting with Winston Churchill • Norway surrenders to Germany • Italy declares war on allies and raids Malta • in response, British forces bomb Genoa and Torino in Italy • France surrenders to Germany and German troops occupy Paris • Soviet Army occupies Lithuania and installs a communist government, then occupies Estonia • General Charles de Gaulle on BBC tells French people to defy the German occupiers • France signs an armistice with Italy • USSR ends the use of an experimental calendar, and returns to Gregorian calendar • Soviet Army attacks Romania and Romania cedes Bessarabia to the Soviet Union • Hitler orders invasion of England (Operation Sealion) • British Royal Navy sinks the French fleet in North Africa • the diplomatic relations are broken between Britain and Vichy government in France • Battle of Britain begins as German forces attack by air for 114 days • Soviet Union annexes Estonia, Latvia and Lithuania • Italian troops invade British Somalia (in the Horn of Africa, near the Gulf of Aden) • Churchill recognizes De Gaulle French government in exile • Alsace Lorraine from France is annexed by the Third Reich (name for Germany from 1933 to 1945) • Greece mobilizes • General George Marshall is sworn in as chief of staff of the US army • the first showing of the high definition color TV takes place in the USA • Crown prince (19 years old) Mihai (Michael, born 1921) succeeds Carol II as king of Romania • Treaty of Craiova (Romania): Romania loses Southern Dobrudja (Cadrilater) to Bulgaria • Italian troops enter Egypt • 4 teens, going down a hole near Lascaux, France, discover 17,000-year-old drawings, now known as the Lascaux Cave Paintings • Japanese troops attack French Indo-China • Germany, Italy and Japan sign a 10 year formal alliance (Axis) • German troops occupy Romania • 40 hour work week goes into effect in the USA • Italy attacks Greece, but Greece successfully resists • Hungary, Romania and Slovakia join the Axis Powers • Romania signs Driemogendheden pact (the Tripartite Pact, or Berlin Pact, a military alliance between Germany, Italy and Japan) • British troops have their first major offensive in North Africa • Germany begins dropping incendiary bombs on London • California's first freeway, Arroyo Seco Parkway, opens •

Solzhenitsyn, 22, marries Natalia, she divorces him in 1950, they marry again in 1957, and finally divorce in 1972.

In **1941** little Corneliu is 9, goes to school, his parents are very concerned, the borders with Bulgaria and with USSR are now much closer to them, and many other events take place in the world: Canada and US acquire air bases in Newfoundland (99 years lease) • Kuomintang forces under orders from Chiang Kai-Shek open fire at communist forces, resuming the Chinese Civil War • British offensive in Eritrea takes place • the first commercial extraction of magnesium from seawater takes place in Freeport, TX, USA • British and Australian troops capture

Tobruk, North Africa, from Italians • British troops march into Abyssinia (Ethiopian Empire) • Japanese armored barges cross Strait of Johore to attack Singapore • Romania breaks relations with The Netherlands • plutonium is first produced and isolated by the American chemist, with Nobel Prize in Chemistry, Dr. Glenn T. Seaborg (1912 – 1999) • German troops invade Bulgaria, then Bulgaria joined the Axis Pact • 50,000 British soldiers land in Greece • Britain leases defense bases in Trinidad (near Venezuela) to US for 99 years • Hitler signs Directive 27 (assault on Yugoslavia) • Pro-German Rashid Ali al-Ghailani grabs power in Iraq and forms a pro-German regime • Churchill warns Stalin of a plan for a German invasion of the USSR • the operation Bestrafung begins - Germany bombers attack Belgrade, Yugoslavia, 17,000 die • Germany bombards Piraeus (port city, 12 km southwest from Athens, Greece • a munitions ship explodes) • Italian held Addis Abeba (Ethiopia) surrenders to British and Ethiopian forces • pact of neutrality between the USSR and Japan is signed • the Kingdom of Yugoslavia surrenders to Germany • Bulgarian troops invade Macedonia in Greece • 100 German bombers attack Athens, Greece • Greece surrenders to Germany • Operation Merkur: Hitler orders the conquest of Crete (the largest Greek island, in the south) • Stalin becomes premier of USSR • Konrad Zuse presents the Z3, the world's first working programmable, fully automatic computer, in Berlin • the first British turbojet flies • Italian army under General Aosta surrenders to Britain at Amba Alagi, Ethiopia • Germany invades Crete, Greece • British troops attack Baghdad, Iraq • the USA declares state of emergency, due to Germany's sinking of the US ship Robin Moor • a German Luftwaffe air raid on Dublin, Ireland, claims 38 lives • Germany bans all Catholic publications • English and French troops overthrow the pro-German Syrian government • Estonia loses 11,000 inhabitants as a consequence of mass deportations into Siberia ordered by Stalin • Turkey signs peace treaty with Germany • Estonians start armed resistance against the Soviet occupation • Finland invades Karelia • Operation Barbarossa: Germany attacks the Soviet Union and occupies the Baltic states • Germany, Italy, Romania and Finland declare war on the Soviet Union • Bulova Watch Co. pays $9 for the first ever network TV commercial in the USA • US forces land in Iceland to forestall Germany invasion • Beirut, Lebanon, is occupied by Free France and British troops • Montenegrins in Yugoslavia start popular uprising against the Axis Powers • the pharmaceutical-grade penicillin is produced in large quantities by Pfizer in Brooklyn, New York, USA • British Prime Minister Winston Churchill launched his "V for Victory" campaign • the USA demand Japanese troops out of Indo-China and start embargo on oil-export to Japan • German army enters Ukraine • more Japanese forces land in Indo-China • The US President Franklin Roosevelt and British Prime Minister Winston Churchill issue the joint declaration that later becomes known as the Atlantic Charter • German troops reach Leningrad • English and Russian troops attack pro-German Iran and Reza Shah Pahlavi (1878 – 1944) of Iran is forced to abdicate throne to his son Mohammad Reza Pahlavi (1919 – 1980) • the blockade of Leningrad (St. Petersburg) by Germany begins • Roosevelt orders any Axis ships found in American waters to be shot on sight • the U.S. Navy is ordered to attack German U-boats • the construction of the Pentagon for the US Department of Defense begins (completed on January 15, 1943) • Hitler orders that for every German killed by Yugoslavian partisans, 100 Yugoslavians to be killed • German army conquers Kiev • General de Gaulle forms the French government in exile in London • nine Allied governments pledge adherence to the common principles of the policy set forth in the Atlantic Charter • German troops start an assault on Moscow: operation Taifun begins • Hideki Tojo (1884 – 1948) regime forms in Japan • Romanian Legionnaires enter Odessa, USSR • Mount Rushmore sculptures are completed in the USA • USA lends Soviet Union $1 million • Germany's drive to take Moscow is halted • Mussolini's forces leave Abyssinia (Ethiopia) • The US troops land on Suriname (north of Brazil) to protect a bauxite mine • Finland joins the Anti-Komintern Pact (Germany, Japan, Italy and others) • Lebanon gains independence from France • USSR begins a counter offensive which causes Germany to retreat, and their troops vacate Rostov • Japanese emperor Hirohito (1901 – 1989) secretly signs declaration of war against the USA on December 1st, 1941 • German siege of Tobruk (port in Libya, near Egypt), after 8 months, ends • Japanese attack Pearl Harbor, Hawaii, USA, on December 7, 1941 • in London, the Dutch government in exile declares war on Japan and Italy • the US and Britain declare war on Japan, and the USA enters the World War II • China declares war on Germany and Italy • Japanese troops land on northern Luzon (the largest island in the north of the Philippines) and overrun the island of Guam, US Territory in the western Pacific Ocean, 2500 km south of Japan • Germany and Italy declare war on the USA • Dutch and Australian troops land on the island Portuguese Timor (south of Indonesia, 500 km north of Australia) • German troops led by the field marshal Erwin Rommel (1891 – 1944) begin retreating in North Africa • Japanese troops land on Hong Kong • Hitler takes complete command of the German Army • Japanese troops land on the island Mindanao (the second largest and the most southern of Philippines) • the first battle of the American Volunteer Group, better known as the "Flying Tigers", in Kunming, China, against Japanese troops • Premier Winston Churchill arrives in Washington, DC, for a wartime conference • Tito establishes the first Proletarian Brigade in Yugoslavia • American forces on Wake Island (US Territory on a coral atoll, north of the Marshall Islands, half way between Hawaii and Japan) surrender to Japanese troops • Japan begins assault on Rangoon, Burma (now Myanmar, west of Thailand) • Japan announces the surrender of the British-Canadian garrison in Hong Kong • Winston Churchill becomes the first British Prime Minister to address a joint meeting of the Congress of the USA, warning that the Axis would "stop at nothing" • Japan bombs Manila, capital of Philippines, even though it was declared an "open city" • Winston Churchill addresses the Canadian parliament.

In **1942** Corneliu is 10, begins to read and write quite well, and also begins to understand some of the big events of this year: the USA and 25 other countries sign a united declaration against the Axis • 28 nations, at war with the Axis, pledge no separate peace • German troops in Bardia, a seaport in Libya near Egypt, surrender • Japanese troops occupy Manila, Philippines • Pan American Airlines becomes the first commercial airline to schedule a flight around the world • the US Joint Chiefs of Staff, in the Department of Defense, is created • Japan invades North-Celebes, Netherland Indies (now North Sulawesi in

Indonesia) • Japan conquers Kuala Lumpur, capital of Malaysia • the first use of an aircraft ejection seat is performed by a German test pilot in a Henkel He 280 jet fighter • Japanese troops invade Burma (now Myanmar, west of Thailand) • Tito's partisans occupy Foca, a small city 200 km southwest of Belgrade in Yugoslavia • the first US forces in Europe during WW II go ashore in Northern Ireland • Italian supreme command demands dismissal of German marshal Rommel • Russian General Timoshenko's troops move into Ukraine • German and Italian troops again occupy Benghazi, Libya • US auto factories switch from commercial to war production • the first Japanese air raid on Java (a southwest island of Indonesia, very densely populated) takes place • the US Congress advises Roosevelt that Americans of Japanese descent should be locked up en masse, so they wouldn't oppose the US war effort • Daylight Savings War Time goes into effect in the US • Hitler's Operation Sealion (invasion of England) is cancelled • Singapore surrenders to Japan • German submarines attack Aruba (a small island in the south of the Caribbean Sea, 50 km north of Venezuela) oil refinery • Japanese troops land on Bali (small island of Indonesia, east of Java) • about 150 Japanese warplanes attack the north Australian city of Darwin • the US President Roosevelt orders detention and internment of all west-coast Japanese-Americans • Japanese troops land on Timor, a southern island of Indonesia (now there is also the separate state of East Timor) • the US President Franklin Roosevelt orders General Douglas MacArthur (1880 – 1964) out of the Philippines, as American defenses collapse • one Japanese submarine fires on oil refinery in Ellwood, 50 km west of Los Angeles, California, USA • the English physicist and radio astronomer James Stanley Hey (1909 – 2000), Fellow of the Royal Society, discovers radio emissions from the Sun • Japanese troops land on Java, the last Allied bastion in Dutch East Indies (now Indonesia) • Japanese forces captures Rangoon, Burma • Dutch colonial army on Java surrenders to Japanese armies • Roosevelt orders men between 45 and 64 to register for non-military duty • the British Arctic convoy PQ13, with war supplies on 19 British, American and Polish ships, departs Reykjavik, Iceland, to Murmansk, USSR, where only 15 ships arrived (during the war about 1400 ships delivered essential war supplies to the USSR) • The US move native-born of Japanese ancestry into detention centers • Tokyo is bombed by American airplanes • a Gallup Poll in the US determines the name WW II for the second world war • Japanese troops occupy Mandalay, the second-largest city of Burma (now Myanmar, northwest of Thailand), 716 km north of Rangoon (now Yangon) • food is rationed in the US • the island of Corregidor (at the entrance of Manila Bay, where American troops were located) and then Philippines surrender to the Japanese Armies • the Battle of the Coral Sea (off the northeast coast of Australia) ends, stopping Japanese expansion • a helicopter makes its first cross-country flight in the USA • Mexico declares war on Germany and Japan • Anglo-Soviet Treaty is signed in London • Battle of Midway (territory of the US, an atoll in the North Pacific Ocean, equidistant between North America and Asia, about one-third of the way from Honolulu, Hawaii to Tokyo, Japan) begins, and this is Japan's first major defeat in WW II, just six months after Japan's attack on Pearl Harbor, Hawaii • USA declares war on Bulgaria, Hungary and Romania • Japanese troops land on the islands Kiska and Attu (2500 km northeast of Japan and 2000 km southwest of continental Alaska), Aleutian Islands, Alaska, USA • German troops march into Sevastopol, a port on the Black Sea, in the southwestern region of the Crimean Peninsula, USSR • the German army is defeated by the British army at El-Alamein, port in Egypt, on the Mediterranean Sea, 106 km west of Alexandria • the US and USSR sign the Lend-Lease agreement during WW II, which gives to the USSR much needed war military assistance from the US • the first V-2 rocket is launched at Peenemunde Army Research Center (Heeresversuchsanstalt Peenemunde), on the Baltic Sea island of Usedorn, 250 km north of Berlin, Germany, and reached 1.3 km • Germany occupies Egypt • Major General Dwight Eisenhower (1890 – 1969) is appointed commander of the US forces in Europe • the US air offensive against Germany begins • Netherland's government in exile (London) recognizes the Soviet Union • the Germans test fly the Messerschmitt Me-262, using only its jet engines, for the first time • German troops conquer again Rostov-on-Don, city at the northeast end of the Sea of Azov, north of the Black Sea, USSR • Hitler's Directive

#45: orders to occupy Stalingrad (now Volgograd), USSR, 500 km northeast of Rostov-on-Don • the first American offensive in Pacific starts at Guadalcanal, the principal island of the Solomon Islands, in the south-western Pacific, 1500 km northeast of Australia • Field Marshal Bernard Montgomery (1887 – 1976) becomes commandant of the British army in North Africa • British premier Churchill arrives in Moscow and meets Stalin • Dwight D Eisenhower is named commander for invasion of North Africa • Premier Churchill travels back to Cairo from Moscow • the US 8th Air Force bombs occupied Europe for the first time • Generalfeldmarschall Fredrich Paulus (1890 – 1957, married Elena Rosetti-Solescu in 1912 (she died in 1949, in Baden)) orders German 6th Army to conquer Stalingrad • Brazil declares war on Germany, Japan and Italy • the Battle of Stalingrad starts: 600 German Luftwaffe's bomb Stalingrad and 40,000 die • Japanese troops land on Papua New-Guinea at Milne Bay, 700 km northeast of Australia • Russian counter offensive begins in Moscow • Cuba declares war on Germany, Japan and Italy • Germany annexes Luxembourg • German troops enter Stalingrad • Japanese planes drop incendiary bombs on Oregon, north of California, USA • British troops land on the island of Madagascar, 500 km east of Mozambique in southeast Africa • Russian troops organize a counter offensive at Stalingrad • launch of the first A-4/V-2 rocket to the altitude of 85 km takes place in Germany • the first salvo of the Russian Katjoesja-rocket destroys a German battalion in Stalingrad • the US and British governments announce the establishment of the United Nations • the first WW II American expeditionary force lands in Africa • last Vichy-French troops in Algeria surrender (Vichy is 400 km south of Paris) • the Soviet Union launches the winter offensive against Germans along the Don front (Don is a 1950 km river in the south of Russia) • 1 million Russians breach the German lines • 3rd and 5th Romanian army corps surrender • German 4th and 6th Army are surrounded at Stalingrad • Japan bombs again the Port Darwin, in the north of Australia • Josip Broz Tito (1892 – 1980) appoints Anti-fascist Liberation Committee in Yugoslavia • the first controlled nuclear chain reaction is done by the Italian physicist Enrico Fermi (1901 – 1954) at the University of Chicago • the US bombers struck the Italian mainland for the first time in WW II •

the first Japanese bombing of Calcutta (now Kolkata, a big city in east India) takes place.

Solzhenitsyn, 24, is an artillery captain in the Russian army for 2.5 years during World War II.

1943 has arrived • Corneliu will be soon 11 years old and now he can understand and talk to his parents about some of the events happening at that very dramatic time: Canadian Army troops arrive in North Africa • the US and Britain relinquish extraterritorial rights in China • Roosevelt and Churchill confer in Casablanca (the largest city in the western Morocco, on the Atlantic Ocean, 300 km southwest of Gibraltar) concerning WW II • the world's largest office building, with air conditioning system, the Pentagon (for the US Department of Defense), was completed • pre-sliced bread sale is banned in the US, to reduce bakery demand for metal parts • Soviets announce that they broke the long German siege of Leningrad (now Saint Petersburg, in the east of the Gulf of Finland from the Baltic Sea, 300 km east of Helsinki), where over one million city residents died • the US ration bread and metal • the Battle of Anzio (a small city on the Tyrhenian Sea, in the southwest Italy, 56 km south of Rome) takes place and Allies are stopped on the beach, by the Germans, until 1944 • British 8th army marches into Tripoli, Libya • the first US air attack on Germany, at Wilhelmshaven (a small coastal town, on the North Sea, 150 km west of Hamburg), takes place • Chile breaks contacts with Germany and Japan • Field Marshal Friedrich von Paulus surrenders to the Russian troops at Stalingrad and the battle of Stalingrad ends with the final surrender of the German 6th Army • shoe rationing begins in the US • Japanese evacuate Guadalcanal • Vietminh forms Indo Chinese Democratic Front in Vietnam • the sea battle in the Bismarck Sea (in the southwestern Pacific Ocean, to the north of the island of Papua New Guinea, 1000 km north of Australia) finishes with the victory of the US and Australia over Japan • the US General-major George S. Patton (1885 – 1945) arrives in Djebel Kouif, (a small town in Tunisia, near Algeria, 230 km southwest of the capital Tunis) • meat, butter and cheese are rationed in the US (meat: 784 grams/week, 2 kilograms for military personnel) • Hitler and Mussolini met for an Axis conference in Salzburg (an old city in Austria, 250 km west of Vienna) • U.S. President Franklin Roosevelt, in an attempt to check inflation, freezes wages and prices, prohibits workers from changing jobs, unless the war effort would be aided thereby, and bars rate increases to common carriers and public utilities • Soviet Union breaks contact with the Polish government exiled in London • 5th German Pantser army surrenders in Tunisia • US 7th division lands on Attu, Aleutian Islands, the first US territory recaptured from Japanese troops • Axis forces in North Africa surrender • Stalin dissolves the Comintern (Communist International, founded by Lenin in 1919 • The United States Army contracts with the University of Pennsylvania's Moore School to develop the ENIAC computer • Argentina is taken over by General Rawson and Colonel Juan Peron • "Pay-as-you-go" US income tax deductions are authorized • British troops invade Pantelleria, Italy, (a tiny island, the ancient Cossyra, 100 km southwest of Sicily, and 60 km east of the Tunisian coast) • Allies begin 10-day bombing on Hamburg, north Germany • the US forces land at Nassau Bay, near the small town Salamaua, Papua New Guinea, 800 km northeast of Australia • the Battle of Kursk (USSR, 400 km northeast of Kiev and 600 km southwest of Moscow) begins, involving 6,000 tanks • the US invasion fleet (96 ships) sails to Sicily, Italy, and US, British and Canadian forces invade Sicily (Operation Husky) • after 8 days of heavy fighting, the greatest tank battle in history ends with the USSR victory over Germany at Kursk, where almost 6,000 tanks took part, and 2,900 were lost by Germany • the Royal Air Force (RAF) bombs Germany rocket base at Peenemunde • 500 allied air forces raid Rome, Italy • the US forces led by General George Patton liberate Palermo, northwest of Sicily, Italy • Benito Mussolini is captured and dismissed as premier of Italy • during the Battle of Troina, (center-east of Sicily, 60 km northwest of Catania), Mount Etna (3350 m, 40 km east of Troina) erupts, sending ash and lava many kilometers into the sky • Bulgarian czar Boris III visits Hitler • US General Patton enters Messina (northeast of Sicily, Italy), completing thus the conquest of Sicily by the Allies • Gromyko is named USSR ambassador in Washington • Japan leaves Aleutian Islands, west Alaska, USA • German occupiers impose 72-hour work (over 10 hours/day, all days) week in occupied countries • Lord Mountbatten (1900 – 1979)

is appointed Supreme Allied Commander in South East Asia • Denmark declares a general strike against German occupiers • arrested former dictator Benito Mussolini is transferred from a prison in La Maddalena (small city in the south of the island Maddalena, northeast of the island of Sardinia, Italy), to a hotel at the ski resort from Campo Imperatore (1700 m) in the Gran Sasso d'Italia massif (in central Italy, 132 km northeast of Rome, 40 km west of Pescara) • Denmark scuttles their warships so as not to be taken by Germany • British 8th army lands in south Italy at Messina (Sicily) • Italy surrenders to the Allies in WW II • US, British and French troops land in Salerno (city on the Gulf of Salerno on the Tyrrhenian Sea, 50 km southeast of Naples (Napoli), Italy) (operation Avalanche) • German troops occupy Rome and take over the protection of the Vatican City • US and Australian troops join in Salamaua, New Guinea, 800 km northeast of Australia • Free French army lands in Corsica (island 250 km southeast of France) •
German paratroopers seize former Italian dictator Benito Mussolini, who was being held prisoner by the Italian government at a hotel on the Gran Sasso massif • having been Generalissimo since 1928, Chiang Kai-shek becomes president of China • Benito Mussolini forms a rival fascist government in Italy • the Russian city of Bryansk (380 km southwest of Moscow, and 400 km northwest of Voronezh) is liberated from German occupation • Soviet forces reach Dnepr river (2200 km, from north (Smolensk), through Kiev, to south (Back Sea)) • Eisenhower and Italian Marshal Piero Badoglio (1871 – (1956) sign an armistice • Allied forces capture Naples (200 km southeast of Rome, Italy) • Averell Harriman (1891 – 1986) is named US ambassador to Moscow • Japanese troops leave the Kolombangara Island, part of the Solomon Islands in southwestern Pacific Ocean, 1500 km northeast of Australia • the island of Corsica is freed by the Free French • Great Britain establishes bases on the Archipelago of the Azores, in the North Atlantic Ocean, 1360 km west of Portugal • Italy declares war on its former Axis partner Germany • streptomycin, the first antibiotic remedy for tuberculosis, is isolated by researchers at Rutgers University, New Brunswick, New Jersey, USA • France arrests the government of Lebanon • Soviet forces liberate Kiev (900 km southwest of Moscow) • American

bombers strike a hydro-electric power facility and heavy water factory in German-controlled Vemork, south of Norway, 300 km west of Oslo • the first US ambassador to Canada, Ray Atherton (1883 – 1960), is nominated • 444 British bombers attack Berlin, Germany • US forces land on Tarawa and Makin Atoll in the Gilbert Islands (in the central Pacific Ocean, 3500 km northeast of Australia, and 4000 km southwest of Hawaii) • Roosevelt, Churchill and Chiang Kai-shek meet to discuss ways to defeat Japan • Lebanon declares independence from the French administration • Conference of Teheran (Iran, 1190 m, 100 km south of the Caspian Sea, 1600 km southeast of Stalingrad (now Volgograd)) between Churchill, Roosevelt and Stalin, takes place • Partisan Tito forms temporary government in Jajce (Bosnia, 200 km east of Belgrade, Yugoslavia) • the battle of Monte Cassino (a rocky hill 130 km southeast of Rome, 520 m, with a historic abbey, Italy), begins • the second conference of Cairo, Egypt: Roosevelt, Churchill and Turkish president Inonu (1884 – 1973), takes place • Yugoslavian resistance forms provisionary government under Dr. Ribar (1881 – 1968) • a military coup takes place in Bolivia • "The International" is no longer the USSR National Anthem • Roosevelt appoints General Eisenhower the supreme commander of the Allied forces in Europe.

In **1944** the little Leu will be 12, and 97 years ago, in 1847, when Mark will be 12, his father died of pneumonia.

Corneliu is questioning his parents about the many events, which dramatically change around him and around the world: General Clark replaces General Patton as commander of the 7th US Army • the first use of helicopters during warfare (British Atlantic patrol) takes place • the US Air Force announces the production of the first US jet fighter, the Bell P-59 • the first mobile electric power plant is delivered in Philadelphia, USA • Churchill and de Gaulle begin a two-day wartime conference in Marrakesh (major city in southeast Morocco, 600 km southwest of Gibraltar) • British Royal Air Force drops 2300 tons of bombs on Berlin • 447 German bombers attack London • 649 British bombers attack Magdeburg (an old medieval city on the Elbe River, 160 km southwest of Berlin, Germany) • Leningrad is liberated from the German blockade, after 880 days, with over

1,000,000 civilians killed • 683 British bombers attack Berlin • 285 German bombers attack London • US invades Majuro, a large coral atoll in Marshall Islands (central Pacific, 4000 km northeast of Australia, and 4000 km southwest of Hawaii) • Allied troops set foot on Japanese occupied territory • Argentina coup by Juan Peron, minister of war, takes place • the first US bombing of Berlin takes place • Anti-Germany strikes in North Italy • Japan begins offensive in Burma (northwest of Thailand) • USSR recognizes Italian Badoglio government • Italian town of Cassino, 2 km east of Monte Cassino, destroyed by Allied bombing • Germany occupies Hungary • Mount Vesuvius (1281 m, 9 km east of Naples, Italy) erupts (the last eruption so far) • Japanese troops conquer Jessami, a small village in East-India, elevation 1200 m • the Soviet Army marches into Romania • British troops capture Addis Abeba, Ethiopia, from Italians • De Gaulle forms a new govern in exile • Allies bomb Bucharest, targeting railroads, and kill 5,000 people • Soviet forces liberate Odessa • diplomatic relations between New Zealand and the Soviet Union are established • Papandreou government in Greece is formed • Messerschmitt Me 262 Sturmvogel, the first jet bomber, makes its first flight • meat rationing ends in the US • Russians recapture Crimea by taking Sevastopol • the Chinese offensive in West-Yunnan (near Burma (now Myanmar) takes place • Generals Rommel, Speidel and von Stulpnagel attempt to assassinate Hitler • the Polish 2nd Army corp captures the convent of Monte Cassini, Italy • the German defense line in Italy collapses • Icelandic voters sever all ties with Denmark • the Japanese advance in Hangzhou, China, northwest of the Qiantang River, 150 km southwest of Shanghai • the Germans pull out of Rome, Italy • the US 5th Army enters and liberates Rome from Mussolini's Fascist armies • King Victor Emmanuel III of Italy (1869 – 1947) abdicates the power and then the throne for his son Umberto II (1904 – 1983, last king of Italy (only for 34 days)) • D-Day: 150,000 Allied Expeditionary Force lands in Normandy, France • the Russian offensive in Karelia (on the border with Finland) takes place • 15 US aircraft carriers attack Japanese bases on Marianas Islands (2000 km southeast of Japan, west of the Mariana Trench, the deepest part of the oceans (-10971 m) • the first German V-1 rocket assault on London takes place • the first B-29 bomber raid against mainland Japan takes place • the US forces begin the invasion of Saipan (part of the Northern Mariana Islands in Pacific, 2500 km south east of Japan) • Iceland declares independence from Denmark • Japanese troops conquer Changsha (on Xiang River, a branch of the Yangtze River, 900 km southwest of Shanghai, China) • the US Congress charters the Central Intelligence Agency • a Russian offensive in the central front sector (Czechoslovakia) takes place • Cherbourg (on the English Channel, northwest of France, 400 km northwest of Paris), is liberated by Allies • more than 2500 people are killed in London and South-East England by German V-1 flying bombs • the United Nations Monetary and Financial Conference at Bretton Woods (12 km west of Mount Washington (1917 m), 250 km north of Boston, USA) starts, establishing the International Monetary Fund and the World Bank • 1,100 US guns fire 4th of July salute at German lines in Normandy (a region in northwest France, on the English Channel, west of Paris) • the first Japanese kamikaze attack on the US fleet near the Japanese Island Iwo Jima (Sulfur Island, only 21 km^2, 1200 km south of Tokyo) takes place • the French General De Gaulle arrives in Washington, DC, USA, and the US General Patton lands in France • there is a heavy Japanese counter offensive on Saipan, occupied by the US troops • the British troops march into Caen (northwest of France, 20 km south of the English Channel, 400 km west of Paris) • the US government recognizes the authority of General De Gaulle • Vilnius (200 km northwest of Minsk) , the capital of Lithuania (south of Latvia, northeast of Poland, west of Russia (now Belarus), is liberated by the Russian troops, which also cross the river Bug, the border with Poland • the Polish troops under general Anders occupy Ancona (east of central Italy • on the Adriatic Sea, 100 km southeast of San Marino, 250 km northeast of Rome) • the US invades the Japanese-occupied island of Guam (8000 km west of Hawaii, 3000 km south of Japan • General Koiso becomes premier of Japan • the US troops occupy Pisa (central west of Italy, 70 km west of Firenze (Florence), 300 km northwest of Rome) • the first jet fighter is used in combat by Germany (Messerschmitt 262) • the first German V-2 rocket hits Great Britain • the first British jet fighter is used in combat (Gloster Meteor) • Turkey breaks diplomatic relationship with Germany • British 8th army reaches the suburbs of Florence (central Italy, 300 km northwest of Rome) • IBM dedicates, in the US, the first program-controlled calculator, the Automatic Sequence Controlled Calculator (known best as the Harvard Mark I) • Churchill and Tito meet in Naples (200 km southeast of Rome, Italy) • Operation Anvil: Allies land on the French Mediterranean sea coast, to liberate Montpellier, Marseille, and Nice • Operation Dragoon: Allied troops land in Provence (southeast of France) • the Russian troops arrive at the Austrian border • the last Japanese troops are driven out of India • the Russian offensive arrives at Jassy and Kishinev, northeast of Romania • Allied troops capture Marseilles, France • King Mihai (Michael) of Romania (born 1921, king 1927 – 1930 and 1940 – 1947) orders his forces to cease fire against Allies and dismisses the pro-Axis premier, Marshal Ion Antonescu (1882 – 1946).

Romania was liberated from the German occupation by the Russian troops on August 23, 1944, and the 12 years old Corneliu will right about 40 years later a very important book about this event. The English translation of this relevant book was published in the US in 2013, by DERC Publishing House, under the title “Roosevelt, Churchill, Stalin and Hitler – their surprising role in Eastern Europe in 1944”

ROOSEVELT, CHURCHILL, STALIN AND HITLER

THEIR SURPRISING ROLE IN EASTERN EUROPE IN 1944

CORNELIU LEU

The front cover of this book.

Back to the events in the second part of 1944: the US 20th Army corp enters Fontainebleau (a commune 55 km southeast of Paris, France, with Château de Fontainebleau (1137)) • the 2nd Tank division under General LeClerc reaches Notre Dame Cathedral (1163 – 1345, 96 m) in the eastern half of Île de la Cité in Paris • General De Gaulle returns to Paris and walks on Avenue des Champs-Élysées.

Buildings on the south side of the Avenue des Champs-Élysées (Elysian Fields), near the Avenue George V (center).

Bulgaria announces withdrawal from the war and the German troops are to be disarmed • an anti-German rebellion in Slovakia takes place • Soviet and Romanian troops enter Bucharest, Romania • the French provisional government moves from Algiers (the capital of Algeria, 1000 km south of France) to Paris • French troops liberate Bordeaux (southwest of France) • Bulgaria government of Bagrjanow resigns •

The western façade of Cathédrale Notre Dame de Paris (1163 – 1345, 96 m), on the south-eastern part of the Île de la Cité, which is considered the center of Paris, in the fourth arrondissement. The three Portals are: Portal of the Virgin, Portal of the Last Judgment, and Portal of St-Anne. The organ has 7,374 pipes, with about 900 classified as historical. It has 110 real stops, five 56-key manuals and a 32-key pedalboard; it is now fully computerized.

French troops liberate Lyon (France, 150 km southwest of Geneva, Switzerland) • a tank division of the British Guards frees Brussels, capital of Belgium, 300 km northeast of Paris • Finland breaks diplomatic contact with Germany • Belgium, Luxembourg and Netherlands sign unity treaty • the first German V-2 rockets land in London and Antwerp (Belgium, 50 km north of Brussels) • Russians march into Bulgaria and Bulgaria declares war on Germany • Allied forces liberate Luxembourg • Roosevelt and Churchill meet in Canada at the second Quebec Conference • the US 5th tank division is the first to enter Germany • Eindhoven (in south of The Netherlands, 150 km southeast of Amsterdam) is free • Armistice between Finland and the Soviet Union is signed (end of the Continuation War) • German Luftwaffe bombs Eindhoven: 200 killed • Soviet forces occupy Estonia and also invade Yugoslavia • Germans crush Warsaw Uprising, killing 250,000 people • British troops land on Greek territory • Canadians free Austria • Soviets march into Hungary and Czechoslovakia • British Prime Minister Winston Churchill arrives in the USSR for talks with Stalin • US takes the Japanese island Okinawa (1500 km southwest of Tokyo) • Tannu Tuva (south of Russia, northwest of Mongolia) is annexed by the U.S.S.R. • German army retreats from Athens, Greece • Riga, capital of Latvia (with Lithuania to the south, Estonia to the north, and Russia to the east), is freed by Russians • the US 1st army begins battle of Aachen (western Germany, 90 km west of Bonn) • Allied troops land in Corfu (western Greece, 100 km southeast of Italy) • British troops march into Athens, Greece • Hungary: Horthy government falls, the Nazi count Szalasi becomes premier • Canadian troops liberate Aardenburg (southwestern Netherlands, 100 km northwest of Brussels) • US forces land in Philippines • the US troops capture Aachen, the first large German city to fall • Tito reaches free Belgrade, Yugoslavia • Sweden announces intention to stay neutral and refuses sanctuary to Germans • pro-German government of Hungary flees • Red Cross wins Nobel peace prize • US bombers based on Saipan (the largest island of the Northern Mariana Islands, 2400 km southeast of Tokyo) begin the first attack on Tokyo • Albania is liberated from Germany control • John Hopkins hospital in the USA performs the first open heart surgery • General De Gaulle arrives in Moscow • British order to disarm everybody in Greece, causes general strike there • the Greek Civil War breaks out in a newly-liberated Greece, between communists and royalists • the Convention on International Civil Aviation is drawn up in Chicago, USA • General Radescu (1874 – 1953) forms the last pre-communist Romanian government, for less than three months • Hizbu'allah (Arm forces for Allah) forms • the US troops land on Mindoro (island in center-western Philippines) • the Battle of the Bulge begins in Ardennes Forest (southeastern Belgium, northern Luxembourg, western Germany south of Aachen and northeast France) • Japanese-Americans are released from the detention camps in the US (in 1988 President Ronal Reagan (1911 – 2004) signed a law which apologized for the internment and paid over $1.6 billions in reparations) • Battle of Bastogne (city in southwest Belgium, at the border with Luxembourg): Germans surround the US 101st Airborne • The US Gen Patton's 4th Tank division turns away the German army at Bastogne • Budapest, Hungary, is surrounded by the Soviet army • King George II of Greece (1890 – 1947, spouse Elisabeth of Romania) abdicates his throne • Hungary declares war on Germany.

In **1945** Corneliu will be 13 on July 21st, but before that, on June 25, his uncle Episcope Grigorie Leu is placed under Romanian Communist Security scrutiny. Mark, in 1848, almost 13, became a printer's apprentice./

Now, as a teen-ager, Corneliu notices every day the fast changes which are taking place around him, and around the world: France joins the United Nations • Allies land on the west coast of Burma (now Myanmar) and conquer the city Akyab (now Sittwe) • British Premier Winston Churchill visits France • Greek General Plastiras (1883 – 1953) forms a new government • the US aircraft carriers attack the Japanese island Okinawa (600 km southwest of the main Japan) • US soldiers led by General Douglas MacArthur (1880 – 1964) invade Philippines • German forces in Belgium retreat in the Battle of Bulge • the Soviets begin a large offensive against the Germans in Eastern Europe • the liberation of Warsaw by the Soviet troops takes place •

Grand Rapids, Michigan, becomes the first US city to fluoridate its water • Swedish ships bring food to starving Netherlands • almost 1000 US Flying Fortresses drop 3000 tons of bombs on Berlin • Roosevelt, Churchill and Stalin meet at Yalta (a Russian resort city in the south of the Crimean peninsula, on the north coast of the Back Sea, 30 km east of Sevastopol, 500 km east of Constanta (Romania)) • US troops under General Douglas MacArthur enter Manila, Philippines • Russian Red Army crosses the river Oder, which forms part of the border between Poland and Germany, in the middle being 100 km east of Berlin • the US 76th and 5th Infantry divisions begin crossing river Sauer, which is in Belgium, Luxemburg and Germany, a left tributary of the river Moselle, and forms a part of the border between Luxemburg and Germany, 200 km west of Frankfurt • Allied planes bomb Dresden, in eastern Germany, 200 km south of Berlin, 135,000 die • the USSR captures Budapest (capital of Hungary, 300 km southeast of Vienna, Austria), after 49-day battle with German troops: 159,000 die • Peru, Paraguay, Chile and Ecuador join the United Nations • Venezuela declares war on Germany • 30,000 US Marines land on the Japanese island Iwo Jima (Sulfur Island, only 21 km^2, 1200 km south of Tokyo) • The Arab League forms in Cairo, capital of Egypt, 1100 km southeast of Athens, Greece • Operation Grenade: the US General Simpson's (1888 – 1980) 9th Army crosses Ruhr, a 217 km river in western Germany, passing by Essen, Bochum, and Dortmund, a right tributary of the Rhine • the US Marines raise the US flag on Iwo Jima (there is a famous photo and statue of this event) • Egypt and Syria declare war on Germany • the US aircraft carriers attack Tokyo • Turkey declares war on Germany • Lebanon declares Independence • the Chinese 30th division occupies Hsenwi, a town in eastern Burma • King Michael of Romania gives in to the Communist government • Finland declares war on Germany • Allies bomb The Hague, Netherlands • the US 7th Army Corp captures Koln (Cologne, 30 km north of Bonn) • the Chinese 38th division occupies Lashio, the largest town in northern Burma (now Myanmar), 200 km northeast of Mandalay • Yugoslavia government of Tito forms • 334 US B-29 Super fortresses attack Tokyo with 120,000 fire bomb • Japan declares Vietnam Independence • the US troops land on Mindanao, the southernmost major island in the Philippines • the USSR returns Transylvania to Romania, from Hungary • Queen Wilhelmina (1880 – 1962) returns to the Netherlands • Würzburg, central Germany (100 km southeast of Frankfurt), is 90% destroyed, with 5,000 dead, in only 20 minutes, by British bombers • 1,250 US bombers attack Berlin • Hitler issues the Nero Decree to destroy all German factories • the first Japanese flying bombs (ochas) attack US Navy ships near the Japanese island Okinawa (1500 km southwest of Tokyo) • the largest operation in the Pacific war: 1,500 US Navy ships bomb Okinawa, Japan • the Japanese resistance ends on Iwo Jima • the US 20th Army corp captures Wiesbaden, central Germany, on Rhein river, 20 km west of Frankfurt • the last German V-1 (buzz bomb) attack on London • the USSR invades Austria • the 3rd Algerian division crosses the Rhein river (a 1233 km river from the southeastern Swiss Alps to the North Sea, passing through the western Germany) • the US forces invade the Japanese island Okinawa • diplomatic relations between the Soviet Union and Brazil are established • Hungary is liberated from the German occupation • General Kuniaki Koiso (1880 – 1950) resigns as the 41st Prime Minister of Japan (for 8.5 months) and he is replaced by the baron and admiral Kantaro Suzuki (1868 – 1948) • the US troops conquer Mulheim, Oberhausen, Bochum, Unna and Essen in the central-west Germany • the 32nd US President Franklyn D. Roosevelt dies (January 30, 1882 – April 12, 1945) • Harry Truman (1884 – 1972) is sworn in as the 33rd President of the USA • the Red Army occupies Wien (Vienna), Austria • American planes bomb Tokyo and damage the Imperial Palace • the US 7th Army and allies forces capture Nuremberg and Stuttgart in southern Germany • the Red Army begins the Battle of Berlin • Benito Mussolini flees from Salò (a small town on the central-west banks of Lago di Garda, 100 km east of Milano), to Milano • diplomatic relations between the Soviet Union and Bolivia and then Guatemala are established • Soviet troops enter Berlin • Allied troops occupy German nuclear laboratory • the US troops in Italy cross the river Po (the longest (652 km) river in Italy, from the Cottian Alps (at the border between France and Italy), flowing eastward along the 45th parallel north, across northern Italy, to the Adriatic Sea, 60 km south of Venezia) • delegates from 46 countries gather in San Francisco for the

United Nations Conference on International Organization • the last Boeing B-17 attack against Germany takes place • the Red Army completely surrounds Berlin • the US and Soviet forces meet at Torgau, Germany, on the Elbe River, 200 km southwest of Berlin • Marshal Henri Philippe Pétain (1856 – 1951), leader of France's Vichy collaborationist regime during WW II, is arrested for treason • Battle of Bautzen (southeastern Germany, near the borders with Czechoslovakia and Poland, 60 km east of Dresden) – the last successful German tank offensive of the war and the last noteworthy victory of the Wehrmacht • the second Republic of Austria forms • Italian partisans capture and execute Benito Mussolini (July 29, 1883 – April 28, 1945) • the US 5th army enters Genoa, northwest Italy, port on the Ligurian Sea, 150 km south of Milano • the Völkischer Beobachter, the newspaper of the Nazi Party in Germany, ceases publication • the US 5th army reaches the Swiss border • the Japanese army evacuates Rangoon in Burma (now Yangon in Myanmar, 300 km west of Thailand) • the Terms of surrender of the German armies in Italy is signed • Venice and Mestre (northeast of Italy) are captured by the Allies • the Red Army attacks the German Reichstag building in Berlin • the US troops attack the German troops near the Elbe river (a 1091 km river from northern Czechoslovakia to the North Sea, 110 km northwest of Hamburg) • Admiral Karl Doenitz (1891 – 1980) forms a new German government • the Soviet army reaches Rostock, north Germany, on the Baltic Sea, 300 km northwest of Berlin • the German Army in Italy surrenders • the Soviet Union takes Berlin: General Weidling (1891 – 1955), the last commander of the Berlin Defense Area, surrenders, Adolf Hitler (April 20, 1889 – April 30, 1945) kills himself • Yugoslav troops occupy Trieste, seaport on the Adriatic Sea, in northeastern Italy, 150 km east of Venezia (Venice) • the 1st Polish armor brigade occupies Wilhelmshaven, a coastal town on the North Sea, in northwest Germany, 150 km west of Hamburg • Allies arrests German theoretical physics Werner Heisenberg (1901 – 1976, Nobel Prize in Physics) • German troops in Netherlands, Denmark and Norway surrender • Admiral Karl Dönitz, leader of Germany after Hitler's death, orders all U-boats to cease offensive operations and return to their bases • Canadian troops move into Amsterdam • Chinese troops counter attack at

Tsjangte, China • German Field Marshal General Von Keitel (1882 – 1946) formally surrenders to the Russian Marshal Zhukov (1896 – 1974) • Victory in Europe Day: Germany signs unconditional surrender, World War II ends in Europe • Czechoslovakia is liberated from the German occupation • Allies capture Rangoon (Burma) from the Japanese • Russian troops occupy Prague, Czechoslovakia • German archipelago of Helgoland (170 ha), in the southeastern corner of the North Sea, 200 km northwest of Hamburg, surrenders to the British troops • the US, USSR, UK and France agree to split occupied Germany, and they declare supreme authority over Germany • The US forces defeat the Japanese forces in the Japanese island Okinawa • The United Nations Charter is signed by 50 nations in San Francisco, USA • The Polish Provisional government of National Unity is set up by the Soviets • Ruthenia, formerly in the eastern Czechoslovakia, becomes part of the USSR • the Labour Party wins the British parliamentary election • the liberation of the Philippines is officially declared • Nicaragua becomes the first nation to formally accept the United Nations Charter • the battleship USS South Dakota is the first US ship to bombard Japan • the first test detonation of an plutonium bomb takes place at Trinity Site, Alamogordo (200 km south of Albuquerque), New Mexico, USA, on July 16, 1945 at 5:30 AM • Potsdam (25 km southwest of Berlin) Conference, with Truman, Stalin and Churchill, holds its first meeting • Declaration of Potsdam: USA, UK and China demand Japanese surrender, but the Japanese government disregards the ultimatum • Winston Churchill resigns as UK's Prime Minister • the US Senate ratifies the United Nations charter 89-2 • the atomic bomb is dropped on Hiroshima (western Japan, 800 km southwest of Tokyo) on Aug 6th, to force Japan to surrender • the US, USSR, England and France sign the Treaty of London regarding the International Military Tribunal • the USSR declares war against Japan and then establishes a communist government in North Korea • the USA drop the second atomic bomb on Japan and destroy part of Nagasaki (western Japan, 1000 km southwest of Tokyo, 300 km southwest of Hiroshima) • Japan announces willingness to surrender to Allies, provided that the status of 124th Emperor Hirohito (1901 – 1989, Emperor for 63 years) remains unchanged • Allies refuse Japan's surrender offer to retain the Emperor Hirohito unchanged • Victory on Japan Day: Japan surrenders unconditionally • South Korea is liberated from the Japanese rule • Aisin-Gioro Puyi (1906 – 1967), the last Emperor of China (the twelfth and final ruler of the Quig dynasty) and ruler of Manchukuo, is captured by the Soviet troops • Indonesia (Dutch East Indies) declares independence from the Netherlands • at the proposal of the US President Truman, Korea is divided on the 38th parallel, with the US occupying the southern area, and the USSR the northern area • Russian troops occupy Harbin (northeast China, 1200 km northeast of Beijing) and Mukden (now Shenyang, northeast China, 600 km northeast of Beijing, and 600 km southwest of Harbin) • the Vietnam conflict begins as Ho Chi Minh (1890 – 1969) leads a successful coup, British troops liberate Hong Kong (southern coast of China, at the South China Sea, 2000 km south of Beijing) from Japan • General MacArthur (1880 – 1964) is named the Supreme Commander of the Allied Powers in Japan • Ho Chi Minh declares Vietnam independence from France • the formal surrender of Japan takes place aboard USS Missouri, and the World War II ends • the first "bug" in a computer was discovered, a moth was removed with tweezers from a relay and taped into the log • Kim Il Sung (1912 – 1994) arrives in harbor of Wonsan, port of North Korea, on the westernmost shore of the Sea of Japan, 150 km east of Pyongyang • German rocket engineers begin work in the US • the US President Harry Truman announces that the atomic bomb secret was shared with Britain and Canada • the Chinese civil war begins, between Chiang Kai-Shek (1887 – 1975) and Mao Tse-Tung (1893 – 1976) • Juan Peron (1895 – 1974) becomes dictator of Argentina • Japanese troops surrender Taiwan to General Chiang Kai-Shek • General Enver Hoxha (1908 – 1985) becomes leader of Albania for 40 years • UNESCO is founded • General George C Marshall (1880 – 1959) is named special US envoy to China • Yugoslavian Socialist Republic is proclaimed • the microwave oven is patented in the US • the Austrian Republic is re-established • the International Monetary Fund is established and the World Bank is founded • the US Congress officially recognizes the "Pledge of Allegiance" • the Ratification of the United Nations Charter is completed.

Solzhenitsyn, 27, is arrested for "disrespectful remarks" written about Stalin in correspondences with a friend. He is taken to a labor camp in Russia for an eight-year sentence.

The year **1946** brings many post war changes, and our Corneliu, now 14, finishes the elementary school, and begins to go to Mircea cel Bătrân High School from Constanța. Mircea cel Bătrân (Mircea the Elder or Mircea I of Wallachia, 1355 - 1418) was ruler of Wallachia from 1386 to 1418. He won some important battles against the much stronger Sultan of the Ottoman Empire Bayezid I (1360 – 1403). At that time, Emperor of the Byzantine Empire was Manuel II Palaiologos (1350 – 1425), and Sigismund of Luxemburg (1368 – 1437) was King of Hungary and Croatia, and, in the last four years, Holy Roman Emperor.

Roma, Italy: The Amphitheatrum Flavium (wrongly called Colosseum, 80 AD, left), the Arch of Constantine (315 AD, right) and a carabiniere wedding event (2011).

Mihai Ralea (1896 – 1964) is the Romanian Ambassador to the US (1946-1948). • First meeting of United Nations General Assembly opens in London (Jan.10) • Winston

Churchill's "Iron Curtain" speech warns of Soviet expansion. The Cold War begins. • The first automatic electronic digital computer, ENIAC, is dedicated at the University of Pennsylvania. • George Balanchine (1904 – 1983, USA) and Lincoln Kirstein (1907 – 1996, USA) establish the New York City Ballet. It makes its home at Lincoln Center in 1964. • Roberto Rossellini's (1906 – 1977, Italy) Neorealist movie, *Rome, Open City,* presents an alternative to Hollywood, with its use of street cinematography, lyrically capturing the despair and confusion of post-World War II Europe. • Vincent du Vigneaud (1901 – 1978, US biochemist, Nobel Prize in Chemistry) synthesizes penicillin. • The US Army makes radar contact with the Moon (400,000 km away) for the first time.

In **1947** Corneliu is 15 and many changes can be observed: on February 10 peace treaties for Italy, Romania, Bulgaria, Hungary, and Finland are signed in Paris. . • On March 12 the Truman Doctrine proposes "containment" of communist expansion. • In June the Marshall Plan is proposed to help European nations recover economically from World War II. . • On December 30, King Mihai I of Romania is forced to abdicate. Then the Romanian Patriarch Nicodim resigns and Justinian Marina takes his place. . • The microwave oven is invented by Percy Spencer (1894 – 1970, US). • John Bardeen (1908 – 1991, American physicist, the only one person to have won the Nobel Prize in Physics twice), Walter H. Brattain (1902 – 1987, American Physicist, Nobel Prize), and William B. Shockley (1910 – 1989, American Physicist, Nobel Prize) develop the transistor. • On St. Nicholas Day, 6 December 1947, Reinhard Gehlen (1902 – 1979, Major General in the German Wehrmacht during World War II, and chief intelligence officer, but dismissed by Hitler for his accurately pessimistic intelligence reports) began to organize a spy ring, codename Nikolaus, with the help of the US Army intelligence and the CIA in Pullach (a southwest suburb of Munich, Bavaria, Germany). Even now, Pullach remains the headquarters of the Bundesnachtrichtendienst (BND), Germany's Federal Intelligence Service.

Solzhenitsyn, 29, begins using a post as a school teacher of mathematics and physics, inside the scientific labor camps in

Russia, as a cover to write. "The First Circle" would later chronicle this time period.

In **1948**, at only 16, the very young Corneliu Leu debuts with the novels and stories “Free Thinking” and “Dobrogea Pages”. Mark Twain, in 1851, almost 16, began working as a typesetter and contributor of articles and humorous sketches for the Hannibal Journal.

At the same time Corneliu is under the Romanian Security scrutiny. . • At the end of February Communists seize power in Czechoslovakia. . • Edwin Land (1909 – 1991, US) invents the Polaroid Land camera.

On March 1**, 1949**, Corneliu’s uncle Episcope Grigorie Leu dies. . • At the end of March, the very young Leu establishes The Writers’ Association, which continues to function. On April 4 twelve nations sign the North Atlantic Treaty establishing NATO.

In **1950**, at 18, Leu’s „Asiziile and other radio-stories” appear. The first modern credit card Diners Club is introduced in the US. The Korean War begins.

When Twain was 18, 97 years ago (1853), he left Hannibal and worked as a printer in New York City, Philadelphia, St. Louis and Cincinnati. He educated himself in public libraries in the evenings.

Solzhenitsyn, 32, is transferred to a labor camp for political prisoners in Russia, where he contracts stomach cancer. It clears in 1954, at 36, after treatment. The ordeal is later published as "The Cancer Ward" and "The Right Hand".

Traces of the Leu family (Grigorie Leu in 1939) on the old foundation walls.

In **1952**, at 20, Leu presents the historical drama serial "The brave's time". On February 6, Princess Elizabeth of York, 25, becomes Elizabeth II, Queen of the United Kingdom, Canada, Australia, New Zealand, South Africa, Pakistan and Ceylon. On February 26, Elizabeth's Prime Minister, Winston Churchill, announces possession of an atomic bomb. On September 11, Corneliu's father, Ion Leu, 58, is interrogated and arrested (1952-1953).

Solzhenitsyn, 35, in **1953**, after serving his eight-year prison term, receives a new sentence: imprisonment for life. Stalin dies on March 5, at 74, after 30 years of dictatorship. On September 7 Nikita Khrushchev (1894 – 1971) takes power in the Soviet Union and starts some reforms.

In **1954**, at 22, Leu's drama in 3 acts "With full speed" is first presented at "Theater at Microphone". Also, his investigation file is opened by the Security on May 4, and he is arrested in the period April 24 – June 23. On February 19, the 1954 transfer of Crimea takes place: The Soviet Politburo of the Soviet Union orders the transfer the Crimean Oblast from the Russian SFSR to the Ukrainian SSR. On February 23 – The first mass vaccination of children against polio begins in Pittsburgh, United States. On February 25 – Lt. Col. Gamal Abdel Nasser (1918 – 1970) becomes premier of Egypt.

In **1956**, at 24, Leu publishes the novel „Devil's Eye" at The Literature Publishing House. On January 17 – USS *Nautilus*, the first nuclear-powered submarine, puts to sea for the first time, from Groton, Connecticut. On January 18–January 20 – the Battle of Yijiangshan Islands (30 km east of the city Taizhou in China and 400 km north of Taipei in Taiwan) takes place: The Chinese Communist People's Liberation Army seizes the islands from the Republic of China (Taiwan). The CIAS (*Comité international d'Information et d'Action Sociale*) is an international, anti-communist network that became a central component of the global anti-communist movement after 1945. There is a unique global nature of CIAS, and the role they played in supporting anti-communist domestic and foreign policies of their respective home governments is remarkable.

Solzhenitsyn, 38, is granted a reprieve from incarceration. He becomes a mathematics and science teacher in Russia..

In **1957,** at 25, Leu brings another novelty: „ The Winter's Tale "- the first live television performance. On January 20, Dwight D. Eisenhower (1890 – 1969) is inaugurated for a second term as President of the United States. The first nuclear-powered submarine, the USS *Nautilus* (1954) logs its 60,000th nautical mile (111,120 km, 20,000 leagues), matching the endurance of the fictional *Nautilus* described in Jules Verne's (1828 – 1905) novel *"20,000 Leagues Under the Sea"* (1869). It is decommissioned on March 3, 1980.

In **1958**, at 26, Leu is very active and publishes another novel, „The golden age", at The Literature Publishing House, the stories „Dobrogea Nights", at the Youth Publishing House, and the play in 3 acts „The family", with which the TV theater is inaugurated. In the first day of 1958 the European Economic Community (EEC) is founded, and the first Carrefour store opens in Annecy, a city in south-eastern France, on the northern tip of Lac d'Annecy, 35 km south of Geneva, Switzerland. On December 18 the United States launches SCORE, the world's first communications satellite.

In **1959**, at 27, Leu publishes the short stories „The blood and the water" at The Literature Publishing House. On January 3 Alaska is admitted as the 49th U.S. state, and on August 21 Hawaii is also admitted as the 50th (and the last so far) US state. On December 1st, the Antarctic Treaty is signed by 12 countries, including the major powers; it is a landmark treaty, which sets aside Antarctica as a scientific preserve and bans military activity on that continent.

In **1863**, after Mark Twain, 28, was a river pilot on Mississippi, a miner in Virginia City, Nevada, and now a journalist at a Virginia City newspaper, the Territorial Enterprise, he first used his pen name.

In **1961**, at 29, Leu publishes the reportages „With our hands", at The Literature Publishing House. On January 20, John

F. Kennedy (1917 – 1963) succeeds Dwight Eisenhower (1890 – 1969) as the 35th President of the United States of America. On February 14, the Element 103, Lawrencium, is first synthesized in Berkeley, California. On June 19 the British protectorate ends in Kuwait, and it becomes an emirate.

Solzhenitsyn, 43, has his manuscript "One Day in the Life of Ivan Denisovich" (about a labor camp inmate) at "Novy Mir" editor Aleksandr Tvardovsky (1910 – 1971, Russian poet and writer). Tvardovsky supports the novel, publishing it in 1962, with the consent of Khrushchev, in a brief period of de-Stalinization. 27 years would pass before the Soviet Union publishes a second Solzhenitsyn novel (in 1989).

In **1962**, at 30, Leu publishes another novel- „A strong family", at the Youth Publishing House. On July 23, Telstar 1 relays the first live trans-Atlantic television signal. Telstar 1, built by Bell Telephone Laboratories, USA, was launched on top of a Thor-Delta rocket at Cape Canaveral LC-17, Florida, on July 10, 1962. It successfully relayed through space the first television pictures, telephone calls, fax images and provided the first live transatlantic television feed.

Mark Twain at 30, in 1865, after moving to San Francisco, writes "Jim Smiley and His Jumping Frog".

In **1963**, at 31, Leu publishes the short story „The second future", The Military Publishing House. On January 8, Leonardo da Vinci's (1452 in Vinci, Republic of Florence, now Italy – 1519 in Amboise, Kingdom of France) *Mona Lisa* (or la Gioconda, 1503 – 1507, Louvre, Paris, France) is exhibited in the United States for the first time, at the National Gallery of Art in Washington, D.C.

Mark Twain at 31, in 1866, takes a trip to Hawaii, as correspondent of the Sacramento newspaper "Alta California", and gives his first public lecture.

Washington, D.C. (1790) in 2007, National Gallery of Art (1937, in the National Mall).

In **1964**, at 32, Leu publishes the novel „The power” at The Literature Publishing House. On May 1, at 4:00 AM, John George Kemeny (1926 – 1992, mathematician, President of Dartmouth College (1769, Hanover (on the Connecticut River, 180 km northwest of Boston), New Hampshire, USA, Latin: Collegium Dartmuthensis, motto: Vox clamantis in deserto (The voice of one crying out in the wilderness))) and Thomas Eugene Kurtz (1928, mathematician, Professor at Dartmouth College) ran the first computer program written in BASIC (Beginners' All-purpose Symbolic Instruction Code), an easy to learn high level programming language which they created. BASIC was eventually included on many computers and even some games consoles.

Twain, at 32, in 1867, travels as correspondent to Europe and the Holy Land, sees a picture of Olivia Langdon (Livy) and publishes “The Celebrated Jumping Frog of Calaveras County, and Other Sketches”.

Paris: Musée du Louvre (1793): a statue representing art, in front of Pavilion Richelieu, in Cour Napoléon (1803). The Louvre is located on the right bank of La Seine, in the 1st arrondissement, and has about 35,000 museum objects, exhibited over an area of 60,600 m^2. With more than 8 millions of visitors each year, the Louvre is the world's most visited museum. The museum is housed in the Palais du Louvre, originally built as a fortress around 1190 under Philip II of France (1165 – 1223, king 1179 – 1223).

Solzhenitsyn, 46, as Khrushchev is ousted, has his plays halted and his unpublished novel "The First Circle" is seized.

Corneliu Leu (left) with Ion Baiesu (1933 – 1992, Romanian writer) at “Luceafarul”.

Chapter 2. The next 25 years – the 2nd stage Leu

In **1965**, at 33, Leu publishes the stories „Ballads” at the Youth Publishing House, and the play in 3 acts „The second love”, premieres at the Constanța Theatre and at the TV Theatre. On March 22 the Romanian ruler changes. On December 5 Charles de Gaulle (1890 – 1970), is re-elected as French president.

Ion Baiesu (first left), Corneliu Leu (second from left), Eugen Barbu (1924 – 1993, Romanian writer, 3rd from left), Fanus Neagu (1932 – 2011, Romanian writer, 4th from left) at “Luceafarul”.

In **1966**, at 34, Leu's play in 3 acts „The beast”, premieres at Radio Theatre and TV Theatre. On January 12, the United States President Lyndon Johnson (1908 – 1973) states that the United States should stay in South Vietnam until Communist aggression there is ended. On July 18, the manned spaceflight *Gemini X* (with John Young and Michael Collins) is launched. After docking with an unmanned spacecraft Agena target vehicle, the astronauts then set a world altitude record of 763 km.

Twain at 34, in 1869, after many lectures across the U.S., meets and is engaged to Livy. He publishes “The Innocents Abroad”, as a subscription book, and it is an instant best seller.

In **1967**, at 35, Leu publishes the novel “Constant Hagiu private life”, at the Youth Publishing House, and establishes the radio station “Radiovacation”. On February 8 France launched its

Diademe-C satellite and on February 15, its Diademe-D satellite into Earth orbit. These satellites were magnetically stabilized, which limited their tractability in the southern hemisphere.

Twain at 35, in 1870, marries Livy, 25, her father buys them a house in Buffalo, New York, close to Niagara Falls, and their son Langdon is born.

In **1968**, at 36, Leu publishes the short stories „The right to love" at The Literature Publishing House, and begins the production and presentation, over several years, of the TV series of author movies „Romantic travels". On January 5 in Czechoslovakia, the Communist Party's Central Committee votes out Antonin Novotny (1904 – 1975) as First Secretary and replaces him with Alexander Dubcek (1921 – 1992). Novotny remains the country's president, but it is the beginning of what will be known as the Prague Spring – a reference to the blossoming of reforms called "socialism with a human face", until the Soviet invasion.

Solzhenitsyn, 50, completes his masterwork, "The Gulag Archipelago", a history of the labor camps in which he served. The book would become a powerful indictment of Russian dictator Joseph Stalin, who used the camps to hold political prisoners, in an attempt to destroy the opposition to the Soviet totalitarian state.

In **1969**, at 37, Leu establishes Eminescu Publishing House and the collection „The love novel" (Mihai Eminescu (1850 – 1889) is one of the best Romantic poet). On March 3 the Apollo program continues with NASA launching *Apollo 9* (with James McDivitt, David Scott, Rusty Schweickart), to test the lunar module.

Twain at 37, in 1872, moves with Livy to Hartford, Connecticut, publishes "Roughing It", daughter Susy is born, but son Langdon, 1 year and 7 months, passes to eternity.

Radulescu Neagu 's caricature that Corneliu Leu turned it into a badge.

In **1970**, at 38, Leu publishes the novel „The woman with blue eyes" at the Junimea Publishing House. This novel has some difficulties with the Security (the secret police). Leu also establishes the TV movie Studio, and begins the production of the first TV Romanian serials and co-productions. On February 11 Japan becomes the fourth country to launch a satellite into orbit. On September 28 Anwar Sadat (1918 – 1981) becomes the president of Egypt.

Twain at 38, in 1873, invents and patents "Mark Twain's Self-Pasting Scrapboo", and publishes "The Gilded Age".

Solzhenitsyn, 52, in 1970, wins the Nobel Prize for Literature (before the publication of "Gulag"), but the Soviet state protests, preventing him from receiving the prize for years. His unpublished manuscripts begin leaking to the West, and Solzhenitsyn's literary fame grows.

In 1971, at 39, Leu produces the feature film „The Siege" at „Romaniafilm". On July 26, as part of the Apollo program, the launch of Apollo 15 takes place.. On July 31 the Apollo 15 astronauts become the first to ride in a lunar rover, a day after landing on the surface of the Moon.

In 1972, at 40, Leu's three acts play „The happy woman" premieres at Bacău Theatre and at the TV Theatre. On January 5 the 37th President of the United States Richard Nixon (1913 – 1994) orders the development of a space shuttle program. In October the First International Conference on Computer Communications is held in Washington, D.C., and hosts the first public demonstration of ARPAnet, a precursor of the Internet.

In **1973,** at 41, Leu establishes „The movies house number 4" and becomes the producer of many movies and great screenings such as: „Cantemir" (1673 – 1723), „Ioanide", „The truth and the power", „Mihai Viteazul" (Michael the Brave, 1558 – 1601), „The actor and the savages", „Ciprian Porumbescu" (1853 – 1883), „The stone country", „The evening event", „The midnight house", "With clean hands", "Felix and Otilia", „The pale light of sorrow", „Uncle Mărin The Billionaire", „The green grass of home", „Alexandra and the hell", „The black chest", „Tănase Scatiu", „The world creation", „The strange agent", „The impossible love", „The Castle of the Carpathians", etc. He also publishes the second edition of the novel „The power" at the Eminescu Publishing House. On June 30 a very long total Solar eclipse visible in North- East of South America, the Atlantic, and central Africa took place. During the entire Second Millennium (1001 – 2000), only seven total solar eclipses exceeded seven minutes of totality. This was the last. Observers aboard a Concorde jet were able to stretch totality to about 74 minutes by flying along the path of the Moon's umbra.

Twain at 41, in 1876, after two years ago daughter Clara was born (1874 – 1962) and they moved to eccentric Nook Farm house in Hartford, publishes "Tom Sawyer".

Solzhenitsyn, 55, in 1973, has the first of the three volumes of "The Gulag Archipelago" published in the west. Alexei Kosygin's (1904 – 1980) Soviet government does not take immediate action. Also Solzhenitsyn marries his second wife, Natalia Svetlova. They have three sons: Yermolai, Stepan and Ignat.

Corneliu Leu (center) with the documentary filmmakers.

In **1974**, at 42, Leu publishes „Theatre" in "Rampa" collection, and the three acts play „The good girl from heaven" in the magazine „The Theater" and premieres at Pitesti Theater. On March 8, Charles de Gaulle Airport opens in Paris, France. On April, the world population reaches 4 billions of people, estimated by the United States Census Bureau.

Solzhenitsyn, 56, is labeled a traitor by the Soviet state-run newspaper "Pravda". He is stripped of his citizenship and deported to West Germany. Solzhenitsyn lives in Switzerland, then continues his exile in Cavendish, Vermont, USA (160 km northwest of Boston), where he completes "The Red Wheel," a series of novels about the formation of the modern Soviet Union.

In 1975, at 43, Leu appears in „Contemporary Romanian literature dictionary", at The Albatross Publishing House. On August 1 the Helsinki Accords, Helsinki Final Act, or Helsinki Declaration was the first act of the Conference on Security and Co-operation in Europe held in Finlandia Hall of Helsinki, Finland, during July and August 1, 1975. Thirty-five states, including the USA, Canada, and most European states except Albania, signed the declaration in an attempt to improve relations between the Communist bloc and the West. The Helsinki Accords, however, were not binding, as they did not have treaty status, but they had a positive impact for the people looking for freedom in the Communist bloc.

In 1976, at 44, Leu produces the TV feature film - „Benchmark 2516", and publishes the novel „This sentimental life" at The Romanian Book Publishing House. In January the Cray-1, the first commercially developed supercomputer, is released by Seymour Cray's (1925 – 1996, mathematician and electrical engineer) Cray Research. In May several elongated comet-like objects were discovered on pictures taken with the UK Schmidt Telescope in Australia. Because of their appearance, they became known as cometary globules, even though they have nothing in common with comets.

1977, at 45, Leu's three acts play „Professor Dignity" premieres at Craiova National Theater and at the TV Theater, his novel „ The woman with blue eyes" has a second edition at The Albatross Publishing House, and he publishes the novel „Dracula's complaint" at The Romanian Book Publishing House. In January the world's first personal all-in-one computer (keyboard, screen and tape storage), the Commodore PET, is demonstrated at the Consumer Electronics Show in Chicago, USA. On January 3 Apple Computer is incorporated.

Twain at 45, in 1880, starts investment in the Paige typesetter, publishes "A Tramp Abroad", and daughter Jean is born.

In 1978, at 46, Leu produces the film „The house between the fields", a co-production „Romaniafilm" and the Romanian TV, and publishes the novel „The price of the love, of the faith and of the hatred" at The Romanian Book Publishing House. On April 10 Volkswagen becomes the second (after Rolls-Royce) non-American automobile manufacturer to open a plant in the United States, commencing production of the Rabbit, the North American version of the Volkswagen Golf, at the Volkswagen Westmoreland Assembly Plant near New Stanton, Pennsylvania (the plant closes in 1992). On April 18 the U.S. Senate votes 68–32 to turn the Panama Canal over to Panamanian control on December 31, 1999.

In 1979, at 47, a very active Leu appears in „Romanian literature Dictionary“, at the Universe Publishing House, publishes the novel „Patriarchs” at The Romanian Book Publishing House, publishes the anthology volume „Commented Theater” at Eminescu Publishing House, publishes the journalistic anthology „Romantic reporter in the country and the world” at Junimea Publishing House, appears in “Romanian literature chronologic dictionary“ at The Scientific and Encyclopedic Publishing House, publishes the stories „Native land ballads” at Ion Creanga Publishing House (Ion Creanga, 1837 – 1889, well known writer and raconteur), and publishes „The novel of a great day” at The Albatross Publishing House. On February 7 the dwarf-planet Pluto (discovered by Clyde W. Tombaugh (1906 – 1997, American astronomer) on February 18, 1930; Pluto's surface is 3.3% of Earth, gravity 6.7% of Earth, temperature -230° C, distance from the Sun 6 billions of km (40 times farther than Earth), it has 5 satellites) enters a 20-year period inside the orbit of the 8th and farthest gaseous planet Neptune (discovered by Urbain Le Verrier (1811 – 1877, French mathematician) and Johann Galle (1812 – 1910, German astronomer; Neptune's distance to the Sun is 4.5 billions of km (30 times farther than Earth), surface 15 Earths, gravity 1.14 Earth, temperature -200° C, it has 14 satellites) on 23 September 1846), for the first time in 230 years.

In **<u>1980</u>**, at 48, Leu's three acts play „The soul of the place” premiers at TV Theater, and he produces the film „The spies circus" at „Romania film". In July Microsoft's Bill Gates (born 1955, he will become the wealthiest man on Earth between 1995 – present (2015, over $82 billions)) agrees to create an operating system for the new IBM Personal Computer. In September, David Bradley (born 1949, engineer) becomes one of the "original 12" engineers working on the project (under Don Estridge (1937 – 1985, electrical engineer)) and is responsible for the ROM BIOS code and for developing the Control-Alt-Delete command. On November 12, as part of the Voyager program, the

NASA space probe *Voyager I* makes its closest approach to Saturn (the sixth gas (mainly hydrogen) planet from the Sun, at 1.5 billions of km (10 times farther than Earth), the second largest after Jupiter, it has a large ring of small satellites, surface is 83.7 earths, density less than water, gravity about the same as Earth, temperature -139° C), when it flies within 124,000 km (about the diameter of Saturn) of the planet's cloud-tops, and sends the first high resolution images of the world back to scientists on Earth.

Twain at 48, in 1883, after two years ago published "Prince and the Pauper", publishes "Life on the Mississippi".

In **1981,** at 49, Leu's play „Dracula" premieres at Sibiu Theater. On March 5 the ZX81, a pioneering British home computer, is launched by Sinclair Research, going on to sell over 1.5 millions of units worldwide. On April 3 the Osborne 1, the first successful portable computer, is unveiled at the West Coast Computer Faire in San Francisco, USA. On August 12 the IBM Personal Computer is released.

Twain at 49, in 1884, publishes in London "The Adventures of Huckleberry Finn" (American edition comes out in 1885), and founds his own publishing company.

In **1982**, at 50, Leu publishes the novel „The Islands" at The Albatross Publishing House. On January 7 the Commodore 64 8-bit home computer is launched by Commodore International in Las Vegas, USA (released in August 1982); it becomes the all-time best-selling single personal computer model.

Clemens (Mark Twain) turns 50, in 1885, publishes the memoirs of Ulysses S. Grant (1822 – 1885, the 18th U.S. President (1869 – 1877)), memoirs now considered a literary classic.

In 1983, at 51, Leu publishes the journalistic reports „Symbols" and „The February night novel" at The Military Publishing House. On January 1st the migration of the ARPANET to TCP/IP is officially completed in the US, and this is considered to be the beginning of the true Internet.

In 1984, at 52, Leu's second edition of „ The novel of a great day" appears at The Albatross Publishing House, and he publishes the novel „The winning soldiers' wounds" at The Romanian Book Publishing House. On January 10, under the 40th US President Ronald Reagan (1911 – 2004), the United States and the Vatican (Holy See) restore full diplomatic relations.

In 1985, at 53, Leu's „The novel of a great character" is published at The Military Publishing House. On January 1st the Internet's Domain Name System is created, and Greenland is withdrawn from the European Economic Community. On January 21 the U.S. President Ronald Reagan is sworn in for a second term in office.

1986, at 54, Leu reestablishes, at „Contemporanul" magazine, the supplement "The Illustrated reality". On January 1st Spain and Portugal enter the *European Community*, which later becomes the European Union. On January 24 the Voyager 2 (launched on August 20, 1977, at Cape Canaveral LC-41, Florida, USA, and still working now (2015)) space probe makes its first encounter (at a distance of 81,500 km) with Uranus (the seventh gas (mostly hydrogen and helium) planet from the Sun, discovered with a telescope (for the first time in history) by William Herschel (1738 – 1822, German-born British astronomer and composer), in 1781, 2.9 billions of km from the Sun (19 times farther than Earth), its surface is 16 Earths, gravity 0.9 of Earth, temperature -200° C, it has 27 satellites).

Corneliu Leu talking at a literary discussion „Contemporanul”.

In **1987** – 1990, at 55 – 58, Leu publishes the trilogy „The Facts, The Century, The Power” at The Albatross Publishing House. On January 8, 1987, the Dow Jones Industrial Average closes for the first time above 2,000, gaining 8.30 to close at 2,002.25 (after 28 years, in 2015, it is over 18,000). On January 2, 1988, The Soviet Union begins its program of economic restructuring (perestroika) with legislation initiated by Premier Mikhail Gorbachev (born 1931, he had begun minor restructuring in 1985).

Twain at 55, in 1890, after publishing, one year ago, “A Connecticut Yankee in King Arthur’s Court”, (King Arthur was a legendary British king, circa 470 – 530), which was extensively criticized, buys all rights in the Paige typesetter. His mother Jane, 87, passes in eternity.

In **1989**, at 57, Leu’s third edition of „ The novel of a great day” appears at The Albatross Publishing House. On January 7 Akihito (born in 1933 in Tokyo, Japan) is enthroned as the Emperor of Japan, followed by the change in the era name from Showa to Heisei on the following day. On December 22nd, after a week of bloody demonstrations, Ion Iliescu (born 1930) takes over as president of Romania, ending the communist dictatorship.

The icon (with Corneliu Leu on the left and his wife Rodica on the right) as votive chapel fresco from the small town Poiana Tapului, in the Bucegi Mountains, 150 km northwest of Bucharest.

Chapter 3. After 57 – the new Leu

In 1990, at 58, Leu establishes The House for Publishing and for Audio, Video and Film Production „Reality", with the publications „Ave", „The Trouble", „The Christian poetry anthology", and also establishes Bishop Grigorie Leu Foundation. On January 1st, Poland becomes the first country in Eastern Europe to begin abolishing its state socialist economy. Poland also withdraws from the Warsaw Pact.

In 1991, at 59, Leu publishes the prose and scenarios „Of horror and of laughter", at the Reality Publishing House, and establishes the weekly radio heading „The mailbox 33". In February Russia has an ambiguous policy towards North Korea, and this fact facilitates the first North Korean nuclear crisis.

Twain at 59, in 1894, after he leaves Hartford, in 1891, to live in Europe, because of financial problems, he publishes "Pudd'nhead Wilson", his publishing company fails, and he files for bankruptcy.

In 1992, at 60, Leu publishes the novel „The Poet as a flower" at the Reality Publishing House, he produces in 1992 - 1993 the European reportage „A rich country with rich peasants", at the „Reality", and also establishes the radio-TV shows with public „Political Cabaret". On January 1st, the 41st President George H. W. Bush (born 1924) becomes the first U.S. President to address the Australian Parliament. On January 2, the first President of Russia Boris Yeltsin (1931 – 2007) ends price controls, resulting in prices of some goods and services becoming 3 to 5 times more expensive. This in effect ends the command economy in Russia.

In **1993**, at 61, Leu's 3 acts play „The success' man" – at the National Radio Theatre. On January 1st, The Dissolution of Czechoslovakia takes place: the Czech Republic and Slovakia separate. Also the European Economic Community eliminates trade barriers and creates a European single market. On January

3rd, Presidents George H. W. Bush (United States) and Boris Yeltsin (Russia) sign the second Strategic Arms Reduction Treaty.

Twain at 61, in 1896, continues for a second year to lecture around the world, to restore his finances, but his daughter Susy, 24, passes to eternity.

In 1994, at 62, Leu publishes The Brancoveanu Anonymous at the Reality Publishing House (Constantin Brancoveanu (1654 – 1714) was Prince of Wallachia between 1688 and 1714). Also Leu (which means lion) establishes the weekly moralistic heading „In the lion's mouth" in the newspapers „Libertatea", „Ordinea", "Azi", „Cronica română", „Albina" and in the monthly program „The life as a show". On January 1st, the North American Free Trade Agreement (NAFTA) is established.

Solzhenitsyn, 76, following the reinstatement of his citizenship in 1990 after the collapse of the U.S.S.R., returns home, settles near Moscow, where he would live the rest of his life.

In 1995, at 63, still strong and very active Leu publishes the novel „The Road to Damascus" at Eminescu Publishing House, becomes a full member of the International Institute Jacques Maritain (1882 -1973, French Catholic philosopher), publishes the essays „The local democracy" at the Reality Publishing House, and also produces the complex shows with live radio broadcasts and TV series „The transition circle dance", „„Do not shoot the government", „The transition bomb", „The elections are coming". On January 1st, The World Trade Organization (WTO) is established to replace the General Agreement on Tariffs and Trade (GATT, established in 1948). Austria, Finland and Sweden act to join the European Union (established in 1993, with origins in 1951 and 1958, when France, West Germany, Italy, Netherlands, Belgium and Luxemburg are the first inner six). The Draupner wave (a single giant wave, 25.6 m, measured at the Draupner platform) in the North Sea in Norway is detected, confirming the existence of rogue waves (which occur where physical factors, such as high winds and strong currents, cause waves to merge to create a single exceptionally large wave).

Corneliu Leu (first from the right) at the registration of the Political Cabaret for radio -TV

In 1996, at 64, Leu's 3 acts play „ The general and the pilfering" at the National Radio Theatre. Also he publishes the novel „The bureaucratic spies" at Eminescu Publishing House, and produces the multimedia complex shows with live broadcasts „We and the Europe", „The change has changed", „Winter Political Story". On January 3rd, Motorola introduces in the US the Motorola StarTAC Wearable Cellular Telephone, the world's smallest and lightest mobile phone to date.

In 1996, at 64, Leu's 3 acts play „ The general and the pilfering" at the National Radio Theatre. Also he publishes the novel „The bureaucratic spies" at Eminescu Publishing House, and produces the multimedia complex shows with live broadcasts „We and the Europe", „The change has changed", „Winter Political Story". On January 3rd, Motorola introduces in the US the Motorola StarTAC Wearable Cellular Telephone, the world's smallest and lightest mobile phone to date.

In 1997, at 65, Leu establishes the National Conference of the Intellectuals from Villages, publishes the essays „Europe's profligate sons" at the Reality Publishing House. His 3 acts play „Dămăroaia Story" premieres at the National Radio Theatre, and he is among the initiators and becomes a founding member of the European Association for Pluralistic Education. On May 11 the IBM's Deep Blue supercomputer defeats Garry Kasparov (born 1963) in the last game of the rematch, the first time a computer beats a chess World champion in a match.

In 1998, at 66, Leu establishes the National Institute of Personalism, then establishes the magazine „Pluralitas", and he appears in "International Author's and Writer's Who's Who" – Cambridge, UK. He also publishes the essay „Did the Romanians have the luck of a revolution?" at the Reality Publishing House. On January 6, the Lunar Prospector US spacecraft is launched into orbit from Cape Canaveral SLC-46 (Florida, USA), around the Moon, and later finds evidence for frozen water, in soil in permanently shadowed craters near the Moon's poles.

In 1999, at 67, Leu appears in "Marquis Who's Who in the World" and in „Cambridge Dictionary of International Biography"; also he establishes „The Movement for the Advancement of the Romanian Village". On January 1st the euro is established and becomes the official currency of the Eurozone, which consists of 19 of the 28 member states of the European Union.

A book launch presented by Fanus Neagu (left) and Mihai Miron (right), with Corneliu Leu (center).

In **2000,** at 68, Leu publishes the essays „Re-introduction to Personalism" at the Reality Publishing House, appears in „International Directory of Philosophy and Philosophers" at B. G. State University – Ohio, USA, and in „International Man of the year 2000-2001" - Cambridge Biographical Centre, UK. He also starts The Foundations Association for Rural Development. 2000 is the last year of the 2nd millennium, and the 100th and last year of the 20th century. 2000 was designated as the World Mathematical Year. On January 14 the Dow Jones Industrial Average closes at 11,722.98 (at the peak of the Dot-com bubble).

In **2001**, at 69, Leu publishes the novel „The winter love" at the Reality Publishing House, establishes, 172 years after its onset, the new series of the journal „Albina" (The Bee), publishes „The Cross Bishops Book" at the Reality Publishing House, and appears in „500 Leaders of Influence"- American Biographical Center. 2001 is the 1st year of the 3rd millennium, and the 1st year of the 21st century. On January 20 George W. Bush (born 1946) is sworn into office as President of the United States.

Twain at 69, in 1904, after finishing to pay off all the creditors (even if he was protected by bankruptcy), suffers the loss of his beloved wife for 34 years, Livy, 59. He begins dictating autobiography and moves to New York City.

Corneliu Leu

Corneliu Leu (first from the left) speaking at the launching of the new edition "The Romanian Albina".

In 2002, at 70, Leu appears in „Encyclopedia on Personalists of the Twentieth Century", publishes the anthology volume „Memories of the Writers' House" at the Reality Publishing House. The magazine „Albina" becomes „The Romanian Albina", a publication of the Movement for the Advancement of the Romanian Village, with a consistent program for the socio-economic development and for the European integration of the Romanian rural. The English translation „The Islands" of the novel „Insulele" (published in Romanian in 1982), is published by „Realpublishers". He starts producing the TV show „The literary café". On February 19, NASA's *2001 Mars Odyssey* space probe begins to map the surface of Mars, using its thermal emission imaging system.

Twain at 70, in 1905, is the guest of Theodore Roosevelt (1858 – 1919, the 26th U.S. President (1901 – 1909)) at the White House, has a banquet for his 70th birthday in New York, speaks frequently, and addresses congressional committee on copyright issues.

Corneliu Leu (left) at a festivity together with academicians Solomon Marcus (born March 1, 1925, mathematician, professor of this author (Michael Dediu) 50 years ago, second from left) and Vasile Tarâţeanu (born 1945, Romanian poet from Ucraine, first from right).

In 2003, at 71, Leu launches in the „Pluralitas" magazine the Diachronic Personalism hypothesis and publishes „Current personalist ideas in C. Rădulescu-Motru's work" (C. Rădulescu-Motru (1868 – 1957) Romanian philosopher). Leu appears in „The Coexistence World Initiative Network Partner Directory", and in „Directory of Philosophy Center USA". He publishes the novel „The Complaints Novel or Dracula's Executioner" at the Reality Publishing House, and "Personalist philosophy studies, methods and hypothesis" in Personalista collection. On January 16, the Space Shuttle Columbia (first flight 1981) is launched on its last flight. On January 23, the last signal is received from NASA's Pioneer 10 spacecraft (launched in 1972, 258.8 kg), some 12 billions of km from Earth, after working for 30 years, 10 months and 22 days.

An award ceremony at Cotroceni Palace (the official residence of the President of Romania), with President Ion Iliescu (the 4th from the left), and Corneliu Leu (the 3rd from the right).

In 2004, at 72, Leu publishes the journalism notes, pamphlets and tablets „In the lion's mouth – or the political chronicle of the years 1992-2004", at the Reality Publishing House. The magazine „Albina Românească" (The Romanian Bee) turns 175 years from its appearance, and with this occasion Corneliu Leu receives The Cultural Merit Order at the level of Grand Officer. He publishes the studies and courses "The journalism beginnings in Romania" at the Reality Publishing House, and the anniversary album „175 years of Romanian press", with facsimile transliterations and comments, at the Reality Publishing House. On January 4, NASA's MER-A spacecraft lands on Mars at 04:35 UTC, and on January 24, NASA's MER-B spacecraft lands on Mars at 05:05 UTC.

In 2005, at 73, Leu launches the concept „Transnational Civil Society'', and the abbreviated English translation „The Novel of a Great Day" appears in „Realpublishers". On January 5, Eris, the largest known dwarf planet in the Solar System, is identified by a team led by Michael E. Brown (born 1965, American astronomer) using images originally taken on October

21, 2003, at the Palomar Observatory. On January 14, the Huygens probe lands on Titan, the largest moon of Saturn.

Twain at 74, in 1909, after last year he moved into the Italian style splendid mansion Stormfield in Redding, Connecticut, where he formed the "Angelfish Club" for young girls, he suffers the loss of his youngest daughter Jean, 29.

In **2007,** at 75, Leu begins the FINAL WORKS series with "Novellas and Stories", then the „Historical Novels" volumes, „Theatre", „Contemporary Novels", „Journalism", „ Studies", „Memoires", and publishes the studies „Civil Society, Meritocracy, Real Democracy" in a homage volume at 75 years. On January 1st, Romania and Bulgaria join the European Union. On June 8, the Space Shuttle Atlantis begins its mission.

Mark Twain at 75, in 1910, visits Bermuda for the last time, and passes in eternity, of a heart attack, on April 21, in his house at Stormfield. He was buried in his wife's plot at Woodlawn Cemetery in Elmira, New York. His only surviving daughter, Clara, placed a monument there. Mark Twain is considered the father of American literature.

In **2008**, at 76, Leu publishes the three acts play „Devil's confessor". On February 7, Space Shuttle Atlantis (first flight in 1985) launches to deliver the European-built Columbus science laboratory to the International Space Station (launched in 1998).

On August 3, 2008, at age 89 and 7 months, the great Russian writer Aleksandr Solzhenitsyn, who significantly contributed to the collapse of the totalitarianism in the USSR and eastern Europe, passes in eternity.

In 2009, at 77, Leu publishes „About meritocracy" or "pale reflection about meritocracy in the nemeritocracy disconcerting shadow" at the Reality Publishing House, and an essay "The human person and the sustainable development pragmatism", accompanied by several case studies produced by Gh. Manea – The Movement for the Advancement of the Romanian Village. 2009 was the International Year of Astronomy. On February 10, a Russian and an American satellite collide over Siberia, creating a large amount of space debris.

Corneliu Leu is proclaimed “Patriarch of Mizil Festival” (Mizil is a small town 100 km northeast of Bucharest)..

In 2010, at 78, Leu publishes the novel „The woman even if she is a queen" co-publishing by the Reality Publishing House and „Signs" Publishing House. The memoir volume „Elective affinities", and the novels „ The woman even if she is a queen", „The Islands" and "The novel of a great day" appear in

"Amazon.com" in the US. The novel „Roma-termini" is published by „Virtual Bing-Bang" Publishing House. In 2010 and 2011 – the first 22 volumes from the series „definitive works" and three English translations are distributed through the electronic book network www.corectbooks.com. In February NASA's Solar Dynamics Observatory (SDO) is launched, and the SDO uses various wavelengths to observe the Sun.

Corneliu Leu with his book of soul: "Roma Termini".

In 2011, at 79, Leu publishes a Romanian and contemporary novel "Prosecutor from X...". at the Reality Publishing House. On January 1, Estonia officially adopts the Euro currency and becomes the 17th Eurozone country..[2]

In 2012, at 80, Leu publishes "The church from ether" at the Reality Publishing House, and "The Romanians and the newspaper – about the beginnings of the Romanian press "Realitatea" at the Reality Publishing House. On March 13, after 244 years since its first publication (1768), the *Encyclopedia Britannica* discontinues its print edition.

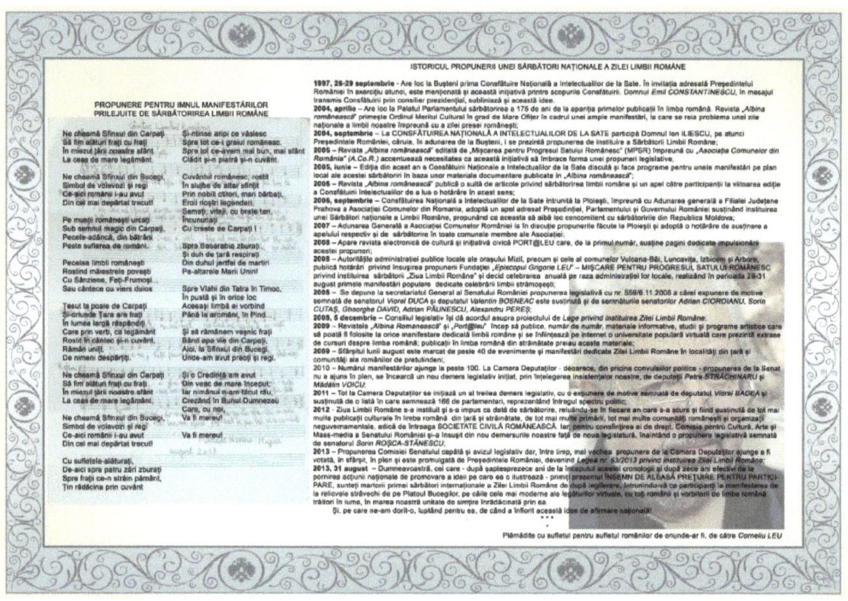

PROPUNERE PENTRU IMNUL MANIFESTĂRILOR
PRILEJUITE DE SĂRBĂTORIREA LIMBII ROMÂNE

Ne cheamă Sfinxul din Carpați
Să fim alături frați cu frați
În miezul țării noastre sfânt
La ceas de mare legământ

Ne cheamă Sfinxul din Bucegi,
Simbol de voievozi și regi
Ce-aici românii i-au avut
Din cel mai depărtat trecut!

Pe munții românești urcați
Sub semnul magic din Carpați,
Pecete-adâncă, din bătrâni
Peste suflarea de români.

Pecetea limbii românești
Rostind măiestrele povești
Cu Sânziene, Feți-Frumoși...
Sau cântece cu viers duios

Țesut la poale de Carpați
Și-oriunde Țara are frați
În lumea largă răspândiți,
Care prin verb, ca legământ
Rostit în cântec și-n cuvânt,
Rămân uniți,
De nimeni despărțiți.

Ne cheamă Sfinxul din Carpați
Să fim alături frați cu frați
În miezul țării noastre sfânt
La ceas de mare legământ,

Ne cheamă Sfinxul din Bucegi,
Simbol de voievozi și regi
Ce-aici românii i-au avut
Din cel mai depărtat trecut!

Cu sufletele-alăturați,
De-aici spre patru zări zburați
Spre frații ce-n străin pământ,
Țin rădăcina prin cuvânt

Și-ntinse aripi ce vâslesc
Spre tot ce-i graiul românesc,
Spre tot ce-avem mai bun, mai sfânt
Clădit și-n piatră și-n cuvânt

Cuvântul românesc, rostit
În slujbe de altar sfințit
Prin nobili ctitori, mari bărbați,
Eroii noștri legendari,
Semeți, viteji, cu brațe tari,
Încununați
Cu creste de Carpați !

Spre Basarabia zburați
Și duh de țară respirați
Din duhul jertfei de martiri
Pe-altarele Marii Uniri!

Spre Vlahi din Tatra în Timoc,
În pustă și în orice loc
Aceeași limbă ei vorbind
Până la aromâni, în Pind...

Și să rămânem veșnic frați
Bând apa vie din Carpați,
Aici, la Sfinxul din Bucegi,
Unde-am avut preoți și regi.

Și o Credință am avut
Din veac de mare început,
Iar nimănui n-am făcut rău,
Crezând în Bunul Dumnezeu
Care, cu noi,
Va fi mereu!

Va fi mereu!

ISTORICUL PROPUNERII UNEI SĂRBĂTORI NAȚIONALE A ZILEI LIMBII ROMÂNE

1997, 28-29 septembrie - Are loc la Bușteni prima Consfătuire Națională a Intelectualilor de la Sate. În invitația adresată Președintelui României în exercițiu atunci, este menționată și această inițiativă printre scopurile Consfătuirii. Domnul *Emil CONSTANTINESCU*, în mesajul transmis Consfătuirii prin consilier prezidențial, subliniază și această idee.
2004, aprilie – Are loc la Palatul Parlamentului sărbătorirea a 175 de ani de la apariția primelor publicații în limba română. Revista *„Albina românească"* primește Ordinul Meritul Cultural în grad de Mare Ofițer în cadrul unei ample manifestări, la care se reia problema unei zile naționale a limbii noastre împreună cu a zilei presei românești;
2004, septembrie – La CONSFĂTUIREA NAȚIONALĂ A INTELECTUALILOR DE LA SATE participă Domnul Ion ILIESCU, pe atunci Președintele României, căruia, în adunarea de la Bușteni, i se prezintă propunerea de instituire a Sărbătorii Limbii Române;
2005 – Revista *„Albina românească"* editată de „Mișcarea pentru Progresul Satului Românesc" (MPSR) împreună cu *„Asociația Comunelor din România" (A.Co.R.)* accentuează necesitatea ca această inițiativă să îmbrace forma unei propuneri legislative,
2005, iunie – Ediția din acest an a Consfătuirii Naționale a Intelectualilor de la Sate discută și face programe pentru unele manifestări pe plan local ale acestei sărbătoriri în baza unor materiale documentare publicate in *„Albina românească"*;
2006 – Revista *„Albina românească"* publică o suită de articole privind sărbătorirea limbii române și un apel către participanții la viitoarea ediție a Consfătuirii Intelectualilor de a lua o hotărâre în acest sens;
2006, septembrie – Consfătuirea Națională a Intelectualilor de la Sate întrunită la Ploiești, împreună cu Adunarea generală a Filialei Județene Prahova a Asociației Comunelor din Romania, adoptă un apel adresat Președinției, Parlamentului și Guvernului României susținând instituirea unei Sărbători naționale a Limbii Române, propunând ca aceasta să aibă loc concomitent cu sărbătoririle din Republica Moldova;
2007 – Adunarea Generală a Asociației Comunelor României ia în discuție propunerile făcute la Ploiești și adoptă o hotărâre de susținere a apelului respectiv și de sărbătorire în toate comunele membre ale Asociației;
2008 – Apare revista electronică de cultură și inițiativă civică PORT@LEU care, de la primul număr, susține pagini dedicate impulsionării acestei propuneri;
2008 – Autoritățile administrației publice locale ale orașului Mizil, precum și cele al comunelor Vulcana-Băi, Luncavița, Izbiceni și Arbore, publică hotărâri privind însușirea propunerii Fundației *„Episcopul Grigorie LEU"* – MIȘCARE PENTRU PROGRESUL SATULUI ROMÂNESC privind instituirea sărbătorii „Ziua Limbii Române" și decid celebrarea anuală pe raza administrației lor locale, realizând în perioada 28-31 august primele manifestări populare dedicate celebrării limbii strămoșești;
2008 – Se depune la secretariatul General al Senatului României propunerea legislativă cu nr. 558/6.11.2008 a cărei expunere de motive semnată de senatorul *Viorel DUCA* și deputatul *Valentin BOSNEAC* este susținută și de semnăturile senatorilor *Adrian CIOROIANU, Sorin CUTAȘ, Gheorghe DAVID, Adrian PĂUNESCU, Alexandru PEREȘ*;
2008, 5 decembrie – Consiliul legislativ își dă acordul asupra proiectului de *Lege privind instituirea Zilei Limbii Române*.
2009 – Revistele *„Albina Romanească"* și *„Port@leu"* încep să publice, număr de număr, materiale informative, studii și programe artistice care să poată fi folosite la orice manifestare dedicată limbii române și se înființează pe internet o universitate populară virtuală care prezintă extrase de cursuri despre limba română; publicații în limba română din străinătate preiau aceste materiale;
2009 – Sfârșitul lunii august este marcat de peste 40 de evenimente și manifestări dedicate Zilei Limbii Române în localități din țară și comunități ale românilor de pretutindeni;
2010 – **Numărul manifestărilor ajunge la peste 100. La Camera Deputaților** - deoarece, din pricina convulsiilor politice - propunerea de la Senat nu a ajuns în plen, se încearcă un nou demers legislativ inițiat, prin înțelegerea insistențelor noastre, de deputații *Petre STRĂCHINARU* și *Mădălin VOICU*;
2011 – Tot la Camera Deputaților se inițiază un al treilea demers legislativ, cu o expunere de motive semnată de deputatul *Viorel BADEA* și susținută de o listă în care semnează 166 de parlamentari, reprezentând întregul spectru politic;
2012 - Ziua Limbii Române s-a instituit și s-a impus ca dată de sărbătorire, reluându-se în fiecare an care s-a scurs și fiind susținută de tot mai multe publicații culturale în limba română din țară și străinătate, de tot mai multe primării, tot mai multe comunități românești și organizații neguvernamentale, adică de întreaga SOCIETATE CIVILĂ ROMÂNEASCĂ. Iar, pentru consfințirea ei de drept, Comisia pentru Cultură, Arte și Mass-media a Senatului României și-a însușit din nou demersurile noastre față de noua legislatură, înaintând o propunere legislativă semnată de senatorul *Sorin ROȘCA-STĂNESCU*;
2013 – Propunerea Comisiei Senatului capătă și avizul legislativ dar, între timp, mai vechea propunere de la Camera Deputaților ajunge a fi votată, în sfârșit, în plen și este promulgată de Președintele României, devenind *Legea nr. 53/2013 privind instituirea Zilei Limbii Române*;
2013, 31 august – Dumneavoastră, cei care - după șaptesprezece ani de la începutul acestei cronologii și după zece ani efectivi de la pornirea acțiunii naționale de promovare a ideii pe care ea o ilustrează - primiți prezentul ÎNSEMN DE ALEASĂ PREȚUIRE PENTRU PARTICIPARE, sunteți martorii primei sărbători internaționale a Zilei Limbii Române de după legiferare, întrunindu-vă ca participanți la manifestarea de la relicvele străvechi de pe Platoul Bucegilor, pe căile cele mai moderne ale legăturilor virtuale, cu toți românii și vorbitorii de limba română trăitori în lume, în marea noastră unitate de simțire înrădăcinată prin ea.
Și, pe care ne-am dorit-o, luptând pentru ea, de când a înflorit această idee de afirmare națională!

* * *

Plămădite cu sufletul pentru sufletul românilor de oriunde-ar fi, de către *Corneliu LEU*

The document showing that Corneliu Leu was the initiator and founder of the Romanian Language Day.

In 2013, at 81, Leu publishes the studies and articles "The Century and the democracy" at the Reality Publishing House, then "On the revolution's altar" at the Reality Publishing House. The novel „Roosevelt, Churchill, Stalin and Hitler – their surprising role.in Eastern Europe in 1944" is published by DERC Publishing House, Boston, Massachusetts, USA. On February 21, American scientists use additive manufacturing to create a living lab-grown ear from collagen and animal ear cell cultures. In the future, it is hoped, similar ears could be grown to order as transplants for human patients suffering from ear trauma or amputation.

At the Museum of Literature, with Corneliu Leu (second from left).

In **2014**, at 82, Leu publishes „The car nr. 13 or the Life like in the movies" – from the series „mysteries from the peaceful town X" – at the Reality Publishing House, also „1,100 pages THE FACTS, THE CENTURY, THE POWER" – at the Reality Publishing House. Florentin Popescu publishes the volume CONVERSATIONS WITH CU CORNELIU LEU - at the Reality Publishing House. On January 1, Latvia officially adopts the euro as its currency and becomes the 18th member of the Eurozone.

Corneliu Leu (right) and Michael Dediu, in 2013.

In **2015**, at 82.5, Leu publishes UNWANTED ANNEXES – mandatory in our earlier life and, sometimes, difficult to avoid even in the present one, that is what joins us through the eye of those who spy on us - RAVEX COMS. On January 1, Lithuania officially adopts the euro as its currency, replacing the litas, and becomes the nineteenth Eurozone country. On January 15, the Swiss National Bank abandons the cap on the franc's value relative to the euro. On March 6, NASA's multi-target orbiter *Dawn* (launched in 2007) enters orbit around Ceres (discovered by Giuseppe Piazzi (1746 – 1826, Italian astronomer) in Palermo, in 1801, is the largest object in the asteroid belt, which lies between the orbits of Mars and Jupiter, 950 km diameter), becoming the first spacecraft to visit a dwarf planet.

Corneliu Leu is married with Rodica, and they have two sons: Vlad and Tudor.

He graduated in Journalism and Foreign Languages.

Let's see now, pour la bonne bouche, a few exciting scientific, medical and technical news:

- experts are trying to reverse-engineer the algorithms of the human brain, by blending data science and neuro science, in attempts to make rapid advances in machine learning and artificial intelligence.

- A new mathematical analysis tool has allowed a deeper understanding of the anatomy of the human head, describing the skull as an extended network structured in 10 modules.

- Researchers have developed a research methodology called Anatomical Network Analysis (AnNA), based on network analysis mathematical tools, for studying anatomy.

- Researchers have developed a statistical technique that sorts out when changes to words' pronunciations most likely occurred in the evolutionary history of related languages. Their model gives researchers a renewed opportunity to trace words and languages back to their earliest common ancestor or ancestors - potentially thousands of years further into prehistory than previous techniques.

- Researchers have achieved the first image fusion of mass spectrometry and microscopy - a technical tour de force that could, among other things, dramatically improve the diagnosis and treatment of cancer. Using a mathematical approach called regression analysis, they mapped each pixel of mass spectrometry data onto the corresponding spot on the microscopy image, to produce a new, predicted image.

This book is connected with a big event, which happens only once per century, for those who use the American style for date: on March 14, 2015 we have 3.14.15 and at 9:26:53; the date/time will correspond to the first 10 digits of the mathematical constant π (pi) = 3.141592653. This is a truly once-in-a-lifetime joyful event for those people lucky enough to be around at this date and time!

Chapter 4. LES GESTES, LE SIÈCLE, LE POUVOIR

LITTERATURE ROUMAINE DEVENANT HISTOIRE EUROPÉENNE DES EXTRÉMISMES DU SIÉCLE PASSÉ ET DE L'EXPÉRIMENT CYNIQUE DU COMMUNISME

12 romans :

« 1100 pages sur LES GESTES d'armes de certains civils pendant LE SIÉCLE des guerres mondiales, ou qu'est-ce que signifie LE POUVOIR »

12 novels :

„1,100 Pages about the HEROIC ACTS of some civilians during the CENTURY of World Wars or what POWER means"

Une série des romans par CORNELIU LEU

Événement littéraire : 12 romans sur LES GESTES, LE SIÈCLE, LE POUVOIR

paru sous cette couverture qui reproduit l'une des typiques peintures proletcultistes d'un auteur mentionné comme « dirigeant politique de la peinture roumaine venu de Moscou et émigré plus tard à l'occident»

At the end of this booklet an ENGLISH INTRODUCTION

En se consacrant, des ses premières livres, comme un auteur des romans historiques ingénieusement construites sur une solide documentation, Corneliu Leu a élargie dans les derniers décennies cette documentation avec la propre expérience sous le régime communiste. Le bien connu auteur roumain a dévoilé les origines ténébreuses de cette idéologie dans les provocations artificielles des services secrètes des grands pouvoirs et des organisations occultes. Ainsi, en donnant toujours une teinte historique à la finesse de l'analyse psychologique des personnages, il évoque de l'intérieur d'une société tombée géopolitiquement sous l'influence et le contrôle bolchevique, le manque de liaison entre ce genre de totalitarisme et les intérêts populaires. La description des destins affectes et la force dramatique des événements qui constituent les actions romanesques démontrent que, de point de vue diachronique le communisme est seulement la forme contemporaine d'un mal permanent qui essaye détruire l'intimité naturelle de la vie humaine. Mais, de point de vue synchronique, se prétendant démagogique à représenter la classe ouvrière, ce communisme ne corresponde ni même aux aspirations de celle-ci.

Ainsi, en polémique avec les fausses motivations révolutionnaires et les expérimentes cyniques auxquels des forces arbitraires ont soumet dans l'histoire l'évolution normale des pays européennes, en cultivant la philosophie d'un bon sens postmoderniste comme permanente aspiration humaine vers une évolution normale, qui refuse les recettes artificielles des intérêts occultes, se développe une dramaturgie attentivement élaborée, en produisant des actions entrelacées avec beaucoup de subtilité métaphorique.

La pénétrante manière d'aborder un tel thème (sur ses profonds aspects de méditation artistique basée sur l'objectivité des réactions humaines en action) de cette série des romans de Corneliu Leu couvre, par les destines typiques des leurs personnages, l'histoire récente du continent : de la beauté d'une *fin de siècle* infiltrée graduellement par les provocations extrémistes, anarchistes et, en fond, militaristes produisant les fissures de sa *belle époque*, aux convulsions des deux guerres mondiales et les effets d'une révolution qui se prétend aussi *mondiale*. Et, dans ce cadre historique, la philosophie appartenant au drame de chaque personnage met l'accent sur les manipulations des intérêts qui essaient dominer l'époque, les malversations politiques, la dégradation de la morale humaine. Ainsi, l'ascension et, après, la chute du pouvoir soviétique dans le monde se transforme dans le symbole du mal qui ne se résume au communisme; c'est la menace d'une agression permanente sur la condition humaine. Agression contre l'intégralité de l'humanisme, ou une vraie religion du mal qui, en but de domination, s'adapte à l'évolution historique comme permanente tentative de dégrader la personne morale en cultivant les caprices de la personne physique.

Plaidoirie contre le crime de *lèse-personne-humaine,* marquée d'une grande force de description et d'expression de la métaphore concernant les injuries envers tout sentiment humaine de liberté, on peut dire que c'est un cycle romanesque marquant pour la première fois dans la prose contemporaine un réquisitoire littéraire, pas seulement du communisme, mais avec des résonances vers tout attaque contre les sincères et naturelles aspirations qui animent les personnes et les communautés humaines du notre monde.

Ces mille pages de prose, écrites de façon artistique originelle, mélangent les drames les plus sensibles à une pensée profonde sur la condition humaine, les événements historiques du « siècle des deux guerres mondiales » à l'analyse psychologique de la personne humaine moderne, les destins de quelques personnages marquants pour l'époque au développement des différentes actions. Tout ceci constitue des sujets différents, inclus dans des morceaux de prose indépendante, qui offre au lecteur une bien choisie satisfaction artistique : chaque titre peut être lu séparément et, en même temps, on le retrouve dans d'autres nouveaux textes, avec les personnages qu'on connaissait déjà. Le parcours des destins est plutôt suggéré que relaté dans une manière classique, évitant la vieille technique littéraire pour laquelle le public contemporain n'est plus patient.

Une manière subtile de suggérer, dans une formule minimaliste, l'évolution des choses et des personnages dans le contexte historique du dernier siècle. Tout cela est décrit fragmenté, comme dans un jeu des vitraux, incitant ainsi l'imagination du lecteur de participer à la reconstitution des faits. Le lecteur moderne, contaminé de « passivité spectatrice », retrouve le plaisir d'antan, à lire les romans de Corneliu Leu et à revivre à coté des personnages de celui-ci. Et ceci se passe de la sorte, parce que la prose moderne de l'auteur offre, par chacun de ses titres, un film, capable de garder vive l'attention du public. Tout son oeuvre incite, grâce aux allégories et métaphores qui y abondent, à la méditation sur la condition humaine et sur les agressions de toute sorte, que l'homme moderne doit vaincre. Telles qualités on fait le signataire d'une chronique littéraire consacrée à un des ces romans d'écrire : « Malgré ses petites dimensions, ce roman mérite au moins deux thèses de doctorat, une en littérature et une en psychologie. Cette bizarre mise sens dessous dessus des perspectives, ce renversement des plans, ce franchissement, voire violation de la logique courante et de la prose traditionnelle, cet anarchique bouleversement des situations, ces changements du tac au tac de personnages et de leurs états d'âme, la belle écriture classique du point de vue du style, d'où est bannie toute vulgarité ou trivialité, font de ce petit livre un grand livre, voire un livre exceptionnel, et nous espérons que la critique de haut vol ne manquera pas l'occasion d'en parler comme il faut. »

De ce point de vue, on peut parler de l'oeuvre de Corneliu Leu, comme d'un premier effet de la philosophie personnaliste, dont il est un connu promoteur, sur la prose des idées qui animent notre époque et même sur la structure du discours romanesque, dans ce présent marqué par plusieurs tentatives antihumaines, de source différente, qui négligent ou même attaquent les libertés de la personne humaine. Ce discours romanesque gagne une telle résonance en deux directions : Premièrement, il touche la sensibilité artistique du lecteur contemporain, préoccupé par son destin et jamais indifférent aux idées qui, quotidiennement, sont exprimées, sans effet artistique, dans les media, en l'éloignant des sens les plus profondes qu'on trouve dans l'art littéraire; deuxièmement, la structure moderne de son roman, qui dépasse ainsi le stage «expérimental», en regagnant les lignes de force, qui caractérisent cette espèce littéraire d'élite, «l'artillerie lourde » de la littérature, avant que le spectateur se plonge dans le plaisir du facile *enterteinement*. Ceci n'est pas au hasard, parce que Corneliu Leu est celui qui, quelques décennies avant, a lancé une nouvelle formule du roman historique, en proposant un espèce de montage présentant en même temps, des fictions ou des faits réels, appartenant aux personnages historiques réels ou imaginaires.

Ainsi, réalisant des romans comme un montage artistique d'insertions de documents réels dans la fiction, ces documents confèrent au texte romanesque plus de réalité et de crédibilité, adressées au lecteur habitué avec le *«non fiction»*.

En prouvant l'efficacité de la formule dans une entière série de romans de thématique antique, médiévale et moderne, qui utilisent de tels insertions bien nuancées, Corneliu Leu présente maintenant, en achevant sa nouvelle série, ses persuasives recherches de renouveler l'architecture du roman et l'expressivité artistique de la prose moderne.

Ceci justifie, peut-être, même le titre presque funambulesque de cette appréciable quantité de prose qui s'est proposée le minimum de pages possibles en comparaison avec les destinées, les sentiments, les méditations, les curiosités, les souffrances, les satisfactions et les effets artistiques qu'elles proposent :

1100 DE PAGINI despre FAPTELE de arme ale unor civili în SECOLUL războaielor mondiale, sau ce înseamnă PUTEREA

Que signifie: **1100 pages sur LES GESTES d'armes de certains civils pendant LE SIÉCLE des guerres mondiales, ou qu'est-ce que signifie LE POUVOIR.**

On peut dire que, la seule chose de manière classique qui est respectée dans ces mille pages, en dehors de la pureté stylistique de l'invention et la fantaisie linguistique, qui caractérisent la composition de la phrase, est la chronologie bien marquée par le premier titre :

« Sur l'autel de la révolution»

C'est l'histoire de la Révolte des paysans roumains dont les plus récents documents prouvent qu'elle a été provoquée par des instigateurs de la police impériale Habsbourgeoise, à la même manière que les autres révolutions nationales ont été provoquées par des services secrets des armées ou des politiques antagoniques, mettant en pratique la méthode de l'export de révolution pour trois siècles des occultes provocations anarchiques dans tout le monde. Placée dans le milieu du journalisme en train de devenir la «quatrième puissance», avec un tendre conte d'amour pour une fille qui touche par son intelligence, l'action décrit, à travers les yeux d'un jeune journaliste en formation, la manière dans laquelle la presse exagère les faits. C'est une allégorie qui avertit, avant la lettre et dans le décor rétro de la fin de siècle, les trucs contemporains, qu'emploient les média pour semer la panique dans la population. Dans la manière de «journal d'un journaliste expatrié» se développe la continuation dramatique du conte d'amour. Une vingtaine d'années de pérégrination à travers l'Europe, où, les guerres et les émeutes font les deux personnages se séparer et se rejoindre. Une panorama d'autres personnages s'impliquant ou souffrant ou arrivant à la déception dans les révolutions qui agitent toute l'Europe, assiégeant, à la fin, en Russie. Où se retrouvent, donc, les deux qui constituent, enfin, une famille ? Cet impressionnant sommet de leur amour se passe dans l'atmosphère «révolutionnaire» qui dénie la famille et toute autre valeur spirituelle qui avait maintenu, jusqu'à présent, leurs sentiments. Et c'est seulement leur admiration réciproque, de la femme pour la complexité des visions de son homme, et de l'homme pour le charme de la monstrueuse intelligence de sa femme, qui leur confère la force de résister dans le milieu toujours menaçant du terrorisme staliniste.

« L'oeil du diable ou que signifie le pouvoir»

Dans une atmosphère des fantasmes balkaniques, correspondant à la période américaine de la conquête de l'Est, se développent les deux tristes expériences de la jeunesse des deux personnages jumelés, deux cousins qui tentent de s'affirmer : L'un devient professeur diplômé et s'inscrit dans un mouvement intellectuel, dirigé par son maître, spiritus-rector, qui est d'un nationalisme modéré, l'autre trouve son chemin dans la gauche syndicale.

« Le barbu incognito»

Apres une grande déception, concernant les compromis politiques de son maître, le professeur se retire de la vie publique, en se dédiant á l'étude et à ses élèves. Il est visité incognito par un mystérieux barbu accompagné par une jeune fille, qui lui propose d'organiser un mouvement populaire des formations sociales et patriotiques, mais refusant les extrémismes lesquelles, soutenues par les pressions étrangères sur la dictature royale, qui étaient en ascension. Celui-ci explique sa manière conspirative d'actionner parce qu'il est un vieux journaliste de gauche, enfui de Moscou où sa femme á été tuée dans les répressions de Staline contre ses critiques de l'internationale communiste. La théorie que le visiteur développe pour obtenir l'adhésion de ce professeur, qui se dit apolitique, est une démonstration historique qui devient la pièce tournante de toute la série, sur la trahison et la manipulation des révolutions de tous les temps, par des intérêts occultes, en suivant, pour des pouvoirs personnels, l'exportation et non l'accomplissement d'une vraie révolution. Hésitant, le professeur écoute les vers révolutionnaires récités par le barbu mystérieux qui se cache de la vengeance staliniste. Et celui-ci continue son chemin main dans la main avec la jeune fille qu'il a adoptée de la famille de sa femme sacrifiée.

« Nuit et Novembre»

Invasion des troupes «alliés» de Hitler. Gouvernement imposé par l'extrême droite, penché sur les crimes politiques. Parmi les adversaires politiques tués, la première victime est l'ancien maître du professeur, le spiritus-rector des modérés. Désolante atmosphère de rébellion, dictature et intolérance dans toute l'Europe, illustrée par les confrontations d'une ville provinciale où sont placés les tanks de Rommel.

« La balle et la pensée »

En passant outre ses vielles désillusions, le professeur, indigné par le crime extrémiste, provoque des réactions dans les milieux démocratiques, ses protestes attirant la vengeance des fascistes qui essayent le transporter dans un camp d'exécution. Son cousin le fait échapper en mobilisant les syndicats et ainsi, la guerre commençant, ils entrent dans une résistance bien intentionnée du point de vue patriotique mais, où se mêlent aussi des provocateurs de l'espionnage soviétique, sous le prétexte des indications de la troisième Internationale Communiste.

« Tête carré ou l'autre face de la médaille »

C'est un des agents du l'NKVD KGB, introduit comme dirigeant imposé par l'Internationale, qui réussit à dévier quelques actions sociales pour des stratégies de l'Armée rouge, provoquant l'emprisonnement des leaders, tandis qu'il s'enfuit en changeant d'identité. Le professeur reste seul avec ses partisans, sans aucune liaison avec le reste du mouvement. Entre-temps, la troisième Internationale supprimée, ses infiltrées se retirent à la centrale de Moscou et, pour un court délai, la gauche roumaine entre dans le mouvement de résistance démocratique. Invité au «centre», le professeur redécouvre le barbu qui l'avait visité autrefois et lui récite des verses révolutionnaires. Celui-ci lui parle d'une collaboration avec les autres parties et le roi, pour un coup d'Etat, en vue d'éloigner la dictature militaire et déclencher une insurrection. Parce que le caractère national de cette insurrection ne convient pas à la stratégie de l'Armée Rouge, qui vient de s'ériger dans la libératrice des peuples, en introduisant leur politique avec les tanks, des actions conjointes de commando NKVD réalisent, avec petites différences de procédure, l'isolation et l'enchaînement sous garde bolchevique des dirigeants du communisme national et, après cette mesure de sureté, l'emprisonnement des dictateurs philo germaniques, en traçant ainsi la route armée qui va imposer leur manière staliniste de mystifier l'idéologie.

« C'est la politique qui commence ! »

La description de qu'est-ce qui se passe dans le cabinet gouvernement où siège le premier ministre intermédiaire, plié aux ordres de Kremlin, explique, dans une certaine mesure, cet occultisme, pendant que le tempérament qui mélange la dictature avec le cynisme idéologique du titulaire de ce cabinet, offre la perspective d'une multiplication de ce type de cabinet et du régime qui est à l'aube. Au niveau des institutions gouvernementales, les actions qui ont provoqué la déroute des vrais travailleurs et le bouleversement des faits à la mairie provinciale, racontées auparavant, on prévoit le gouffre entre les aspirations populaires et la nouvelle classe des «hommes de l'appareil bureaucratique» asservis la dictature, faussement nommée: «prolétaire». Ceci souligne leur caractère toujours militaire, avec une propagande bien enrégimentée et absolument démagogique du point de vue de la foi politique, qui, malheureusement, précède cette espèce de cynisme politique, généralisé dans la démagogie pragmatique contemporaine, en niant la nécessité, ou l'efficacité des doctrines.

« Le pouvoir »

Sauvés par l'insurrection, les leaders échappés de la condamnation capitale sont reconnus comme dirigeants de leur ville portuaire et imposés par une grande manifestation populaire à la mairie. Le gouvernement des technocrates militaires, dont la priorité est la cible des armes vers Berlin, n'échappe pas à une certaine réaction. Parmi les sous-secrétaires existait, déjà, des infiltrés. Retourné de Moscou, celui surnommé «Tête carré» a la mission, dans le staff du Ministère de l'Intérieur, de détourner ce qu'il y est de spontané vers la stratégie générale d'occupation rouge, dissimulée par les accords de Yalta et Téhéran. Ainsi, la Gendarmerie reçoit l'ordre absurde d'occuper la mairie, en obligeant les nouveaux venus la quitter. La déroute et l'état d'absurde se généralisent même pour ceux qui ont à en profiter. La psychologie des tous devient paradoxale. Les commandants des gendarmes ne connaissent pas la source de l'ordre, les extrémistes de la vielle administration les incitent à tuer les résistants, la condamnation capitale menace de nouveau les leaders installés et la foule qui les avait installé ne comprend rien. Les provocations et les manipulations qui sont détectées cachent leurs directions en soulignant l'occultisme de leurs origines. Le suspense d'une anarchie générale domine, tandis que le professeur mobilise les villages des alentours, en isolant les gendarmes qui se retirent dans le brouillard, menaçant tout l'avenir.

« Ca c'est la vie sentimentale »

Le destin d'un homme capable qui, pauvre enfant, fait de grands efforts à s'instruire scientifiquement. Ayant de la présence d'esprit, des manières, celui-ci tente de valoriser la vie dure qu'il est obligé de vivre. Un «carriériste» de bonne qualité, de type Rastignac, qui commence une formation universitaire presque parfaite, détruite d'un seul coup par le commencement de la seconde guerre mondiale, qui le transforme dans un tellurique soldat, condamné aux tranchées où il est blessé et à la vie de caserne, qui n'a pas besoin des ses tentatives de devenir un vainqueur intellectuel. Interrompu, mais pas encore vaincu, il essaye sa chance dans la nouvelle vie civile, marquée par les slogans de la politique révolutionnaire, en adaptant, sans difficultés, ses méthodes cyniques correspondant à la vie dure d'autrefois, pour parvenir parmi les dirigeants politiques communistes. De sang froid, il agit sans scrupules, mais ses désillusions montent et démontre ce qu'on a nommé dans un titre antérieur «l'autre face de la médaille» : Le manque total et même le mépris des valeurs morales qu'il a héritées dans l'ancienne société et devant lesquelles il s'est préparé à les respecter, ou utiliser un vrai et subtile art pour les éluder. Il sent, ainsi, à côté du primitivisme de ceux formés à diriger pour Staline, les «masses prolétaires», les mêmes humiliations qu'il avait vécu dans le tellurisme des tranchées et des casernes. Une flamboyante histoire d'amour avec une étudiante bien éduquée qui le séduit par le charme d'une «monstrueuse intelligence», complète le roman d'un couple d'élite, abandonné par leur destinée dans le monde du carriérisme primitif des «apparatchiks» du parti communiste d'instruction militaire. La surprise de ce roman est la parution du barbu présenté autrefois comme venu incognito chez le professeur, ou en action clandestine pendant la guerre. La jeune femme est aujourd'hui, la fille adoptive de la famille de sa femme après l'exécution de celle-ci et formée par le barbu comme une copie du charme de la «monstrueuse intelligence» de sa toujours regrettée épouse. Pour échapper au KGB qui le chasse de la même manière qu'ils on chassé Trotski et les autres, il vit en clandestinité dans les montagnes, parmi les travailleurs des forets qui ont construit la bibliothèque d'un monastère comme refuge pour ses archives sur la vraie conception de «manu militari» dans le soit disant Parti Communiste, en démontrant l'impossibilité d'une vision démocratique dans ce mouvement et ses antagonismes avec les intérêts de la classe ouvrière.

« Le temps de la liberté de s'exprimer »

Pendant les premières années du gouvernement communiste, engagés dans la construction socialiste, le professeur et son cousin ont des fonctions au niveau des préfectures, le dernier devenant même chef dans une région. Quand le régime s'établie par la consolidation des pays satellites de Moscou, incommode par sa pensée moins doctrinaire, mais son vieux stage de leader syndical ne permettant pas d'être éloigné, celui-ci est congédié de l'exécutif pour une importante fonction formelle á l'étranger. Le professeur avec sa pensée libre, qui a dérangé plusieurs fois les «disciplinés» de la commande de mentalité militariste, dévient, ainsi, un suspect par sa pensée à la bourgeoise. Il sera sanctionné à la fin et impliqué dans un des dossiers contrefaits qui l'accusait de favoriser l'ennemi de classe. On le retrouve, à la fin, déporté dans un camp, accablé par la mort de sa femme et l'état psychologique déprimant dans lequel tombe leur fils adolescent.

« Le politruque »

C'est le surnom que le professeur gagne dans le camp où sont emprisonnés, condamnés juridiquement ou en détention abusive, des milliers de personnes de toute catégorie politique. Ce sont, soit des représentants de la lutte de classe, des ennemis, publics ou soupçonnés de communisme ou appartenant au perfide slogan : ceux qui ont «nui aux libertés du peuple». Il est surnommé ainsi en reconnaissant sa culture marxiste et matérialiste dialectique. Même le commandant, expérimenté flic dans son comportement d'une extrême et insensible placidité, le respecte quand ils discutent en secret. Tandis que les simples gardiens, cruels et abusives d'habitude, ont peur de dévoiler devant lui des rituels religieux, qu'ils ont gardé et que leurs instincts les font se dévoiler devant d'autres prisonniers. La vue panoramique de la faune de ce champ fait de toute sorte de victimes possibles dans le communisme : ennemis, anciens alliés, simples soupçonnés, possibles adversaires des dirigeants, même innocents et leurs propres membres, se fait des deux perspectives : La fenêtre étagée du cabinet d'où surveille l'oeil placide du commandant, et l'observation fiévreuse, face à face et souffrant la peine commune, du professeur. De temps à autre, criminelles disparitions ou douteux suicides, qui, étrangement, après la mort de Staline, se multiplient. À ce moment, le professeur découvre des intimités maladives du commandant qui reconnaît son comportement brutal par le désir de ne penser à rien tandis que, bénéficiant de sa sélection comme ouvrier fidèle au Parti, est arrivé à un salaire assez important. Mais, les exagérations des ceux qui ont multiplié les crimes pour effacer leurs propres abus de l'époque staliniste, l'ont indigné, en troublant sa placidité. Le professeur comprend ainsi l'ascension de celui surnommé autrefois «tête carré» et est sauvé par isolation au secret. Dans cette terrible isolation, le professeur découvre un paralysé qui ressemble au barbu d'autrefois. Mais celui-ci refuse catégoriquement à reconnaître ceci, en se prétendant un moine accusé d'avoir favorisé un autre, un très chassé personnage qui a disparu. Et le moine insiste sur cette disparition en suggérant que personne n'a pas eu la satisfaction de trouver le chassé pour le livrer au Staline... Mais, quand il est en train de rendre son âme, en s'élevant de sa paralysie, il récite les connus vers révolutionnaires.

« Les blessures des soldats vainqueurs »

Le survivant de cette catégorie des personnages est l'ancien leader syndical et dirigeant dans les premières années de la construction socialiste. En se retournant de la haute fonction internationale avec laquelle il a été en même temps récompensé et exilé, isolé et oublié, il se sent comme un sommet entouré du néant dans lequel ils ont disparu tous ceux qui ont vécu et lutté autour de lui et, en n'ayant pas d'héritiers directs, s'intéresse de ce qu'est est devenu l'enfant du professeur et, à la suite, d'un autre proche, un enthousiaste combattant qu'il a formé. Ainsi, il commence un périple dans la région où il s'est affirmé autrefois et qu'il a gouverné vers «le rêve d'or du communisme». Mais, d'une perspective objective, il constate la destruction de son idéal. Reconstituant la décadence morale de la société qu'il a eu l'impression de servir, en se considérant son soldat vainqueur, il se sent un vaincu dont les blessures ne pourront jamais guérir. Ces sont les douze titres qui composent ce millier de pages de prose dense, par gestes et aventures, par étude psychologique et débat sur la condition humaine, par histoires d'amour et destinées dramatiques, en tentant en permanence une solution romanesque moderne pour dépasser le stade d'une simple reconstitution et pour devenir, par son contenu allégorique, un permanent à propos

de la contemporanéité. On peut dire, même, en évaluant le talent moraliste de l'auteur : Un avertissement à la philosophie politique du cynisme contemporain, argumenté avec beaucoup d'art et de fantaisie.
En usant de tels échos sentimentaux, paraboles dans la construction de l'action, allusions dans l'invention artistique et méditation sur lės possibles parallélismes dans le temps, Corneliu Leu continue, par ce considérable ouvrage, l'expérience novatrice de son cycle des romans historiques, en perfectionnant l'incitante formule de roman métaphore, dont l'action se passe dans un temps historique, mais avec son discours tout á fait contemporain.

AN ENGLISH INTRODUCTION

As part of the ***Corneliu Leu definitive*** works, these twelve books make up the cycle ***1,100 Pages about the Heroic Acts of some civilians during the Century of World Wars or what Power means***.

On the Altar of the Revolution is, in chronological reading order, the first. The other eleven books are: ***Devil's Eye or What the Power Means**, **The Bizarre Incognito**, **Night and November, The Bullet and the Thought, Square Head or the Obverse of the Medal,The Politics Begin, The Power, This Sentimental Life, Time for Free Speech, Political Activist (or The Propagandist), The wounds of Victors.***

A symbolic novel that describes how the Austro-Hungarian imperial police infiltrated among the Romanian peasants and incited them to the 1907 revolts, *On the Altar of the Revolution* alludes to the contemporaneous instigations of the Soviet Union's and other secret services' spies that led to the 1989 Romanian revolts. Likewise, by taking the book's main character through the inner circles of illustrious personalities of the day, like Mussolini, Lenin, to Rockefeller, Trotzky and others, all while unveiling their forsaking of their ideals for the purpose of exporting the revolution, the author suggests a parallel with the contemporaneous Bilderberg group and other similar, assumed components of the "occult" that lead from behind the scenes the political destiny of humankind.

The first chapter, "the mission of the superpowers", is actually the history of the 1907 Romanian peasants revolt that new evidence reveals was triggered by instigators from the Habsburg police. This strategy of exporting a revolution and provoking anarchy had been employed for at least the last 300 years by various secret services belonging to different armies or to antagonistic politics, and materialized in many prior or subsequent revolutions. The author proposes a new interpretation of the period's history, by finding a common denominator between the autocratic emperor Frantz Joseph and the revolution's advocate Karl Marx: both are master-minds of exporting anarchy in different countries, for the purpose of domination. The emperor adopts Karl Marx's concept of exporting revolution, concept used by the British secret services, and implements it in his own expansion strategy.

Anchored in the world of press at the time when it was solidifying its role as the fourth power in the state, and following a tender love story that extends the dreams of youth into the destiny of an intelligent, clear-minded couple, the novel reveals, through the eyes of a rooky journalist, how the press manipulated and was manipulated to exacerbate and/or distort the facts. It is an allegory that warns, "avant la lettre" and set in the retro décor of the end of the XIX century-beginning of the XX, of present day practices of using the mass media to instigate and to induce panic among population.

Another section of the novel describes the European continent affected by the political turmoil preceding the fall of the empires shortly before WWI, but from a different perspective than commonly accepted interpretation of the events; the same light is shed on prior revolutions and on the Sarajevo coup which is supposed to have triggered the conflagration.

While the story takes the reader through several countries of the old continent that had been shaken by social unrest for over a decade, it concurrently follows the dramatic development of the love story. This emotional saga of love and dedication is remarkable by the subtle description of what becomes an allegory of the birth and endurance of the most defining human sentiments. The romantic spontaneity of the genuine love at first sight is marked, in time, by the tragic fate of the classical symbols, as they are touched by the "occult" that resonates even in the modern novelistic characters. In the last part of the book the two lovers, having endured and survived the vicissitudes of the wars and revolts that separated them, unexpectedly reunite in the fledgling Soviet Union, along with others that are either active participants in the revolution or victims thereof.

The climax of their love story is set in the midst of the absurd dictatorial suspicions, the leftist exaggerations, the destruction of the family and spiritual values – the very values that kept their love alive. And only their mutual admiration – woman's for the complexity of her man's visions and aspirations, and man's for his woman's charismatic sensibility and intelligence – is what gives them the strength to surmount the Stalinist terrorism which is threatening their lives and which overtly proceeds to eliminate its opponents.

Couverture d'un autre cycle de l'auteur :
LES ROMANS HISTORIQUES

Le chemin vers Damas
Le bon voisin
Le bourreau de Dracula
L'anonyme des Brancovans
Le roman d'un nuit de février
La femme même reine

The Bucegi Mountains and part of the town Poiana Tapului, in front of Corneliu Leu's window.

Chapter 5. DER BEHAARTE, INCOGNITO

von Corneliu Leu

Übersetzung: Dr. Gabriela Căluţiu Sonnenberg

Lektorierung: Mag. A Elke Barbara Müller

1.

Valentinas altes, von ihren Eltern vererbte Haus war der Grund warum sie und Alexe, zwei arme und fleißige Studenten, die bei ihren Lehrern an der Uni als Tutoren sehr geschätzt waren, am Ende doch auf die akademische Laufbahn verzichteten und in die Provinz gingen, wo sie immerhin unter einem sicheren Dach leben konnten, ohne jemandem einen Groschen Miete zu schulden.

Das Haus verkam, da die Alten sehr früh verstorben waren, noch ehe sie ihre Tochter als Ärztin erleben konnten. Doch die beiden legten Hand an und wenn auch langsam, sie renovierten es gründlich. In der kleinen Gemeinde sprach sich diese gute Nachricht schnell um. Sie waren fleißig und zuverlässig und so kam es, dass bald die Bauern morgens, noch vor ihrem Gang zum Viehmarkt, gleich ihre Kranken mitsamt Geschenken, in Form von fetten Hühnern, an den Beinen zusammengebundene, sonstige gefiederte Tiere, beziehungsweise ein Maß Maismehl, Eier oder ein Käselaib mitbrachten. Auch die ferne Verwandtschaft bekam ihren Anteil und wurde obendrauf von Valentina medizinisch behandelt, umsonst, denn sie hatte nicht vergessen, dass sie durch viele von ihnen während ihrer Studienzeit unterstützt wurde.

Der Zaun war immer noch derselbe wie früher, üppig überwuchert von Jasmin und Klette, genau so wie zu jener Zeit, als sie zusammen mit dem jungen Drăgan gesehen wurde, der damals noch auf der Suche nach Arbeit war. Ähnlich erging es auch der Pforte, die später, beim Ertönen eines dem Stargesang nachempfundenen Pfiffes, sie nach draußen rief. Die Ellbogen auf den Zaun abgestützt hörte sie ihm nachdenklich zu und ihr Gesicht zeigte mehr Weisheit und Treue als Liebe. Lediglich das

schicke, emaillierte Schild mit der Bezeichnung „Doktor Valentina Alexe" vermittelte den heimlichen Stolz von zwei ehemals armen Kindern, die in der großen Universitätsstadt auf den Ruhm einer akademischen Karriere verzichtet hatten, um eben hier ein bescheidenes, ehrliches Leben zu führen. Denn Valentinas Gründlichkeit machte die Runde, vor allem bei Prüfungen, während Alexe, abgesehen von seiner Tutorenstelle beim großen, legendären Geschichteprofessor, auch die Studentengruppe der fortgeschrittenen Partei führte, in dessen Kreise er mit den gewagtesten, emanzipiertesten Persönlichkeiten und erstklassigsten Intellektuellen Ideen austauschte.
Dafür ersann er nun in ganz eigener Manier persönliche Rache. Er wandelte seinen ganzen Frust in Arbeit um, indem er sich beim Hausrenovieren so richtig rein kniete und austobte, denn natürlich machte er alles selbst. Ja, er half sogar dem Meister beim Bau seiner makellosen, weißen, mit großen Fenstern versehenen Praxis. Innerhalb von zwei Jahren gelang es ihm, sämtliche Lehrer, Agronomen, Verwalter und Beamte der Umgebung in eine ordentliche Gruppe zusamme zu bringen, die ihrem Rang als sich als Apostel verstehende Intellektuelle durchaus Ehre machte. Nicht einmal die alltäglichen Sorgen und auch nicht die Geburt seines Sohnes vermochten es, seine Aufmerksamkeit von den wichtigen Zielen der höheren Ebene abzuziehen. So war es auch nicht verwunderlich, dass eben der berühmte Professor ihm die Ehre erwies, auf der Taufe seines Sohnes als Pate zu erscheinen, denn es herrschte eine Selbstverständlichkeit unter ihnen vor, die keineswegs an unverdientes Emporkommen denken ließ. Gestützt auf ihre ehrliche Denkweise, auf Bildung und Moral, wuchs auch der gute Ruf seiner Organisation. Die Bürger schauten zu ihm hoch, seine entschlossene Art die Ideale der Agrarpartei (rum. *Partidul* Sămănătorist) auf die Bedürfnisse der Bauern anzuwenden und die Tatsache, dass er selbst dem bescheidenen Umfeld derselben entsprungen war, schafften Vertrauen. Natürlich gab es viele Genossen innerhalb von reicheren, aktiveren Parteien, die sich über ihn lustig machten. Als gestandene Geschäftsleute, die ihren obskuren Aktivitäten in der durchaus glamouröseren Grauzone der Gesellschaft nachgingen und diese gern als politische Raffinesse oder Wahlvorteile weiterverkauften, verschmähten

diese ihn und seine Parteigenossen, doch das interessierte ihn herzlich wenig.
Es war dies auch eine Genugtuung für die beiden Dorfintellektuellen, die es immerhin geschafft hatten, nachdem sie in einfachen, perspektivelosen Umständen aufgewachsen waren, sich aus eigener Kraft nach oben zu verdienen. Ihre einzige Chance hatten sie genutzt und, als sie alleine auf der Welt geblieben waren, bestärkten sie sich gegenseitig weiter und lernten begierig und trotzig immer mehr dazu. Inmitten einer vielfältigen und feindlichen Umgebung schafften sie es jedes Mal aufs Neue, selbst dann wenn die Situation hoffnungslos erschien und ihre Ressourcen praktisch erschöpft waren. Am stärksten war jedoch das Gefühl des Zusammenhalts, die unglaubliche Kraft ihrer jungen Liebe, die sie schon als Teenager zusammenschweißt hatte. Nur dieser Liebe hatten sie die Tatsache zu verdanken, dass sie die härtesten Prüfungen heil überstanden hatten und an solchen Stellen Fuß fassten, wo sie spürten dass sie es zu etwas bringen konnten, wo sie aus sich etwas machen konnten. Dieses Gefühl ist bei armen, intellektuellen Paaren gar nicht selten; oft werden sie für ihr Leben dadurch geprägt, denn es schafft eine echte Kommunikation, die sie zu einer fast geschlossenen, unglaublich festen Einheit wachsen lässt, deren eigentlicher Halt im absoluten, bedingungslosen Vertrauen liegt.
Auf dieser Weise besaß Alexe im Umgang mit den Menschen eine gewisse Ausstrahlung, die sich in aufmerksamen, ausgeglichenen Gesten äußerte, eine Art, die nur durch festen Halt in der Familie zu erreichen möglich ist; Valentina, mit zierlicher Gestalt und ernster Miene, strahlte eine ähnliche Ruhe aus, denn sie spürte an ihrer Seite die Schulter eines rechtschaffenen Mannes, an dessen Entwicklung sie persönlich mitgewirkt hatte. Dazu kam, dass er mit ihr intim verbunden war, so dass sie fast das Gefühl hatte, als wären die beiden auf ewig füreinander vorbestimmt. Alles beruhte auf ihren gemeinsamen Erfahrungen und auf der Tatsache, dass sie, ganz allein auf sich selbst gestellt, immer zusammen gehalten hatten.
Ihre Suche war ein gemeinsames Unterfangen, denn das, was er unter den Männern tat, bewirkte sie bei den Frauen. Jene waren verschwiegen und scheu, so wie es am Lande üblich ist, doch ihre Hilfe nahmen sie gerne entgegen. In ihrer Rolle als Ehefrau, enge

Vertraute, Partnerin und beste Freundin ihres Mannes erfüllte sie ganz selbstverständlich und ohne darauf herum zu reiten die Rolle der modernen Frau.

Genau diese Eigenschaft seiner Frau half ihm ganz besonders, als er die große Enttäuschung mit der Partei des Professors einstecken musste. Den damals, in dem Krisenjahr, nach dem politischen Umsturz, als der König Karl seinen Sohn und dessen Regenten wegfegte um sich selbst auf den Thron zu katapultieren – zugegeben, er machte es auf einer etwas abenteuerliche Art – war noch nicht voraussehbar, dass er sich später als Diktator entpuppen sollte. Um ein Zeichen zu setzen und als Warnung an die Politiker bildete er eine neue Regierung. Und er war schlau genug, um berühmte Persönlichkeiten in sein Boot zu holen, wie zum Beispiel den bereits legendären Professor für Geschichte, den er kurzerhand zum Premierminister machte.

Ob der König davon profitiert hat bleibt umstritten, aber ganz sicher erfuhr Alexes′ Anerkennung sozusagen einen heftigen Aufschwung unter diesen neuen Umständen. Die lokalen Intellektuellen hatten jetzt, plötzlich, nach langer Unterdrückung und Demütigung vonseiten der kleinbürgerlichen Krämerklasse, einen neuen Helden. Alle sahen in ihm schon den zukünftigen Bürgermeister, wenn nicht sogar etwas noch noch Größeres, jemanden auf höherer Kreisebene. Das Unheil war aber leider, dass, bedingt durch die Eigenheiten der frisch gebildeten Koalition, der lokale Verwaltungskreis ausgerechnet der Gegenpartei zugeteilt wurde, einer Partei, die kein Interesse an Studentenwählern zeigte, sondern eher dem Metzgerbaron zugeneigt war.

Darüber verlor Alexe kein Wort. Er wurde lediglich stiller, trauriger. Man konnte förmlich sehen wie ihn düstere Gedanken umkreisten. Misstrauisch, reizbar, benahm er sich wie ein beleidigter Mensch, dessen tiefste Gefühle enttäuscht wurden. Seinem Mitstreiter erklärte er wortkarg, dass er sich ab sofort nicht mehr mit Politik befassen wolle. Nur Valentina kannte ihn gut genug, um das Ausmaß seiner Enttäuschung zu erahnen. Als ihr bewusst wurde, wie sehr er sich quälte, nahm sie den Zug und erschien an der Tür des geliebten Mentors in der Großstadt, samt vorschriftsmäßiger Beigabe, so wie man es von anständigen Verwandten aus der Provinz erwartet.

Als sie zurückkehrte, umarmte sie ihn ganz lange und teilte ihm mit, dass er Recht behalten hatte. Das war das einzige was sie tat, während sie sanft sein Gesicht streichelte. Sie schämte sich, ihm zu sagen, dass der Professor ihm mitteilen ließ, in der Politik müsse man viel Geduld haben. Anders gesagt, viel schlimmer als die pathetischen politischen Reden, die der Professor in kleinen, privaten Kreisen zu halten pflegte, war die Feststellung, dass selbst er, als stark bewunderter Held in die Knie gezwungen wurde und sich seine eigene Ohnmacht angesichts der politischen Machschaften eingestehen musste. Er hatte sich auf die Gegnerseite geschlagen besiegt vom verdorbenen System und machte dazu noch einen tiefen Knicks vor dem doch so bösartigen König.

Valentinas Umarmung nahm einfach kein Ende, denn damit zeigte Alexe wie ihr Zweigespann, trotz unbarmherziger, widrigster Umständen immer stabiler und stärker wurde, ausgehärtet von den argen Witterungen des Lebens. Ihre vollkommene Einheit gewann dadurch mehr Halt, denn diese Schicksalsschläge kamen ja von außen, sie waren eigentlich nur weitere Proben, die ihre Liebe auf den Prüfstand setzten, überhaupt gar nicht wichtig genug, um ernst genommen zu werden.

Alexe war ein sturer Agnostiker, der sich gern mit Atheismus-Demonstrationen befasste, manchmal nur deshalb, um sich selbst zu beweisen, dass er mit seinen intellektuellen Ambitionen immer noch die Kleinlichkeit des Alltags Anderer, die es besser als er im Leben hatten, besiegen konnte. Also bedankte er sich nicht einmal beim lieben Gott für das wunderbare Geschenk, eine derart liebe- und verständnisvolle bessere Hälfte geschenkt bekommen zu haben. Aber er fand Zuflucht im warmen Nest seiner Familie, von Liebe umgeben, so dass selbst er, als purer Rationalist, sich gezwungen sah zu gestehen, dass ihr Vertrauen zueinander fast religiöse Züge aufwies. Ihre geheimnisvolle Einheit gewann enorm an Bedeutung, denn sie schöpften immer mehr Kraft aus der Quelle des intellektuellen Bündnisses, das sie so stolz machte. Es war ihr einziger und alleiniger Verdienst, diese Vollkommenheit erreicht zu haben.

2.

Der Mann, den Valentina eintreten ließ, nachdem sie ihm das Tor aufgehalten hatte, strahlte etwas Beeindruckendes aus; seine Haltung war irgendwie stolz, aber auch eigenartig zurückhaltend. Er trug Kleider von guter Qualität, aber sie waren ein klein wenig abgewetzt.

„Was soll dieser Behaarte da?“ – fragte sich Alexe, als er Valentinas unerklärliche Aufregung und Begeisterung registrierte, eine Herzlichkeit die er sonst bei ihr nur in bestimmten Fällen erlebte, wenn sie etwas Erfreuliches ankündigte.

„Hier ist jemand für dich!“

Und, obwohl der Mann in einem sehr gemäßigten Ton sprach, konnte man die bestimmenden Akzente in seinen Worten erkennen:

„Ich heiße Anton Celaru, mein Herr, und ich bin absichtlich an diesem Bahnhof ausgestiegen um sie zu treffen! ...“

Gewiss klang sein Name recht beeindruckend, vor allem wenn er ihm durch seine klangvolle Stimme Audruck verlieh, doch Alexe konnte seinen ersten Eindruck nicht loswerden, nämlich den, dass es sich hier um einen recht behaarten, wilden Sonderling, vielleicht auch um einen Vagabunden, handeln konnte. Also beließ er es beim „Haarigen” und schaute ganz interessiert auf seinem weichen, krausen Vollbart, der einer faltigen, von Unruhen gezeichneten Wange entsprang, die ihn entfernt an seinen Cousin Drăgan erinnerte.

„Als ich sie mit Valentina kommen sah“ – sprach er und meinte damit die ungewöhnliche Freundlichkeit, die er bei seiner Frau gespürt hatte – dachte ich es handele sich um einen meiner Neffen, der auch so eine, hm… Ausstrahlung hat.

„Eine wilde Ausstrahlung, nicht wahr!“ – erwiderte der Fremde amüsiert: „Sie meinen wohl den Drăgan, oder nicht?!“

„Sie kennen ihn?“

„Nicht persönlich; aber gehört habe ich von ihm... Ich weiß, also... So wie ich auch von Ihnen gehört habe!“

Bereits angezogen befand sich Valentina eigentlich auf dem Weg zum Krankenhaus, doch sie kehrte noch einmal zurück ins Haus und legte ihre Tasche weg. Wohlgemerkt kein schickes Accessoire, sondern um ihren „Werkzeugkoffer“ handelte es sich, denn er enthielt alles, was man für dringende Notfälle braucht. Dann widmete sie ihre Aufmerksamkeit dem Mädchen, welches sich in Begleitung des Haarigen befand. Liebevoll wie eine Mutter half sie ihm aus dem Oberkleid und begleitete es ins Nachbarzimmer, wo der kleine Paul auf seinem Hochsitz am Tisch saß. Mit Lätzchen um den Hals gebunden wartete der Kleine darauf, dass ihm sein Vater die Butter aufs Brot schmierte. Es war der Tag, an dem der Vater dran war, was dem Kleinen sehr gefiel, denn an solchen Tagen saßen sie unter sich wie anständige Männer und er aß aufrichtig alles auf, wie es sich gehört, ohne, wie bei seiner Mutter, zu quengeln.

Die Ankunft des Behaarten um diese fast heilige Stunde störte die Familienidylle; Valentina, auf ihrem Weg aufgehalten, agierte instinktiv nach dem Muster der selbstverständlichen Gastfreundschaft, welches ihr im Blut lag, übermittelt von Generation zu Generation. Sie streichelte den Kopf des Mädchens, um ihr die Scheu zu nehmen und platzierte sie am Tisch vor Alexes´ Gedeck, ihrem Sohn gegenüber.

„Es ist sehr gut so“ vertrieb sie die Zurückhaltung des Mädchens „ schau nur wie er sich freut, dass du mit ihm zusammen isst. Ich freue mich, ja, das freut mich sehr“ brabbelte der Kleine in sein Lätzchen.

Alexe versuchte nicht einmal sein stolzes, väterliches Lächeln zu verbergen und blickte etwas überrascht zu dem Mädchen hinüber, das sich unter Valentinas liebevoller Betreuung sehr wohl zu fühlen schien.

„Das ist meine Nichte. Sie hat das Schuljahr mit „hervorragend” abgeschlossen. Als Belohnung nehme ich sie jetzt mit in die Ferien ans Schwarze Meer und dann fahren wir noch eine Runde durchs Land; so sind wir auch bei Ihnen hier angelangt“ meinte der Behaarte so, als ob er sich erklären müsste „Ich, in der letzten Zeit...“

Doch, als ob sie die guten Schwingungen gespürt hätte, näherte sich Valentina mit zwei Kaffees und meinte locker, ihrer weiblicher Intuition folgend:

„Ach, lassen Sie das; trinken Sie erst einmal was und nachher können sie sich in Ruhe unterhalten. Wegen Paul machen Sie sich bitte keine Sorgen; schauen Sie nur, wie er vor Freude regelrecht aufblüht!“

Durch die offene Tür konnte man das Mädchen sehen, die sich Valentinas Art kleine Butterbrote aufzuschmieren und aneinander wie Zinnsoldaten anzureihen schon angeeignet hatte und fleißig weitermachte; der Bub lachte glücklich. Wie beiläufig, nebenbei, bemerkte Alexe erneut und mit Freude die Gabe seiner Frau, die einfachsten alltäglichen Aufgaben in kleine Festgesten zu wandeln. Sie tat dies mit einer Hingabe, die alles um sie herum in ein warmherziges, fast heiliges Licht tauchte, und das sogar dann, wenn Fremde in der Nähe waren.

3.

„Also, selbst wenn sie meinen Cousin nicht persönlich kennen, sie wissen schon welche Denkweise er vertritt“ versuchte Alexe das Gespräch weiter zu knüpfen und nebenbei merkte er, dass sein Gegenüber doch wesentlich kleiner war so wie es sein erster Eindruck gewesen war. Wenn er nicht diese freche Räuberhaltung gehabt hätte, könnte man ihn leicht in der Menge übersehen, dachte er sich. Er war kein Riese, wie Drăgan, aber durch seine unglaubliche, wirre Mähne, durch die Art wie er seinen reich verzierten Schafsfellrock auf den Schultern trug und die provozierende Pose, die er offensichtlich gerne einnahm, flößte er Respekt ein, vielleicht mehr als sein Cousin. Es war, als ob er unentwegt etwas zu verteidigen hätte, immer bereit dazu, einem unsichtbaren, vermeintlichen Feind schlagfertig Paroli zu bieten. So kam auch sofort die Antwort auf Alexes´ Frage wie aus einem Gewehr geschossen.

„Eben das ist es, Herr Lehrer, dass ich ihn kenne und von ihm vieles gehört habe, doch weiß ich immer noch nicht genau was er im Schilde führt, obwohl ich mir das sehnlichst wünsche!“

„Und Sie sind zu mir gekommen, um das zu erfahren“ stellte Alexe fest und machte sich daran, ihn auf eine kleine Enttäuschung vorzubereiten. Dann erwähnte er die etwas abgekühlte Beziehung, die er schon immer zu seinem Cousin hatte, von der Zeit an, als dieser in verschiede Gerichtsverfahren involviert war, als die Leute vom Hafen offen rebellierten und hingingen, um ihn zu verteidigen. Ihn, Alexe, hatte er immer zur Seite geschoben, als ob sein Cousin ihn für irgendetwas Ungewisses bestrafen wolle.

„Nein, hierher bin ich gekommen, um in erster Linie Sie kennen zu lernen. Ich will auf Tuchfühlung gehen, denn ich bin der Meinung, dass Sie ein Patriot sind“ kam genau so unerwartet die

Antwort aus dem vom dicken Schnurrbart überwucherten Mund, begleitet von heftigem Ein- und Ausatmen, genauso wie das aufwühlende Wesen seines Trägers.
„Sie halten Drăgan nicht für einen Patrioten?“ unterbrach er die Logik der Diskussion; aber es gelang ihm nicht, den Anderen zu provozieren, denn man konnte schon erahnen, dass er ein ganz klares Konzept verfolgte und kaum erwarten konnte, es zu erläutern:
„Ich könnte Drăgan zu meinen Fittichen zählen, wenn ich wüsste ob ich selbst einer von ihnen bin. Aber ich hatte nicht die Gelegenheit, seine Bekanntschaft zu machen, mein Herr, weil ich bis vor einigen Jahren im Ausland war, und seitdem ich zurück bin steckt er in diesem Prozess fest... „ Plötzlich schien er sich selbst zu trösten: Na ja, er hat seine Leute, die Gewerkschaften, die ihn stützen. Ich habe mich zurück ins Land geschlichen, lieber Herr und ich suche die Nähe der Menschen, die mit mir etwas gemeinsam haben, Menschen mit denen ich was Neues beginnen kann... Stattdessen, in dieser Bewegung, wo Alles Allen gehört und geteilt wird, gibt es viel zu viele Diversionen, die ich den Leuten erklären müsste, sie informieren und auf dem Laufenden halten...
„Sie sprechen von Drăgans Bewegung?“
Der Mann erhob sich abrupt, ging zum Arbeitstisch, wo Alexe für gewöhnlich entweder las, Kontrollarbeiten korrigierte oder sich Notizen machte und richtete seinen Zeigefinger demonstrativ auf ein Titelblatt, nachdem er die anderen Bücher zur Seite schob. Es war klar, dass ihm der Roman bekannt war, denn er erkannte ihn alleine vom flüchtigen Blick auf die Kante.
„Ich sehe, Sie haben hier „Die Beichte eines Besiegten” von Panait Istrati, deswegen erlaube ich mir, Ihnen direkt ins Gesicht zu sagen: ich weiß nicht, ob es sich hier noch um eine Bewegung oder um etwas Anderes handelt. Die Sache hat sich gespalten; es sind schmerzhafte Teile über, die nie wieder richtig zusammengefügt wurden. Alles wächst in absurdem Maße, nimmt eine Gestalt an, die ich am liebsten korrigieren möchte“ sprach er und stöhnte, bewusst seinen Atem zügelnd. Dann protestierte er lauthals: „Weil nicht einmal Sie an das gute Ziel glauben, mein Herr; nur zu gerne möchte ich wissen, ob Drăgan versteht warum ich die landesinternen Probleme so betone und

nicht die internationale Komponente!... Ich habe da ein paar ernste Bedrohungen erkannt, mein Herr..."

So seltsam wie sie gekommen war, ebbte sich die aufgebrauste Stimmung wieder. Aus unerklärlichem Grunde war der Haarige auf einmal sehr böse über das, was er zu sagen hatte, was Alexe wiederum zu einer weiteren Frage veranlasste:

„Und ich, wie kann ich Ihnen dabei helfen, wo sie mich mit dem Patriotismus so durchbohren?"

Der Mann blätterte das Buch durch, seine Aufmerksamkeit aber war auf seine eigenen Gedanken ausgerichtet:

„Sie haben ein Recht, mich danach zu fragen, denn ich befürchte, dass Sie dieses Buch auf völlig andere Art als Drăgan deuten; und ich sollte die Dinge hier nicht durcheinander bringen. Also, ich frage nach Patriotismus, weil ich nur schwer begriffen habe, dass ich eigentlich ein Patriot bin. Vielleicht bin ich sogar ein Nationalist, was ich nicht gewesen bin als ich das Land verließ, eben um als Internationalist zu fungieren. Aber meine Frau wurde in Russland umgebracht, mein Herr, von Stalin. Wir haben dort zusammen gearbeitet, auf der Dritten Internationale. Wir waren die Vertreter der Cristescu-Plăpumaru-Partei, falls Ihnen das bekannt klingt. Warum wir uns nicht mit Anderen vermischten, die auf anderen Wegen gekommen waren, werden Sie gleich verstehen; vielleicht besser als Drăgan, der, ich mag es so zu glauben, wahrscheinlich Beziehungen zu ihnen pflegt. Darum sehe ich mich gezwungen zu riskieren, den Leuten reines Wasser einzuschenken."

„Das tut mir leid – erwiderte Alexe und ihm dämmerte es langsam, worum es da eigentlich ging „ich habe das Gespräch auf Drăgan gerichtet, da er mein Cousin ist. Aber glauben Sie mir bitte, wir müssen uns nicht unbedingt über ihn unterhalten... Im Grunde weiß ich nicht, ob ich momentan wirklich über meinen Patriotismus reden möchte... Im Gegenteil, das Thema liegt mir eigentlich überhaupt nicht" fügte er entschlossen zu.

„Ich kenne Ihre Enttäuschung!" – versicherte ihm in Befehlston der Haarige, aber gleich darauf kriegte er sich wieder ein: „Ich habe Ihren Fall aufmerksam verfolgt; vielleicht denken Sie, ich habe mich da in etwas eingemischt was mich nichts angeht... aber die Arbeit in der Illegalität verlangt von uns durchaus auch so etwas" ergänzte er als Entschuldigung „und ich wäre nicht hierhergekommen, um Sie zu provozieren, wenn ich nicht die

Gewissheit gehabt hätte, dass ich selbst nicht viel mehr als ebenso ein Enttäuschter bin. Ich selbst bin mehr als Sie enttäuscht, mehr als Panait Istrati in der Rolle des Besuchers des ersten Arbeiter- und Bauernstaates. Für mich gilt, wie ich schon sagte: sie haben meine Frau schlicht und einfach getötet; sie hätten mich genauso gut umbringen können, doch ich war bereits außer Landes; denn sie hatten uns die ganze Zeit über unter Beobachtung gehabt, wissend dass meine Frau solche Zweifel hegte... Herr Lehrer“ warnte er ihn in belehrendem Ton „ich habe Ihnen Vieles zu sagen; wollen sie wissen warum ich sie aufgesucht habe, oder wollen Sie zuerst hören wer ich bin und vor wem ich auf der Flucht bin?“

„Ich habe Nachmittagsunterricht; geplant hatte ich, diesen Morgen mit meinem Sohn zu verbringen, aber wie ich sehe übernimmt ihr Mädchen meine Rolle hervorragend, also...“ rechnete sich Alexe die Lage aus und überlegte schnell; am Ende gab er dem momentanen Impuls nach, sich aus der Politik heraus zu halten und erwiderte in unerwartet entschlossem Ton, als ob er seinen Cousin Drăgan vor sich gehabt hätte:

„Sagen Sie mir, warum Sie mich suchen. Vielleicht haben sie den Falschen gefunden, dann wäre ja unser Problem schnell gelöst.“

Merkwürdigerweise fühlte sich sein Gegenüber gar nicht beleidigt. Er mahne nur, indem er auf Panait Istratis´ Autorenfoto zeigte, welches ihn mit dicker Hornbrille auf der Rückseite seines berüchtigten Buches abbildete:

„Gut; eines muss Ihnen jedoch klar sein: ich habe die Pistole im Nacken. Stalin verzeiht nicht.“

„Und weiter? Sie appellieren an meinen Patriotismus, um Hitler zu dienen?“ äußerte er erneut seinen Verdacht und wiederholte die ablehnende Antwort, die er auch bei der vorausgegangen Einladung, der Legion beizutreten, gegeben hatte.

„Ich bin ein Mensch der niemandem mehr dienen will, mein Herr (möglicherweise habe ich das noch nie gewollt, aber ich hatte mich getäuscht, also, ich wurde besiegt, wie Panait Istrati das sagt). Ich habe einen anderen Weg entdeckt.“

„Mit der Pistole im Nacken?“

„Mit!... Trotzki hat sich ausgerechnet in Mexiko versteckt, und selbst dort ist er nicht in Sicherheit! Ich, um Ihnen die Wahrheit zu sagen, verstecke mich bei den Waldarbeitern und Baumfällern, und ich habe sogar eine Operation ohne Narkose über mich ergehen lassen, um nicht mehr zu hinken. Darf ich Ihnen jetzt sagen, warum ich Sie aufgesucht habe? Schauen Sie, ich gebe es gerne zu: der Ausflug mit dem Mädchen ist nur ein Vorwand; ich habe mir schon viele konspirative Vorgangsweisen angeeignet. Ich bin auf der Suche nach Menschen, Herr Lehrer. Ich vertrete eine Bewegung, die auf die falsche Bahn geraten ist und jetzt suche ich Leute, die mir dabei helfen können, sie in die richtige umzuleiten."

„Patrioten."

„Unbedingt. Wir sind zu sehr untergangen. Es gibt einige Kameraden auf dieser Welt, die meine Meinung teilen. Oder besser gesagt, teilten, denn Stalin hat einige davon erschießen lassen."

„Also, wenn ich sie richtig verstehe, benötigen Sie Leute wie mich, um die Kommunisten zu locken; aber ich habe mich sogar von Drăgan distanziert, trotz enger Verwandtschaft."

„Vielleicht zog er sie dahin. Ich sehe die Lage anders."

„ Zu den Legionären?"

„Nein. Obwohl..."

„Warum schweigen Sie? Was wollten sie weiter sagen?"

„Ich war einmal gar nicht so weit davon entfernt. Und Sie, immer an die Armen denkend, kamen vorbei und dann hörte ich ihren Führer Codreanu den Gewerkschaftern über die Gefahr des Bolschewismus vorreden, aber damals verstand ich nicht viel von diesen Dingen. Ich werde es Ihnen erklären. Aber jetzt ...verlangen Sie von mir, Ihnen meine Gründe zu nennen; ich bin nur vom Thema abgewichen, um Ihnen zu beweisen, dass ich es damit ernst meine. Den Rest erkläre ich Ihnen später, falls Sie dann noch Zeit und Interesse haben."

Etwas an dieser unaufdringlichen Hartnäckigkeit gefiel Alexe. Trotz Mähne und bewusst fahrlässiger Körperhaltung machte sich dieser Mann keine Mühe zu imponieren, er wagte seine Unsicherheiten offen auszusprechen, ganz im Kontrast zu dem wirren Zustand seiner Kopf- und Barthaare.

„Die Dinge radikalisieren sich, Herr Lehrer und sie erscheinen in einem völlig neuen Gewand!... Sie zeigen ihr wahres Gesicht, nicht das, welches uns die Propaganda pro oder contra auftischt. Um Ihnen klar zu machen, warum ich Sie besuche, müsste ich bei der politischen Lage beginnen, die durch unseren Karl den Zweiten eindeutig zur Festigung seiner eigenen Machtposition gesteuert wird. Doch dazu zur späteren Stunde, denn in ganz Europa hat schon der offene Kampf für die Diktatur angefangen. Zuerst versuchten die Amerikaner die Finanzdiktatur zu etablieren, indem sie der Krise - die viele bankrotte Kapitalisten in den Selbstmord trieb - die Schuld für alles gaben; aber Hitler erhob sein Haupt und begann auf eigene Faust zu morden, oder denselben Kapitalisten das Eigentum zu entwenden, was ja ungefähr auf das Gleiche hinaus geht, denn er beschuldigte dafür dieselbe Krise. Denken Sie daran, was war Mussolini gestern und was ist er heute. Denken Sie an Lenin, der als Krimineller galt, weil er die russische Zarenfamilie erschießen ließ, was ja von einer kommunistischen Revolution auch nicht anders zu erwarten war. Bloß, seit Stalin an die Macht gekommen ist, erschießen sich die Kommunisten gegenseitig, oder sie nehmen an uns Rache, wir Revolutionäre aus anderen Ländern, die Auslandsfreiheit wollen. Er tut das, um seine persönlichen Vertrauensleute in die Schlüsselpositionen einzusetzen und damit eine Pseudorevolution zu forcieren, die einzige, die ohne Freiheit zustande kommt. Neulich hat sich Maniu mit den Legionären zusammen getan, weil diese jungen Kämpfer einen beträchtlichen Bekanntheitsgrad erreicht haben, dadurch, dass sie gewaltige Rache für die Armut ihrer Eltern nahmen; sie nahmen Hinrichtungen innerhalb ihrer Organisation vor, nach Hitlers´ Art, der sie dabei ermutigte; sie haben sicherlich vom Fall des Apothekers Stelescu gehört, oder nicht?... Was Karl angeht, ich garantiere Ihnen, dass er zum Diktator wird, da er dem Goga eine Regierung schenkt, einem der bloß über zwei Parlamentsmitglieder verfügt. Das Land braucht eine patriotische Union, mein Herr, die das Ziel im Fokus behält! Das ist das, was ich suche. Ich bin nicht vaterlandslos, wie Trotzki, um nach Mexiko flüchten zu müssen. Ich habe ein Land, dem ich Unrecht getan habe, aber ich möchte betonen, dass meine linke Überzeugung nicht der Fehler daran war; erst dadurch habe ich den patriotischen Sinn erkannt, der durch die Vereinigung mehrerer ehrenhafter Kräfte zustande kommen und etwas bewirken kann. Dies könnte für uns zu einem Ergebnis führen: eine patriotische Union, mit möglichst wenig Einfluss aus dem Ausland. Ich bin davon fest überzeugt. Und eines möchte ich noch hinzufügen: Ihre Enttäuschung mit dem Professor ist auch meine Enttäuschung. Denn er, auch wenn er es wohl in einer etwas romantischeren Art machen würde, er würde sich der Sache der Bauern schon widmen, denn er war einer der Wenigen, die nicht durch Auslandsinteressen „verunreinigt" wurden. Was jedoch Argetoianu angeht, dessen Vertreter praktisch Ihren Posten kassierte, über ihn kann man nicht dasselbe sagen! In Sachen Politik ist er hartnäckig und rücksichtslos. Zum Beispiel, der Verzicht auf Sie, im Kader des Herrn Professors, hat ihn überhaupt nicht gestört. Nicht wahr, dass ich Recht habe?"

„Aus Ihrer Sicht haben Sie schon Recht, aber ich bin aus der Politik heraus."

„Sie werden sehen, Herr Lehrer, dass man aus der Politik nicht einfach rausgehen kann; schon die Enthaltung jeglicher Meinung ist bereits eine politische Handlung."

„Daran sollten Sie sich nicht so festklammern."

„Doch, das tue ich; ich habe lange überlegt und ich kann darauf gar nicht verzichten."

„Ich mag es, mit ihnen zu reden, aber ich glaube, Drăgan wäre für Ihre Sache viel nützlicher als ich – sprach Alexe aus Überzeugung – und ich versichere Ihnen, was sie im Fall ihrer Frau durchgemacht haben flößt mir eine Menge Respekt ein."

„Soll ich das als Aufforderung zum Gehen verstehen?"

„Nein, ganz und gar nicht, im Gegenteil, Herr Celaru. Bitte bleiben Sie noch. Ich sagte nur, dass ich keine Politik machen will, nicht dass ich Ihnen nicht nahe sein möchte. Bitte verweilen Sie noch, denn ich bin Ihnen dankbar für alles, was Sie mir erzählen. Mit meinem Cousin streite ich oft, seit er auf dieser radikalen Schiene reitet; so hatte ich nicht einmal die Gelegenheit, ihn mit Panait Istratis´ bitterer Abrechnung mit dem Kommunismus bekannt zu machen, um ihm eine Lektion zu erteilen."

„Bedenken Sie aber, dass ich ein gefährlicher Geselle bin, Mein Herr; ich werde verfolgt, seien Sie gewarnt."

„Wie Sie meinen. Mir ist die Politik viel zu klar, um noch Angst vor einer eventuellen Kontamination zu empfinden."

„Keine Angst, ich verlasse Sie noch bevor Ansteckungsgefahr von mir ausgehen kann."

„Lassen Sie uns anders vorgehen: Sie bleiben, aber Sie behandeln mich, als wäre ich politisch unbedarft. Ich weiß, ich kann das gut, so habe ich auch Andere die mir gefolgt sind irregeführt. Ihr Besuch ehrt mich sehr, es ist eine erhoffte Gelegenheit viel mehr zu erfahren, als das, was hier einem einfachen Intellektuellen zugänglich ist" rutschte ihm in einem Augenblick der Schwäche doch noch die Wahrheit raus. Sein Verplappern bewies, dass er noch vom ursprünglichen Studentenstolz erfüllt war, den ihm während der Studiumszeit sein Professor an der Uni eingeimpft hatte; diese Eigenschaft war zweifelsohne eine gute Fähigkeit seines früheren Mentors; diese konnte ihm immer noch keiner übel nehmen, selbst wenn er inzwischen einige gravierende Fehler begangen hatte.

„Ich bin kein Intellektueller, lieber Herr, dieses Glück hatte ich nicht. Ich bin ein Autodidakt" sprach der Behaarte, indem er seine lange Wolljacke ablegte und das offen getragene Hemd zum Vorschein kommen ließ, als ob er jeder Witterung mit seiner breiten Brust trotzen wolle „Ich fühle mich zu den Intellektuellen hin gezogen, aber ich kenne meine Grenzen sehr wohl, den mein Lernen war chaotisch und unsystematisch. Doch die Politik hat mich vieles gelehrt, denn man muss dabei sein, um etwas verstehen zu können, so etwas kann man nicht aus einem Buch herauslesen. Wenn es nach den Büchern ginge, dann könnte ich Ihren Professor als Nationalist bezeichnen, doch die Legionäre sind auch Nationalisten. Trotzdem stehen sie sich frontal gegenüber und bekämpfen sich sogar heftig, um gleich darauf wieder Frieden zu schliessen. In solchen Fällen bleiben ehrliche Menschen, wie Sie, oft auf der Strecke. Ich habe schon seit längerer Zeit darauf gewartet, Ihre Reaktion diesbezüglich testen zu dürfen."

„Dachten Sie, ich würde zu den Legionären überlaufen?"

„Selbst das wäre möglich gewesen."

„Ich reagiere nicht. Das habe ich Ihnen bereits gesagt: ich habe aufgegeben."

„Schauen Sie, ich kann Ihnen nicht einfach sagen, dass der Mensch nicht aufgibt, sondern bloß seine Meinung ändert; Sie müssen begreifen, wer ich bin; es ist viel ehrlicher so" erwiderte der Haarige hitzig und seine Brust schien sich durch die Hemdöffnung noch mehr zu bäumen, als mache er seinem Ärger mehr Luft. Er schien wie von einer äußeren Kraft getrieben, um seine Seele protzig und theatralisch frei zum Vorschein zu bringen.

4.

„Als ich jung war, fing ich mir eine Bleivergiftung ein, Saturnismus, bekannt als Druckerleiden. Aus diesem Grunde trug ich ein paar Jahre lang die Brust offen, bis ich geheilt wurde und man mir den Soldatenrock verpasste. Aber, seitdem sie meine Frau umgebracht haben, ist meine Krankheit zurückgekehrt; vielleicht reagiere ich so auf das Blei, das ihren Körper durchbohrte, vielleicht wiederum bereitet sich mein Körper auf eine Portion Blei vor, die noch auf mich zukommen wird“ sprach er etwas rätselhaft, eher zu sich selbst. Es dauerte eine ganze Weile bis er sich beruhigte und sich wieder klarer ausdrückte, doch seine Rhetorik mäßigte sich nicht „Ich war Geselle und später Arbeiter an der Constantin Mille Druckerei, für die Zeitung „Die Wahrheit”... Gott, was war das für ein Mensch!... Was für ein Chef, was für ein Poet!... Und dann begann er plötzlich ein Gedicht vorzutragen: *Sie sagten: der Stärkere siegt immer,/ Die Herrschaft der Faust von oben bis unten,/ Der Fortschritt lebt dem Kampf inne und, eine nach der anderen/ Eure Illusionen werden mit lautem Getöse stürzen!...* er hatte eine blumige Schrift, die lediglich von meinem Meister entziffert werden konnte; und ich habe bei ihm alles gelernt, denn der große Chef hielt große Stücke auf mich... Was für ein Poet, mein Herr, was für ein Mensch!... Als bei mir die Krankheit diagnostiziert wurde, nahm er mich aus der Bleiwerkstatt raus; er hatte gerade ein eigenes Telegrafenbüro aufgemacht. Weißt Du, was es damals bedeutete, einen Telegrafen zu haben? ... Er hatte Korrespondenten überall, unmittelbare, wie kein anderer!... Er arbeitete wie in Paris... Um mich vom Blei fern zu halten half er mir dabei, den neuen Beruf zu erlernen, denn es war ein sauberes Arbeitsumfeld und ich war schlau genug, um die Telegramme entziffern zu können und sie in sauberer Schrift umzuschreiben... Wäre ich dort länger geblieben, wen sie mich bloß nicht für die Armee rekrutiert hätten, dann hätte er mich sicherlich später zum Redakteur befördert, obwohl ich ihn damals, 1907, ziemlich geärgert habe ... Viel zu spät habe ich das verstanden. Erst als ich von meiner Frau erfuhr, was die Franzosen, die ja für ihre unorthodoxe, nicht wirklich linke Orientierung berüchtigt sind, denn sie pfeifen auf die innenparteiische Disziplin und streben eine freie, saubere Revolution an – was also diese Franzosen unter dem Begriff „Revolutionsexport”, beziehungsweise „Importrevolution” verstehen ... Aber zu der Zeit konnte ich die

Lage noch nicht klar deuten. Ich befand mich in der Phase der Wissensakkumulation, des Informationenaneignens; ich las unglaublich viel, alles was mir in die Hände kam, ununterbrochen, nächtelang. Massenweise gedruckte Worte, so wie früher, in der Druckerei. 1921, als wir die Partei gründeten, wurde ich dazu ausgesucht, um zusammen mit Cristescu nach Moskau zu gehen. Sogar die Professoren und die Anwälte unserer Partei – denn es gab damals auch Intelektuelle, glaube mir, nicht nur Offiziere mit russischem oder deutschem Drillhintergrund, die als Agenten infiltriert wurden - selbst die beteuerten dass ich extrem belesen war. Aber was ich ihnen an Lesestoff voraus hatte war die Literatur der Revolution, deswegen ... Später, als ich meine Frau kennen lernte, die anständig an der Sorbonne studiert hatte, wurde mir klar, welches Chaos, welche Unordnung in meinem Kopf herrschte... Vielleicht ist das der Grund warum ich nicht vorher das erkannt hatte, was ich an der Seite meiner Frau entdecken durfte. Allmählich begann ich zu verstehen, auch dank der Hilfe des französischen Professors, der mit uns in Moskau verkehrte, da er sich zu den restlichen Kommilitonen überhaupt nicht hingezogen fühlte. Ich verstand, dass sich meine Frau an der Sorbonne mit den Gauchisten politisch engagiert hatte und dadurch mit einem völlig anderen Ansatz an die Internationale herangewachsen war... Na, jetzt habe ich Dir in einem Atemzug alles gesagt, jetzt bist du deutlich besser im Bilde. Vor einem wie Dir werde ich mich nicht verstecken, obwohl Du mit mir nicht über Politik diskutieren willst. Aber ich mag die Art wie Du mein Angebot abgelehnt hast. Und selbst wenn Du mir durch Dein Nein die Möglichkeit gibst, meine wahre Identität und meine Rolle innerhalb dieser Bewegung zu verschweigen, jetzt, wenn ich sie hier, in meiner Heimat zu retten versuche, werde ich Dir trotzdem erzählen, welche Pläne ich habe, um dies zu erreichen... Ich bin über Deine Enthaltung nicht verärgert, bin seit einer ganzen Weile unterwegs und habe viele getroffen, die sich mir nicht anschließen wollten. Viele davon sind wie Du, Menschen bei denen ich etwas mehr Verständnis als bei Arbeitern wie diesen aus Drăgans´ Gruppe erwartet hatte, ordnungsliebende, berechenbare Kameraden, die treu ihrem Anführer folgen. Ich rede hier von unserer Arbeiterbewegung, die von eh und jäh, die deren Bedürfnissen entspricht und sich nicht von hinten durchschieben und steuern lässt, so wie es sich bei allen

Revolutionen ereignet und wie ich damals zu ahnen begann... Den es gibt eine dunkle Macht im Außen, die sie provoziert!... Ja, das habe ich schon 1907 geahnt, als ich mich überzeugen konnte, dass viele der rebellierenden Bauern von ein paar Deutschen und weiteren Fremden provoziert wurden, lauter Unbekannte, die irgendwie punktgenau vor Ort waren, von jemanden auf Befehl aus der Bukowina gebracht waren und überhaupt keine Verbindung zu den Unstimmigkeiten im ländlichen Bereich hatten, die später als Grund für den Aufstand genannt wurden. Im Klartext, der Bauernaufstand wurde von Ausländern eingeleitet, die speziell zu diesem Zwecke ins Land geschickt wurden, von den Provokateuren des Imperiums entsandt; und unsere Armee sollte sie aufhalten, nicht die Bauern!... Ich sagte Dir bereits dass ich damals gegen meinen geliebten Chef rebellierte, weil er Hand in Hand mit den Hintermännern der vorhin erwähnten Provokateure arbeitete, und er verbreitete Lügen, indem er die Behauptung drucken ließ, der rumänische Soldat würde den rumänischen Bauern verprügeln...Dies half mir später bei der Verarbeitung der These dieses französischen Professors und stützte auch die Ideen, die mir meine Frau aus Ihrer Erfahrung in gauschistischen Studentenkreisen vermittelte ... Hach!... Meine Frau war sehr klug; sie hatte ein brillantes Gehirn und war imstande, hervorragende Schlüsse zu ziehen; manchmal kam sie auf unerwartete Erkenntnisse, die keiner zuvor erahnt hätte. Zuweilen waren es einfache Beobachtungen, die einen wie Blitze aus heiterem Himmel trafen, denn sie besaß einen erstaunlich scharfer Blick fürs Detail, welcher bei so einer zierlichen Frauengestalt sehr ungewöhnlich war ... Andere, die meisten, bemerkten diese Gabe nicht einmal!... Manchmal entdecke ich bei diesem Mädchen genau ihre Art, den Dingen auf den Grund zu gehen. Sie hat wohl ihr Talent geerbt, denn selbst wenn sie auf den ersten Blick scheu erscheint, verfügt sie über eine angeborene Weisheit und Ruhe und kann ihre Umgebung ganz genau beurteilen. Sie ist die Tochter ihrer Schwester. So vererben sich manchmal die Charakterzüge, sie springen quer zu den Neffen über oder zu seitlichen Blutverwandten; nicht immer machen sie sich bemerkbar, aber erstaunlich deutlich sind sie manchmal zu erkennen. Die genetische Folge ist nicht unbedingt eine Gerade, sie bricht auseinander, springt zu einem Ast, von Zweig zu Zweig ...Schau Dir ihre Stirn an, so groß, offen, etwas gewölbt, sie ist genau wie die ihrer Tante ... die Stirn meine geliebten Frau!... Ihre Mutter, die Schwester meiner Frau, hat nicht so eine Stirn; aber ein Onkel der beiden, der Pope ist, von dem habe ich ein Bild gesehen, und der hatte genau diese Stirn. Vielleicht hat ihnen der Vater das vererbt, von ihm habe ich nur ein Bild aus der Wehrdienstzeit gesehen, und da trug er eine Mütze tief über die Augen herunter gezogen ... Meine Frau war sehr intelligent; und sie hatte ein logisches Denken, die Ihresgleichen noch sucht. Wenn mir das Schicksal hold ist... Siehst Du, ich sage nicht, „möge mir Gott helfen" denn ich weiß, dass Du nicht religiös bist, so wie ich auch, damals, als ich jünger und radikaler war... wenn es mir also hilft, mir einige Jahre gewährt, um ihre Schritte zu lenken, wird sie eine wunderbare Zukunft haben!... Die Sache mit dem lieben Gott werde ich Dir noch erklären, aber nicht jetzt; die einfachen Menschen, mit denen ich zusammen arbeite, sind ehrlich und benötigen Ihn. Da unsere Politik für sie gemacht wird, werde ich Lenins´ Blödsinn nicht beachten und auch nicht Stalins´ Glaubensabfall, der so typisch für Seminarschüler ist, denn mich interessieren mehr die Menschen mit denen ich zusammen den Kampf organisieren kann. Und diese einfachen Menschen bekämpfen den lieben Gott nicht, sie haben Ihn gerade nötig... Wie soll ich Dir sagen, von ihnen habe ich gelernt, Ihn auch zu brauchen ... Es verhält sich wie mit dem Patriotismus, bei dem ich später angelangt bin und ziemlich ausgelaugt war, erst nachdem ich realisierte, wenn diese einfachen Menschen, die wir emanzipieren wollen, keine Patrioten sind, dann bedeutet das es gibt keine Heimat!... Also, schau, diese Idee von Vaterlandsliebe eint uns. Genauso ging es mir, ehrlich gesagt, als ich mich entschied, zu Dir zu kommen, weil Du ein Republikaner bist; besser gesagt, Du hast etwas Radikales, Entschlossenes, das mich berechtigt, Dich aufzusuchen... Na!... nun habe ich Dir meine wahre Meinung zum Patriotismus gesagt, etwas wovon Dir Dein Professor wahrscheinlich in generellem Sinne gesprochen hat, vielleicht nicht so realitätsnah, obwohl ich mir sicher bin, dass er auch daran fest glaubt: sein Glaube ist sicherlich sehr groß. Aber die Menschen sind sehr unterschiedlich. Du, zum Beispiel, glaubst an einem Patriotismus, der Dich nicht von der Monarchie abhängig macht. Ich übrigens auch; aber für mich ist Patriotismus mehr mit der Bewegung der rumänischen Arbeiterklasse verbunden, weil sie diejenige ist, welcher die größten Hindernisse im Wege stehen und die am schnellsten reagieren muss. Nicht von außen muss man den Arbeiter überzeugen, hier habe ich es geschafft, wie ich Dir bereits sagte, meine Grenzen zu erkennen. Aber es gibt eine Tradition bei uns, eine Eigenart der Arbeiter dieses Landes, die für ihre Bedürfnisse bis zum Äußersten gehen wollen. Dies ist eine ehrliche Bewegung; sie entspringt dem Instinkt und der Not, selbst wenn Andere sie im Interesse anderer Ländern mit ihren Geheimdiensten manipulieren... Sie ist ehrlich und sauber; sie ist „natürlich", würden die Anthropologen sagen, also sie reiht sich in die Evolution ein. Und ich, nachdem ich begriffen habe wie gefährlich Infiltrationen sind, bin sogar verpflichtet, sie zu fördern. Sogar verteidigen muss ich sie vor den Unterschlagungen der Ausländer. So kam ich darauf, dass ich letztendlich ein Nationalist bin. Und, um ein genaueres Ziel zu nennen, ich gebe die Idee einer Partei nicht auf!... Eine Partei die mehrere Kräfte zusammen eint, mit Menschen die verschiedene Glaubensrichtungen haben. Zum Beispiel, Du..."

„Ich glaube an gar nichts mehr; das habe ich Dir schon gesagt. Ich will mir nicht einmal mehr diese Frage des Glaubens stellen. Ich habe einen Beruf, eine Familie, ein paar Freunde, soweit..."

„Aber Du hast auch Überzeugungen" – beteuerte der Behaarte: „Du wünschst Dir Emanzipation, eine Bereinigung der Gesellschaft, eine die am obersten Ende, bei dem gekrönten Kopf beginnt, Du willst..."

Alexe gab ein Zeichen und änderte seine Körperhaltung; es war möglicherweise unbewusst, doch es zeigte seine Verwirrung und die Befürchtung, dass der Behaarte womöglich wieder eine viel zu komplizierte Theorie über eine vermeintliche dunkle Macht, die unsere Schicksale aus dem Schatten lenkt, anfangen würde. Mit seinem rational geprägten Denken hielt er die Theorien seines Gesprächspartners für ausgesprochen unrealistisch und dachte sich, dass dieser viel zu viel Sachen durcheinander brachte, so chaotisch wie er die Dinge darstellte. Da ihm mehr die systematische Art am Herzen lag, unterbrach er seine Rede:

„Herr Celaru, ich höre Ihnen gut zu; sagen Sie mir was Sie wollen, denn es interessiert mich wirklich; ich schwöre Ihnen, dass es mich interessiert und dass ich Ihre ehrliche Meinung schätze. Aber bitte argumentieren Sie mir sachlich und appellieren sie nicht an meine Gefühle, um mich für Ihre Sache

zu gewinnen... Ich sagte Ihnen bereits, dass mich mein Cousin Drăgan auf Distanz hält, wegen der Art wie ich denke und wegen meiner Vorliebe zur Analyse.“
„Ach, Drăgan!... Mit ihm ist es ganz anders. Ihn muss ich sehen, um ihn besser zu verstehen. Das heißt, zu sehen, ob er richtig begreift und nicht durch seine eigenen ideologischen Überzeugungen die Tatsachen verdreht...“
Um seine Gedanken zu ordnen, agierte Alexe instinktiv wie der klassische Lehrer, der sanft die Aufmerksamkeit seiner Schüler auf Bereiche lenkt, die ihnen bekannt sind:
„Jawohl; das interessiert mich schon: Wie sind Sie auf diese ideologischen Uneinigkeit, die Sie erwähnen, überhaupt gekommen?... Ich stimme Ihnen zu, dass sich die Arbeiter um einen Gruppenführer wie Drăgan gern organisieren und ich mag die Bezeichnung, die Sie dafür gewählt haben, dieses „natürliche”. Heißt es, dass Sie auch Menschen trafen, die eine künstliche Revolution befürworten?“
„Und wie!... Die Mehrheit derer, die zur Revolution aufrufen, wünscht sich eine künstlich verursachte, die bestimmten verdeckten Interessen dienen soll. Eine natürliche würde aber den Herzen der Menschen entspringen. Unserer Pflicht als eineige wenige Auserwählte, die noch einen klaren Überblick behalten haben, besteht darin, dieses vorhandene Gleichgewicht zu schützen... Normalerweise wird diese Rolle von den Theoretikern übernommen, aber dann mischen sich die Geheimdienste mit ihren Provokationen ein, infiltrieren falsche Helden, die von anderen Regierungen bezahlt werden und...Was sollen wir noch um den heißen Brei herum reden, Lenin wurde von den Deutschen bezahlt, um die Russen dazu zu bringen, sich geschlagen zu geben; danach bezahlte er sogenannte Revolutionen, um weitere Länder auf seine Seite zu gewinnen. Die Unzufriedenheit der Bevölkerung ist eine natürliche Reaktion, aber alles Übrige...“
„Verstehe ich Sie richtig, ihrer Meinung nach wurde der Rest durch ein paar niederträchtige Handlungen einer machthungrigen Welt verursacht?“
„Exakt!...“ rief er entzückt „Siehst Du, deswegen wusste ich, dass ich Dich treffen muss, obwohl ich nicht geahnt habe, dass auch Du zu diesem Schluss gekommen bist!“

„Diese Tatsache ist mir erst seit kurzer Zeit klar geworden; erst seitdem ich Hitler und Mussolini beobachte, nachdem ich Panait Istratis´ Werk las. Sie haben das wahrscheinlich noch vor mir gewusst... „

„Verschone mich mit diesem „Sie"" – befahl ihm der Behaarte, der sich schon an seiner eigenen Erinnerung erfreute - "Mein Lieber, wir sprachen über das, was meine Frau gewusst und gelernt hat und über Ihre systematische Denkweise. Dadurch, dass sie sich im Kreise französischen Linkstheoretiker ein Bild über die Intervention der Engländer bei der Entstehung der französischen Revolutionen machen konnte fiel es ihr überhaupt nicht schwer, meine Unzufriedenheit und Angst in Moskau zu verstehen. Denn die Geschichte ist viel komplizierter; ich hatte sie hier kennen gelernt, als sie Studentin war; aber dann ging sie auf die Sorbonne und ich wurde nach Russland geschickt. Als ich sie wieder traf, war ich ziemlich verwirrt und es gab nicht viele Kameraden mit denen ich frei darüber sprechen konnte... Denn ich merkte, dass diejenigen, die Stalin nahe standen, nach und nach mehr an dem Wiedererlangen der ehemaligen imperialistischen Macht Russlands, unter der Führung des Väterchens-Zar, interessiert waren als an die Befriedigung der wahren Bedürfnisse der Menschen, die inzwischen nur noch durch Terror beherrscht wurden... Genau das hat auch Panait Istrati gemerkt, als er durch Mutter-Russland zur Erkundungsreise geführt wurde, da die hofften, dass er einen Lobesgesang als Buch veröffentlicht, so wie es die Anderen auf den Kongressen gemacht haben... Sie taten das, weil es in ihrem nationalen Interesse war, aber uns konnten sie nicht überzeugen, denn wir waren dort, um nach Wegen für unsere eigene Arbeiterklasse, in unseren jeweiligen Heimatländern zu suchen, verstehst Du?... Nicht nur ich; wir hatten diesbezüglich schon mehrere Gespräche untereinander geführt und manche von uns verstanden sich schon mittels verstohlener Blicke, wir Fremde, auf dem Komintern. Doch Stalins´ Spürnase blieb das nicht verborgen, er schickte ein paar davon nach Sibirien und andere ließ er hinrichten. Meine Frau gehört zu den Gefallenen; ich hatte das Glück, zu jenem Zeitpunkt, mich im Ausland zu befinden. Natürlich kehrte ich nicht mehr zurück. Sie suchten eine Weile nach mir, verfolgten mich durch ganz Europa, so wie sie auch andere suchten, um sie dann bei den westlichen Regierungen zu enttarnen, auf der Stelle zu ermorden oder zuerst entführten und dann nach Russland zu bringen, wo sie ihnen „vorbildliche" Prozesse inszenierten. Später, irgendwann, entspannte sich die Lage und man vergaß mich... Aber jetzt, als sie bemerkten wie Panait Istrati sie mit Verzögerung enttarnen konnte, nachdem er nach Rumänien zurückgekehrt war, realisierten sie, dass auch ich ein Rumäne bin. Nun haben sie ihre Leute hierher geschickt, um uns beide zu liquidieren... Ich war beim „Cartea românească" – Verlag, in Bukarest, als die „Beichte eines Besiegten" veröffentlicht wurde... Konnte mich freilich nicht offen zeigen, aber ich hielt mich versteckt, um ihn beobachten zu können. Panait Istrati schrieb mit einer Hand Autogramme, doch die andere Hand hielt er auf dem Tisch, in der Nähe seiner Pistole!... Gekleidet mit dieser dicken Wolljacke, die ich mir von einem Legionär geben ließ, hielt mich die Polizei für einen selbstverständlichen Gegner des Schriftstellers... Denn früher, auf dem Foto das Stalins Ceka-GPU-Agenten von mir von über die rumänische Staatssicherheit erhielten, hatte ich ein völlig anderes Erscheinen, mein Herr: ich war ein schlanker, wohlerzogener Junge, trug einen kurzen, ordnungsmäßigen Haarschnitt, war stäts glatt rasiert und erschien in einem ordentlich gebürsteten Sakko, gekleidet wie der typische Bürokrat, ohne große Ambitionen, ein Cinovnic im wahrsten Sinne des Wortes. Und ich hinkte, wegen eines Splitters, der in mir seit Kriegszeiten im Bein steckte. Ich musste eine schwere Operation über mich ergehen lassen, und, nachdem man mir einen Stab ins Bein pflanzte, übte ich ganz lange, bis mir das unauffällige Gehen wieder gelang. Dennoch wollte ich mich dadurch auf keine Fall selbst verraten. So wie ich jetzt aussehe, würde mich niemand mehr erkennen, deswegen kleide ich mich bewusst wie die „Schwarzen Kutten". Inzwischen habe ich mir viele Tricks und Ausweichmanöver beigebracht. Wie viele Jahre sind vergangen, seitdem Du vom Professor enttäuscht wurdest? Fast vier, nicht wahr?... Nun, das sind genau die Jahre, die ich gebraucht habe, um mich zu überzeugen, dass ich mit Dir ohne jegliche Befürchtung offen reden kann..."

Er verlor erneut den Faden. All die Dinge, die er ihm möglichst schnell sagen wollte, vermischten sich erneut. Anhand seiner didaktischen Methode bemühte sich Alexe weiter, ihm das zu entlocken, was ihn interessierte. Nun stellte er sogar fest, dass ihn immer mehr Sachen faszinierten, Themen die er niemals mit Drăgan hätte besprechen können. Denn dies interessierte ihn ganz gewiss, es entsprach seiner eingefleischten Gründlichkeit, seiner Tendenz zur sachlichen Information und zum tief eingehenden Nachdenken. Der Versuch, ihn für einen bestimmten politischen Kampf zu begeistern war ihm hingegen völlig egal:

„Reden Sie weiter. Ich höre zu."

„Mein Herr, Du lehrst Geschichte, hast Du Dich jemals gefragt, warum die Franzosen in den Jahren 1786 und 1848 die größten Revolutionen in Europa schafften, um später ihre eigenen revolutionären Regierungen in Imperien umzuwandeln?!... Ich werde Dir das kurz erklären. Es ist meine Schlussfolgerung. Sie hat sogar meine Frau überrascht, obwohl sie viel besser als ich informiert war und einen tieferen Einblick in die Geschehnisse zu haben meinte" – kehrte er kurz zu seinem persönlichen Drama zurück, das ihn regelmäßig aufwühlte und ihm ein nervöses, zweimaliges Zucken auf die Stirn brachte, als ob er eine unsichtbare Fliege davon jagen wollte – „Weißt Du warum sie so begeistert war? Weil ich derselbe Mensch war, der früher nicht erkennen konnte, welche Manipulation mein damaliger Chef verübte, als er in seiner Zeitung von elftausend ermordeten Bauern berichtete, anstatt zu informieren, dass der Telegraf – an dem ich saß – von Provokateuren sprach, die von außerhalb der Landesgrenze, aus Cernauti, eingeführt wurden, um die hungrige Bevölkerung aufzuhetzen... Verstehst Du?..."

Er verstand. Er verstand, dass der Behaarte ein fieberhaftes Verlangen verspürte, sich endlich frei aussprechen zu dürfen, nachdem er sich so lange Zeit immer nur verstecken musste und zum Schweigen gezwungen war. Es war stärker als sein Ich; im Laufe seines leidenschaftlichen Versuchs, alles auf einmal, in einem Atemzug zu erklären brachen alle Dämme des Schweigens. Alexe wurde klar, dass er das tiefe Vertrauen dieses Mannes gewonnen hatte.

Aber zwischen diesem grenzlosen Vertrauen und der Gefahr einer Ansteckung an dessen Enthusiasmus, welcher mehr einer Obsession als einer kühlen Überlegung entsprang, lagen Welten. Alexe bevorzugte die Ruhe und die beidseitige Kommunikation; der leidenschaftliche Funke sprang nicht zu ihm über.

5.

- „Also, mein Herr, nachdem sowohl 1786 wie auch 1848, blutige, erbitterte Kämpfe und die Guillotine gebraucht wurden, um die berühmten, radikalen Revolutionäre and die Macht zu bringen, als sogar ein neuer Kalender eingeführt wurde, um neue Zeichen der Zeit zu setzen, als die neue Republik stand, die nach Meinung der Revolutionäre dem allgemeinen Wohl dienen sollte und den Bedürfnissen der Mehrheit entsprach, drehten die Franzosen das Ruder in den Wind und erfanden plötzlich einen völlig neuen Monarchen, so einen Napoleon. Das ist die Wahrheit: sie fingen immer mit „Liberté-Egalité-Fraternité" an und am Ende des Liedes sang dann ein noch schlimmerer Autokrat als die Könige davor, denn sie wechselten vom Königreich zum Imperium!... Kannst Du mir das erklären?!... Such nach allen möglichen Antworten und Du wirst immer wieder erkenn müssen, dass sie alle unlogisch, völlig unpassend zu einer Revolution und zu den zwei Napoleons sind... Und dennoch haben die Franzosen das getan; und die Bevölkerung, all diejenigen die davor rebellierten, die Gavroches, Sansculotten, die Bonettes die auf den Barrikaden fielen und die hervorragenden kartesischen Gehirne, die dem Denken wahre Tempel gebaut hatten, die Straße und die Menschenversammlungen auf den Plätzen, um die Guillotine, sogar die Carvounardes, die sich im Ausland abgesetzt hatten, alle akzeptierten diese ehemaligen Beamten, Direktoren, Konsuls die ihnen sofort wieder den imperialistischen Absolutismus servierten!... Warum? Zweimal innerhalb von sechzig Jahren führten die Franzosen eine republikanische Revolution, um sich dann prompt doch für ein Imperium zu entscheiden; in der selben Zeit, beschäftigte sich England, dieses Imperium durch und durch, mit der Verursachung und Manipulierung derselben französischen Revolutionen. Die Schachzüge sind von beiden Seiten, durch die jeweiligen Geheimdienste der zwei Länder sehr gut vorbereitet. Denn siehe da, mein lieber Herr: wo genau schrieb fleißig Marx an seinem Manifest, innerhalb von zwei Jahrzehnten, noch vor der Kommune von Paris, wenn nicht in London, wo er über einen Lebensstandard verfügte, den er in Deutschland niemals hätte erreichen können?... Und seine Theorie wurde ausgerechnet den Franzosen schmackhaft gemacht, um Napoleon den Dritten den Aufstieg an die Macht zu ermöglichen, und nicht dem Gespenst des Kommunismus, dem er zusammen mit Engels eine goldene Zukunft prophezeit hatte!... Welch andere Logik kann so einer Revolution zu Grunde gelegt werden, wenn nicht eine, die sich auf ein geheimes Kalkül stützt und Menschenopfer auf den Barrikaden verursacht?!...“

„ ...Es gibt eine einzige Erklärung; sie bestätigt in Hülle und Fülle meine Theorie, die besagt, dass die französischen Revolutionen von England exportiert wurden, nachdem sie dort detailgenau vorbereitet wurden. Dadurch sollte England auf dem europäischen Festland Fuß fassen, um später über den Kontinent zu herrschen. Erst beim dritten Versuch, als sich England mit Bismark verbündeten und den letzten Napoleon stürzten, ging diese Strategie auf. Diese Theorie ist im Umlauf und ich verschreibe mich auch, eben weil sie die einzige ist, die dieses wiederholte Aufbauschen der Franzosen erklärt. Die Franzosen, lieber Herr, haben durch ihre Napoleons imperialistische Tendenzen übernommen, um dem fremden Druck, wie zum Beispiel dem englischen, etwas entgegen zu halten. Das ist alles, aus diesem Grund musste die Menschheit solch schrecklich blutige Revolutionen über sich ergehen lassen. Provokation und Gegen-Provokation, nicht mehr. Dies ist, um es in Seemansworte zu fassen, die Tide die das Schiff wiegt, auf dem sich unsere Menschheit befindet und sich belügen lässt, von Machtinteressen beherrscht!... Ich, der große Revolutionär, glaube nicht mehr an die Revolution!... Ich glaube nur noch an arme Menschen, die Ihre Rechte sowohl von den Einen, wie auch von den Anderen mit den Füssen getreten sehen, Menschen die kämpfen, um sie wieder zu erlangen!... Nach der Großen Französischen Revolution, die sich in Napoleons große Chance zur Autokratie verwandelte, hat England den Kampf nicht aufgegeben. Ausgerechnet England, geprägt vom berühmt-berüchtigten Konservativismus, bereitete die größte Links-Provokationen in Europa vor. So entstand die Erste Internationale und man legte den Schwerpunkt auf den grenzüberschreitenden Kommunismus, um die Aufmerksamkeit vom Patriotismus abzulenken. Aber umsonst, denn letztendlich wurde Europa mit Imperien übersät: Das französische, das deutsche, das türkische, das russische, nicht zu vergessen das österreich-ungarische, eine Multinationale noch dazu, die von der Konfusion der internationalistischen Ideen profitierte und dadurch nur die Macht von Franz-Josef stärkte. Aus diesem zuletzt genannten Hause entstand die Diversion, die ich noch persönlich im Jahre 1907 beobachten konnte. Also hat er sich das Rezept zur geheimdienstlichen Provokation, welches im Moment von Moskau perfektioniert wird, sehr gut angeeignet... Die Idee einer Revolution ist wie eine Welle der Diversion, die am Ärmelkanal beginnt, über den Kontinent schwappt und immer weiter wogt, vom Provokateur zum Provozierten wird sie weitergegeben: Frankreich übernimmt von England, Deutschland von Frankreich, Russland von Deutschland und wir, die ganz kleinen, schwanken von Einem zum Anderen, oder lassen uns einen kleinen König geben, der manch einer größeren kaiserlichen Familie angehört... Die Revolution ist bloß ein Zustand für naive Menschen, die von Hunger und Unzufriedenheit getrieben werden; man kennt sie auch als Umstand, den man geschickt ausnutzen kann, um einige gekrönte Köpfe loszuwerden, um Platz für andere zu schaffen. Für die Politiker bedeutet sie eine kontinuierliche Herausforderung, die Anstrengung und Energie kostet und für sie persönlich einen bestimmten Profit abwirft. Es ist eine Investition in Dominierungspolitiken, die sich von Westen nach Osten rollen, die von Land zu Land überschwappen, und jedem als Instrument zur Durchsetzung eigener Interessen nutzt. Wie? Durch Auslösen einer Revolution im Nachbarland, Richtung Osten, um später selber dahin nachzurücken. Seitdem diese Methode vor drei hundert Jahren durch den englischen Parlamentarismus eingeführt wurde, wird sie munter von allen benutzt. Es wurden sogar geheime Institutionen geschaffen, die finanziert werden, um diese Situation zu kontrollieren. So hat sich im Jahre 1848 Napoleon der Dritte an die Macht katapultiert, um später über geheime Organisationen seine Macht nach Deutschland und Italien zu erweitern...Und wenn man erzählt, dass Lenin, zum Zeitpunkt seines Wegtransports mit dem gepanzerten Zug, über ein Angebot der Deutschen Geheimdienste verfügte, welches ihm Dutzende von Millionen Goldmark versprach, um aus den Soldaten Revolutionäre zu machen, die ihre Waffen wegwerfen und sich freiwillig ergeben, warum soll denn nicht auch die andere Variante wahr sein, nämlich die, wonach man ihn genauso gut nach England hätte bringen können, um eine Provokation vorzubereiten, die zu einer europaweiten Kommune führen sollte, die man damals in der Propaganda als „Gespenst des Kommunismus" bezeichnete. Wäre es nicht möglich, dass Engels seinen Freund Marx mit Geldern des Geheimdienstes des Großen Albions gefüttert hat? Schließlich sind die dazugehörigen perfiden Machschaften und Organisationen nicht umsonst in die Geschichte eingegangen! Frankreich, unterstützt von den Geheimdiensten der zwei Napoleons, hätte sich im Zivilkrieg durchsetzen und nach Russland schielen können, um sich in etwas grober Manier die gewünschten Gebiete beim Frieden von Brest-Litovsk zu holen. Es wäre gar nicht so abwegig wenn die Deutschen ausgerechnet den bezahlten, der in ihrem Namen diese Abmachung unterschreiben sollte. Ich behaupte also dass Lenin von den Deutschen in der Schweiz rekrutiert und bezahlt wurde, um mit dem gepanzerten Zug zu kommen und die kommunistischen russische Revolutionäre vorzubereiten, die nichts anderes als hitzige, fahnenflüchtige Soldaten waren und durch Versprechen von Land und Boden weiteren Soldaten des Zaren den Seitenwechsel schmackhaft machen sollten. Somit hätten sie endgültig im Sinne der Invasoren das System destabilisiert... Die kommunistischen Führer aus Moskau, die habe ich gekannt; sie sind so: umgedrehte Militärs, die früher auf der Seite des Zaren gekämpft haben und jetzt für die Deutschen den Weg frei gemacht haben. Als sie dann später zur Rolle der leitenden Partei aufgestiegen sind zahlten sie selbst um die Revolution weiter zu reichen, exportierten ihre Ideen und Provokationen und festigten dadurch ihre eigene Macht weltweit. Nun sind sie an den Punkt angelangt, an dem sie sich gegenseitig bekämpfen. Buharin enttarnte Lenin als Verräter der Revolution zu Gunsten der deutschen territorialen Übermacht, aber Lenin erklärt ihn zum Verräter und beseitigt ihn anschließend. Genauso wie in Paris, als die Revolution in der Phase der ausländischen Ambitionen angelangt war; da begannen sich ihre Helden in internen Konflikten zu verwickeln und torpedierten sich gegenseitig. Genau das passiert auch hier, in Rumänien, sie hetzen andere gegen mich auf. Eine zynische Kraft führt die Revolutionen auf Zwischenländerebene, indem sie die Nationen verschlingt und blutige Diktaturen installiert. Es ist wie eine Walze, die von einem bösen Wind geschoben wird. Leider hat sich diese Walze in der immensen Größe Russlands etwas verirrt und beginnt nun rückwärts zu rennen; der Revolutionenexport wütet in alle Himmelsrichtungen, um überall dort zu gewinnen, wo Unzufriedenheit in Rebellion mündet… Ich weiß ganz genau, denn, wie ich Dir schon sagte: ich war mit Cristescu bei Lenin... Der war gerade dabei, eine neue Internationale zu gründen und benötigte Vertreter verschiedener Parteien, die mit wahlberechtiger Stimme auf einer Versammlung seine Vorschläge segnen sollten. Viele, die als Vertreter anderer Länder galten waren nichts anderes als seine ehemaligen Soldaten oder hatten eine Zeit lang als Provokateure, genau wie er selbst, gedient. Wir waren anders, hatten einen anderen Hintergrund, unter Berücksichtigung der Legalität!... Wir hatten gerade einen Kongress gehabt, der uns gewählt hatte, eine Partei, die sich darauf vorbereitete, die Kandidatenliste für das Parlament bekannt zu geben und, nicht in letzter Linie, eine Partei die uns die Vollmacht gab, an diesem internationalen Treffen teilzunehmen und unserem Mandat entsprechend zu wählen... Wir waren in der Tat die Delegation einer Partei, unter der Führung von Cristescu, genauso wie ihre Delegation Lenin als Fürer hatte. Und Plăpumaru nahm kein Blatt vor dem Mund; er sprach zu ihm deutlich: “Also, aus demokratischen Gründen stehen die Dinge bei uns nicht so, Vladimir Ilic!... Lassen Sie uns aus gleichberechtigten Positionen heraus verhandeln. Ich vertrete eine legale Partei in einem unabhängigen Land, Sie vertreten eine andere, in einem größeren, mächtigeren Land; wir diskutieren, verhandeln und finden eine gemeinsame Lösung”!... Jawohl, wir waren damals im internen, hitzigen Gefecht gestählert und vertraten eine Arbeiterklasse und nicht irgend eine Anhäufung von Spionen, die es galt, herumzukommandieren!... Zug um Zug schnitten sie uns ab. Die Leichtbeeinflußbaren zogen sie auf ihre Seite und überzeugten sie, zu ihren Dienern zu werden. Uns, die Resistenten, entfernten sie; ein paar von den Hartnäckigsten töteten sie... Genauso, wie die schlimmsten Kapitalisten, schreckten sie vor nichts zurück, um ihren Gewinn zu maximieren. Wer genau sollte gewinnen? Eine Handvoll Menschen, genau so klein wie die Gruppe, die auf den revolutionären Plakaten als feindliche Minderheit verteufelt wurde und die es zu beseitigen galt. Das waren leere Floskeln, sie benutzten sie nur, sagten sie nur, um die große Masse auf ihrer Seite zu haben... Auf diese Art und Weise werden die Völker niemals siegen. Und ich begreife, dass man ganz andere Interessen verfolgt als das Wohl der Mehrheit, der Provozierten. Ich will etwas für diese Mehrheit der Rumänen tun, sie schützen... Du weißt, was ich tun möchte, Herr Lehrer“ – jetzt wurde er wieder fordernd - „was wäre, wenn wir erneut eine repräsentative Partei bilden könnten?... Ich würde dieses Land zu einer Art Schweiz erklären, die keiner mehr berühren dürfte!... Ich meine“ – er lachte herzhaft, als ob er jemandem einen Streich spielen wollte – „ich würde ihnen beweisen, dass ich nicht umsonst die kommunistische Theorie studiert habe, die diese Schurken bloß zu propagandistischen Zwecken, auf Papier, missbrauchen. Ich würde das durchsetzen, was uns angeht, das Prinzip des Selbstbestimmung der Völker, dieses Prinzip, welches diese verlogenen Führer so gern priesen!... Ich würde so laut schreien, dass alle Nationen dieser Welt mich hören könnten – erhitzte er sich – so dass es niemand mehr wagen wärde, mir zu widersprechen!... Ehrenwort; ich habe einen Brief in diesem Sinne an Titulescu geschickt. Die Volksfront, die ich gründen will, muss möglichst umfassend sein...“

6.

Alexe erinnerte sich wie er ihm zusah als er gegangen war. Das Mädchen an der Hand, machte er sich auf dem Weg zum Bahnhof. Ab und zu bleib er stehen, sprach mit dem Kind, fuhr ihm mit der Hand durchs Haar oder über die Kleider oder gab ihr etwas zu halten , aber er machte es immer in gespannter Haltung, aufmerksam und irgendwie sorgfältig: als ob er sich andauernd umsah, ob ihn jemand beobachtete, als fürchte er, dass jemand ihm folgte. Dann setzte er seinen Weg fort.

Trotzdem, als am Abend darauf Drăgans´ Leute in Begleitung des Mädchens auftauchten, wurde ihm klar, dass ihm wohl sämtliche Vorsichtsmaßnahmen nichts genutzt hatten. Das Mädchen wiederum war ruhig und ausgeglichen, als ob es schon einmal so etwas durchgemacht hätte.

„Das Mädchen hat es noch geschafft, Herrn Drăgan etwas mitzuteilen, aber dann drangen die in das Gewerkschaftshaus hinein und die Chefs wurden vorgeladen, um ihre Erklärungen abzugeben, oder wer weiß was noch... Also blieb sie bei uns und sie erzählte uns von Ihnen; wir verstanden, dass wir sie hierher bringen sollen und es war irgendwie auch nachvollziehbar, schließlich sind Sie, Herr Lehrer, der Cousin von Herr Drăgan. Was nun? Überlassen wir Ihnen das Kind? Das Mädchen will das so!...“

Alexe schaute ernsten Auges auf das Mädchen und verstand ihre Notlage, obwohl sie ihn nicht mit dem Ausdruck einer Bitte, sondern eher einer Herausforderung ansah. Als würde sie sagen „zeig mal was Du für ein Mensch bist!”. Ohne sich sicher zu sein, ob er das Richtige tat, hörte er sich selbst etwas zögerlich sprechen, so als handle es sich um sein eigenes Kind:
„Natürlich bleibt sie hier. Und dann flüsterte er noch unmerklich: Aber, Drăgan, was hat Drăgan gesagt?“
„Nun, das ist es eben, er kam nicht mehr zu Wort, weil die sich ganz plötzlich hinein stützten, so stürmisch wie sie es seit den Streiks von ´33 nicht mehr getan haben. Er konnte nur noch schnell seine berühmte Rede anfangen, nach dem Motto „Angriff ist die beste Verteidigung”, die im Normallfall am Ende zur Einigung führt... Doch die hatten diesmal keine Lust, selbst der Kommissar sagte, es sei ernst, weil den Chefs aus Bukarest ein Verrat gemeldet wurde, und nun fahnden alle nach einem großen Bolschewiken. Drăgan beschimpfte sie aufs Übelste und schrie „ihr wisst, dass wir keine Bolschewiken sind”, dann ging er mit, um seine Erklärung abzugeben und denen aus Bukarest weiter zu drohen, mit einer wichtigen Information, die er angeblich hat... unter uns, ehrlich gesagt, sogar die Bullen waren sichtbar verängstigt, die kamen ja auch so plötzlich, wie aus dem Nichts, als wären sie schon lange auf der Lauer gewesen... Das Mädchen kann also bleiben, oder nicht?...“
„Selbstverständlich. Aber bitte sagt Drăgan... Richtet ihm aus, er soll mich aufsuchen... Er soll...“
„Geht in Ordnung. Leben Sie wohl, Herr Lehrer!“ – die Leute hatten es eilig. Man sah ihnen die Freude an, sich von der Aufgabe mit dem Mädchen befreit zu haben.
Er blieb, den ersten Blicken des Mädchens ausgesetzt, verunsichert und sprachlos. Ihr Blick durchbohrte ihn fragend und er fühlte sich verpflichtet, etwas zu sagen:
„Na?...“
„Kann ich mit Paul spielen, so wie gestern?“ – fragte sie und zeigte auf den Kleinen, der etwas verwirrt da stand.
„Klar kannst du; zieh deinen Mantel aus und...“ – ihm fiel ein, dass er etwas tun musste, um ihre Verklemmung zu vertreiben.
Dann geschah ein kleines Wunder. Es war der Zauber, der plötzlich eintrat, als das wohlerzogene Wesen, welches diesem ungewöhnlich ernsten und doch kleinen Kinde inne wohnte,

endlich sein unsichtbares Schutzschild beiseite legte und sich erlaubte, endlich wieder Kind zu sein. Schnell und ordentlich lief sie zum Kleiderständer und hängte ihren Mantel hin, dann rannte sie zum Jungen und fing an ihn zu umarmen und zu küssen, als wäre er der Träger ihrer ganzen, lang ersehnten Hoffnung. Es war die Seele, an die sich ihr umherirrendes Kinderherz lehnte, um Halt und Trost zu finden.
Alexe war zu Tränen gerührt, doch er traute sich nicht noch irgendetwas zu fragen.
Später erst, als Paul eingeschlafen war, kam das Mädchen scheu zu ihm, als wüsste es dass er ihr jetzt zuhören wollte. Wie ein Erwachsener, der sich für die kurze Verschnaufpause, die er sich erlaubt hat, entschuldigen will, fing sie das Gespräch an:
„Mein Onkel hat mich gelehrt, falls ich einmal von ihm getrennt werden soll, muss ich unbedingt an den Ort zurück kehren, wo ich zuletzt mit ihm zusammen war, damit er weiß wo er mich findet. Das habe ich auch Onkel Drăgan gesagt. Er wird mich abholen; seien Sie unbesorgt!“
Er brachte es nicht übers Herz, ihr seine Zweifel daran mitzuteilen. Stattdessen lenkte er sich mit Tischdecken ab, weckte den Jungen und lud die Kinder zum Essen ein. Danach spielte er gelassen mit allen beiden. Für eine kurze Zeit schien die Welt wieder in Ordnung zu sein und alle Sorgen waren vergessen.
Viel später, als Valentina nach Hause kam, fand sie alle drei, selig in einem Bett schlafend.

7.

Am Tag darauf hatte er vormittags Unterricht. Dadurch dass die Bereitschaft im Krankenhaus anderwärtig vergeben war konnte Valentina zu Hause in ihrer Praxis arbeiten und sich um die Kinder kümmern. Sie dachten, wenn gleich nicht der Behaarte vorbei kommen könne, obwohl das Mädchen immer noch fest davon überzeugt war, wird vielleicht Drăgan erscheinen:
„Sie glaubt an diesen Bolschewiken, der komischerweise an Gott zu glauben scheint!“ – sprach Alexe.
Aber Valentina widersprach ihm diesmal, denn sie war auch gläubig, trotz ihres medizinischen Studiums und der rationalistisch-darwinistischen Orientierung, die sie in den

Gesprächen mit ihrem Mann vertrat. Es schien, als hätte sie durch die Geschichte dieses Menschen eine andere Sichtweise erlangt:
„Er glaubt!...Wahrscheinlich eben weil er sich vor den wahren Bolschewiken, die seine Frau umgebracht haben schützen will..."
„Hm, „die Wahren"!" spottete Alexe „Ich frage mich dann, wieso sie eine von denen sein konnte?"
„Ich frage mich nur" gestand ihm Valentina gerührt „was sie wohl gefühlt haben muss, als sie merkte, dass ausgerechnet die Bolschewiken sie hinrichteten."
Nachdenklich wie durch eine schwere Bürde bedrückt gab Alexe zu:
„Eine schreckliche Welt; schlimmer noch als unsere. Ich muss leider den berühmten Satz zitieren: „Quo vadis, Domine?!"... Immerhin, du warst die Erste, die bei seiner Ankunft gespürt hat, dass er eine Botschaft mit sich trug. Ich kann ihm nicht helfen, ich will das gar nicht" legte er seine Position fest „aber man merkt, dass er nicht nur eine starke Lebenskraft, sondern auch einen Sinn des Lebens ausstrahlt!... Wie dem auch sei" entschied er sich, so als ob er auf einer Idee beharrte, die sie sowieso nicht verstehen konnte „wir müssen dem Mädchen helfen. Egal was Drăgan dazu sagt, das weißt du besser als ich!... Dein Herz weiß es" sagte er noch und küsste sie so, als würde er ihr die gesamte Macht über ihr kleines Universum anerkennen wollen, über ihre kleine Welt, die nur ihnen gehörte, wo sie sich alleine, aber geborgen fühlten und in Partnerschaft herrschten, wie unter einem schützend Dach, das sie vor der Außenwelt abschirmte.
Im Gegenzug zu seiner festen Entschlossenheit überkam ihn eine Welle der Zärtlichkeit, die ihn dazu brachte, das gerade aufgewachte Mädchen auf die Wange zu küssen, als wäre es schon seit eh und jäh Teil der Familie gewesen:
„Dein Onkel wird schon kommen; bis dahin" wenchselte er geschickt das Thema „bleibst du bei uns und bist Paulchens Schwester."
„Sobald er sich befreien kann, kommt er sicher" erklärte das Mädchen in festem Ton „doch es könnte auch passieren, dass sie ihn umbringen, hat er mir gesagt..."
„Vergiss es, wenn er Dir das gesagt hat. Es ist nicht wahr."
Alexe versuchte, sie zu beruhigen, aber das Mädchen ließ nicht locker:
„Es gibt einen Rothaarigen, ich kenne ihn!"

„Woher kennst du ihn?“
„Ein Rothaariger, der schlechtes Rumänisch spricht, ich habe ihn gesehen!...“
„Wann hast du ihn gesehen?“
„Zuerst in Iassi. Der Onkel wurde an einem Ort erwartet, bei einer Gewerkschaftsversammlung, genauso wie gestern Herr Drăgan auf ihn wartete. Wir hatten uns auf die Seite gestellt und schauten den Menschen zu, die gerade rein kamen. Dann sah ihn mein Onkel. Sofort gingen wir weg und kehrten nie wieder zurück. Mein Onkel sagte zu mir, dass er ein sehr böser Mensch sei. Wir stiegen in den Zug ein und setzten unseren Ausflug fort, genauso wie mein Onkel und ich vereinbart hatten, wenn ich gute Noten in der Schule kriege...“
„Daran hast du dich gehalten.“
„Habe ich; aber ich will nicht dass mein Onkel...“
„Das will ich auch nicht“ versicherte ihr Alexe, in gleichem Masse von ihrer kindischen, aber auch ernsthaften Einstellung beeindruckt „wir werden weiter nach Drăgan suchen und erfahren...“
Doch Drăgan gab kein Zeichen und Alexe bereute jetzt, seine Männer, damals als sie das Mädchen brachten, nicht besser befragt zu haben. Jetzt war er in einer Sackgasse gelandet, wusste nicht, wo er mit seinen Nachforschungen anfangen sollte, um herauszufinden was wirklich mit dem Behaarten passiert war und wo er sich eventuell befinden konnte. Die Ungewissheit dauerte so lange bis er von einem gerichtlichen Schnellverfahren erfuhr, in das Drăgan involviert war. Also traf er die Entscheidung, sich als Zeuge zur Verfügung zu stellen.
„Drăgan ist damit nicht einverstanden – brachte ihm sein Anwalt die Antwort. Als er sich nicht abwimmeln ließ, sprach er zu ihm noch deutlicher: Er will nicht, dass Sie ihn in Schwierigkeiten bringen. Er befürchtet, dass Sie die Sachen ganz anders sehen und glaub, es wäre besser, sie von der ganzen Sache fern zu halten.“
„Gut, aber ich weiß, dass der Mensch, der für diese Verhaftungen verantwortlich gemacht wird, kein Bolschewik ist. Er ist kein Bolschewik, er ist kein ausländischer Agent, er ist mehr das Opfer; das kann ich bezeugen; seine Frau wurde von Stalins Männern umgebracht; er selbst...“

„Wir verfolgen eine andere Verteidigungsstrategie; wir beschuldigen nicht einmal die Polizisten, dass sie unter dem Vorwand einer angeblichen Flucht geschossen hätten; wir behaupten lediglich, dass auf einen Unbekannten geschossen wurde und niemand hat genau gewusst, warum der überhaupt da, auf unserer Gewerkschaftsversammlung war..."
So erklärte ihm der Anwalt in groben Zügen sein Plädoyer und nahm an, dass er viel mehr wusste als er, aber er bat ihn, sich seiner juristischen Logik zu unterwerfen. Nun war Alexe verwirrter denn jäh, denn er begriff allmählich, dass die Sache viel komplizierter war als er gedacht hatte. Es sah so aus, als ob der Mensch, der ihm so lebendig die Geschichte aller Revolutionen erklärt hatte, wenn gleich auch ein bisschen skurril in seiner Darstellung gewesen war, erschossen wurde. Der Mann, dessen Frau bereits umgebracht wurde, war jetzt auch tot. Und ausgerechnet Drăgan wurde festgenommen und dafür verantwortlich gemacht.
Als er all dies begriff, wurde ihm klar, dass er ab sofort erst recht einen Grund in den Gerichtssaal zu gehen hatte. Also wartete er geduldig darauf, bis der Prozess aufgerufen wurde.
Doch als Drăgan und seine Gruppe in den Ring gebracht wurden traf ihn der vorwurfsvolle, unerbittliche Blick seines riesenhaften Cousins wie ein Messer. Danach wandte er ihm demonstrativ den Rücken zu. In seinem Inneren meinte Alexe schon seine donnernde Stimme zu hören: „Wenn du nicht sofort verschwindest und es auch wagst etwas zu sagen, werde ich ...!!!..."
Die Festgenommenen wurden vorgestellt. Danach übernahm der Verteidigungsanwalt das Wort. Der Staatsanwalt widersprach ihm, sie stritten. Der Kommissar legte seinen Bericht vor. Merkwürdigerweise schien sich der Polizist besser mit dem Anwalt als mit dem Staatsanwalt zu verstehen. Er schwor, dass der Erschossene eher zufällig von Ihnen festgenommen wurde; und zwar neben dem Gewerkschaftssitz, nicht innen im Gebäude. Er beschrieb den Typen als suspekt, bewaffnet, rothaarig und er sagte, er hätte rumänisch mit einem komischen Akzent gesprochen. Mehr wusste er auch nicht, denn der Mann trug keinen Ausweis bei sich, was ja auch der Grund seiner Festnahme gewesen war. Eigentlich hatten sie vor, ihn auf eine Vernehmung in das Revier mitzunehmen, nachdem sie alle

Festnahmen fertig erstellt hatten, die von ihren Chefs in Auftrag gegeben wurden. Er betonte, dass seine Gefolgsleute keineswegs in die Richtung geschossen hatten, wo sich der spätere Verletzte befand, sondern zur anderen Seite hin, wo sich ein weiterer Verdächtiger versteckt hielt. Letzterer war anschließend spurlos verschwunden, was die Aufklärung der Lage noch komplizierter machte, denn mann vermutete dass eben dieser Vermisste den Rothaarigen erschossen hatte.

Als die Beschuldigten den Ring verließen, warf Drăgan seinem Cousin Alexe noch ein paar böse, vorwurfsvolle Blicke zu. Dieser kam zurück nach Hause und verhielt sich still; zuerst streichelte er den Kindern über die Köpfe und wartete auf Valentina, um sie über die ungewisse Lage in Kenntnis zu setzen und um ihr seine Besorgnis über die weitere Anwesenheit des Mädchens in ihrem Hause mitzuteilen. Er fühlte sich umso mehr verantwortlich für das Kind, nachdem der Behaarte womöglich tot war. Und von Seiten seines Cousins Drăgan war anscheinend auch keine Hilfe mehr zu erwarten.

Am nächsten Tag, als die Zeitungen von einem unbekannten Toten berichteten, der während einer Razzia von einem anderen Unbekannten erschossen wurde, erinnerte sich Alexe wie das Mädchen „Herrn Drăgan und seine Gewerkschaft" erwähnt hatte und fragte es noch einmal:

„Woher weißt du wer Drăgan ist?"

„Mein Onkel hat mir das gesagt, als er mich zu ihm schickte. Das ist meine Mission „ beteuerte sie, als sie merkte dass er sie ernst genommen hatte „Mein Onkel wartet immer in seinem Versteck und ich gehe vor, um die Lage zu testen. Auch bei Ihrer Frau haben wir das so gemacht. Ich ging vor, als sie am Tor war; sofort erkannte ich, dass sie gut war, weil sie mich mochte..."

„Ach so!... Das hat sie mir nicht erzählt" versuchte er sich aufzumuntern, obwohl er ein bisschen besorgt war.

„Ja, ich sagte ihr, dass mein Onkel mit Ihnen etwas besprechen möchte und er will wissen, ob sie alleine sind oder ob jemand bei Ihnen war."

„So fragst du immer?"

„Ja. Mein Onkel ... geht so vor." antwortete sie sanft und nahm sich dabei ziemlich ernst „Er macht das so, weil der Rothaarige, der schlecht rumänisch kann, ihn verfolgt, um ihn zu töten. Ich habe ihn in Iassi gesehen, das habe ich Ihnen schon gesagt; und ich habe ihn noch einmal gesehen, in Bukarest, als mein Onkel wieder ein Treffen mit jemand anderen vereinbart hatte!...“

„Wie hast Du ihn gesehen?“

„Mein Onkel hatte mich geschickt; er erklärte mir wie er aussieht und schickte mich an einen Ort, um zu sehen ob er dort war.“

„Und, war er dort?“

„Es waren viele, die saßen an vielen Tischen, denn es war ein Restaurantgarten, wo mein Onkel verabredet war, aber er vermutete dass auch der Rothaarige davon wusste. Der wusste es wirklich und war uns auf den Fersen, also bin ich gegangen...Und ich habe ihn erkannt. Ich vertraue Ihnen, deswegen sage ich Ihnen die Wahrheit, weil auch mein Onkel mir sagte, dass ich Ihnen trauen kann“ sie hatte wieder diesen erwachsenen Ausdruck im Gesicht „Ich habe ihn erkannt.“

„Und, was hast du getan?“

„Er war sehr nahe und ich habe mich erschreckt. Ich lief zu meinem Onkel und habe ihn gebeten, wegzulaufen, denn ich hatte Angst... Nicht wegen mir, aber für meinen Onkel fürchtete ich mich; ich habe ihn sehr lieb und will nicht, dass ihn diese Feinde umbringen. Aber mein Onkel ist stärker und schlauer als sie. Sie können ihn nicht töten. Und er hat viele Leute, die ihn schätzen und beschützen.“

„Wohnst du bei ihm?“ – fragte Alexe, um nicht an das Drama denken zu müssen, welches das Mädchen nicht einmal erahnte.

„Nur im Sommer, in den Ferien. Er hat eine große, riesige Bibliothek. Er lebt umgeben von Büchern; die hat er alle gesammelt; aber ich kann ihnen nicht sagen, wo das ist. Das darf ich nicht verraten. Dort kommen die Bösen nicht hin; nur Menschen, die ihn sehr sehr gut kennen. Ich kann kaum erwarten, dass wir wieder dorthin zurückkehren, denn dort...“

Doch den Satz beendete sie nicht, denn plötzlich sprang sie voller Freude hoch und fing an zu schreien:

„Es ist mein Onkel, mein Onkel; er ist gekommen; ich kenne seine Pfeifen; mach auf, es ist sein Zeichen!...“

So wurde Alexe Zeuge einer berührenden Szene. Als Vater kannte er sehr wohl die Verbundenheit seines Kindes und konnte somit die ganze Freude nachvollziehen. Als er den Behaarten ins Haus begleitete, sprang ihm das sonst scheue Mädchen wie befreit entgegen. Jegliche Angst und Unsicherheit, die sie den fremden Erwachsenen bis dahin zeigte, fiel von ihr ab als sie den

Menschen sah, dem sie so viel vertraute und den sie bedingungslos liebte. Unter solchen Umständen verschmelzen die Altersgrenzen und die gesellschaftlichen Zwänge und zum Vorschein kommt die pure Verbundenheit, die allen menschlichen Beziehungen zu Grunde liegt und sie so verzaubert. Denn die Liebe ist stärker als alle Altersgrenzen; das Kind ist die Freude des Erwachsenen und der Erwachsene bedeutet Schutz und Geborgenheit für das Kind. Es war, als ob sich vor seinen Augen das Heiligste dieser Welt offenbarte, das Edelste überhaupt, die pure Liebe....

Der kleine Paul reagierte zum ersten mal mit Eifersucht und hopste auf seinem Hochstuhl hin und her, denn er war es nicht gewohnt, dass sich die Streicheleinheiten und die gesamte Aufmerksamkeit der Erwachsenen nicht auf ihn, sondern auf jemand anderen richteten. Ein bisschen war er auch enttäuscht als er sah, dass das in seinen Augen so große Mädchen auch nur ein liebeshungriges Kind war, so wie er. Und das passierte vor den Augen seines eigenen Vaters! Erst als der Onkel und die Nichte anfingen ein Gedicht aufzusagen, beruhigte sich der kleine Bengel und fing an mit seinen kleinen Händchen begeistert zu klatschen. Die Freude des Wiedersehens spiegelte sich in den Versen: *Die Herrschaft der Faust von oben bis unten... Eure Illusionen werden mit Getöse stürzen...*

Als er ihn so fröhlich sah, beruhigte sich Alexe, denn er verstand, dass er sich ab sofort keine Sorgen mehr machen musste. Er lächelte dem Behaarten zu. Dieser nahm den Kleinen in seine Armen und sprach mit gebrochener Stimme, während er mit den Tränen kämpfte:

„Heute ist mein Rachetag. Doch ich weiß immer noch nicht wie ich es ohne mein Mädchen soweit gebracht hätte. Sie tröstet mich über den Tod meiner Frau hinaus!... Hab′ keine Angst; wir werden gleich verschwinden. Sobald sich das Mädchen beruhigt.“

Corneliu Leu (left), his wife Rodica (right) and Sophia Dediu, at Leu's home, in 2013

8.

Mit diesem Mädchen war es eine lange Geschichte, eine Geschichte die Alexe sehr berührte. Der Behaarte drückte das Mädchen fest an sein Herz und sprach bedrückt, vielleicht auch weil er sich an die ganz schwierigen Situationen erinnerte, die er in der letzten Zeit durchgelebt hatte. Kurz gesagt, er war wieder in der aufgewühlten Stimmung, die den Eindruck machte, als wolle er viel zu viel auf einmal erzählen wollen. Seine Lippen kamen dem Druck von Innen kaum nach:
„Sobald sie sich beruhigt, gehen wir... Bis dann sag´ ich Dir nur eins; ja, ich sage Dir, eins musst Du noch wissen; da ich Drăgan nicht treffen konnte und ihn leider trotzdem in Schwierigkeiten brachte, bitte ich Dich zumindest mir zuzuhören... Ich sag´ Dir nur wie es war und dann gehe ich... Fürchte Dich nicht vor Unannehmlichkeiten, auch wenn Du etwas in den Zeitungen gelesen hast“ flüsterte er ihm zu, doch dann überlegte er es sich anders und wechselte das Thema: „Sie wissen nicht wie ich aussehe; ich habe Dir gesagt, dass ich in Ihren Fahndungspapieren völlig anders abgebildet bin. Deswegen

schicken sie Spione im voraus: um in Erfahrung zu bringen, auf welchen Versammlungen ich erscheinen werde, eben um meine Tarnung auffliegen zu lassen. Sie wollen mich identifizieren!“ er sprach dieses „identifizieren” in einem gewissen Unterton aus, etwas zynisch, und lächelte schelmisch dazu: „...Tja, wie es aussieht, habe ich ihren Spion diesmal schneller identifiziert. Ich machte es so gut, dass er jetzt nicht einmal mehr atmet!... Du hast gelesen... – und er stockte wieder – Also lassen wir das; es geht gar nicht darum; vielmehr geht es um Deine Sicherheit, und dass wir gleich von hier verschwinden sollten.“

„Ihr müsst nicht gehen“ beruhigte ihn Alexe als er langsam ruhiger wurde und das Thema wechseln konnte „Ich sprach gerade mit dem Mädchen über ihr Versteck, da wo es so viele Bücher gibt; doch sie wollte mir nicht sagen, wo das ist....“

„Nun, wenn Trotzki ausgerechnet in Mexiko beschützt werden muss“ fühlte er sich zu einer Erklärung verpflichtet, schließlich hatte er Alexes´ Leben in den letzten Tagen ziemlich stark aufgemischt „schütze ich mich auch, zumindest in meinem Heimatland, wo ich meine Aktionen planen kann. Ich will diese Partei umorganisieren, genauso wie es am Anfang war, als wir alle daran glaubten; ich werde sie von russischen Agenten säubern, das habe ich Dir geschworen. Denn die Armen benötigen eine Partei; Agenten muss es wohl schon immer gegeben haben, auch damals. Aber damals hatten wir einen Nădejde, einen Morun, einen Constantin Mille; wir hatten die Studenten, die das lateinische Alphabet mitbrachten, und nicht diese Komitee-Propagandisten, die russische Filme zeigen und Rascolniken-Sekten, die... Die haben nicht einmal eine Kultur, außer Lenins Broschüren... Die sind nicht besonders fähig, das weiss ich auch; aber die GPU stärkt ihnen den Rücken!... Cristescu, meine ich, will nicht mehr politisch aktiv sein. Er lehnt meinen Vorschlag ab, so wie du. Hab´ keine Angst, ich versuche nicht, Dir mein Konzept aufzuzwingen; du kannst Dich selbst überzeugen, was da läuft. Auch ich habe nachgedacht und ich respektiere Dich und Deine Entscheidung, denn Du bist besser als viele andere. Ich meine, Du bist klug genug um Dich selbst zu überzeugen, mehr sage ich dazu nicht. Und wenn nicht, dann nicht... Genau wie Cristescu, den ich respektiere, weil er zu mir sagte: „Hör zu, ich komme nicht mehr, weil ich da nicht mehr reden kann; sobald ich das Wort ergreife, noch bevor man richtig verstehen kann was ich sage, wird man mir den russischen Stempel aufdrücken und ich werde als Stalin-Getreuer beschimpft; doch du weißt ganz genau, dass ich nicht einmal Lenins Mann sein wollte!”... So sprach er zu mir und ich muss das akzeptieren, selbst wenn es mir nicht gefällt. Ich wollte Dir das unbedingt noch sagen, damit Du mich verstehst. Und nun, selbst wenn Du vielleicht glaubst, dass ich Dich in Gefahr gebracht habe, werde ich weg gehen, damit Dir nichts passiert. So wie ich bereits bei unserem letzten Treffen sagte: ich kämpfe gar nicht gegen die Legionären, denn auch sie sind aus der Armut des Landes entstanden, doch es spielt eine große Rolle mit welcher Gruppierung sie verbandeln. Ich habe Codreanu in Iassi kennen gelernt, als er im Namen unserer Gewerkschaften sprach, eben um deren Macht von den Russen und von Lenins chaotischen Truppen fern zu halten. Er redete genau aus diesem Grunde, um diese Agenten, diese bolschewistischen Provokateure zu enttarnen und um unseren ehrlichen Gewerkschaftleuten zu helfen. Also verstehe ich warum sich Maniu mit Codreanu verbündete; ich verstehe nicht warum die nicht begreifen, dass sie sich an Hitler ausliefern und sich gegenseitig erschießen; soviel!... So, das ist, was ich Dir noch sagen wollte... Aber es musste gesagt werden, versteht Du? Das alles wollte ich Dir und Drăgan gleichzeitig sagen. Aber jetzt musst Du es an ihn weiter leiten, damit er versteht warum wir eine etwas breitere patriotische Front aufbauen müssen. Ich werde verschwinden; für eine Zeit lang muss ich untertauchen, aber glaube mir, ich gebe den Kampf nicht auf!... Ich werde mich nicht geschlagen geben! Wie gesagt: auch die Armut hat eine Partei verdient, die ihre Rechte vertritt...“

Mit diesen Worten zeigte er seine Entschlossenheit, doch es schimmerte auch ein Hauch von Paranoia durch. Es zeigte ein unnatürliches, groteskes Verhalten, sprang von Euphorie zu tiefster Betroffenheit über, war mal bittend und dann wiederum befehlend, wechselte von Zärtlichkeit zu Aggression, er war einfach nicht stabil. Sein offen getragenes Hemd, die drohende Haltung, mit ausgestreckter Brust, die bewusst verwegene Art den Mantel auf den Schultern zurück zu schieben, all das zeugte von seiner tiefen Betroffenheit und von seiner gefährlich instabilen Lage. Die grauen Haare seiner Brust vermittelten den Eindruck, dass vielleicht seine Zeit schon durchgelaufen war.

„Meine Bleivergiftung ist wieder da“ erreichte er wieder sein leidliches Thema, und zeigte auf seine Hemdöffnung „doch diesmal verdanke ich es nicht dem Bleidampf der Druckerei, sondern der vergifteten Luft aus Kreml, wo sie uns in ihren vorgerasteten Druckmuster hinein zu drücken versuchten. Um ihnen zu entkommen, musste ich jahrelang so herum spazieren; ob Sommer oder Winter, bei Schnee und Regen, ich war immer barhäuptig und meine Brust war immer sichtbar... Verrückt, nicht wahr? Nun, das bin ich auch, wie denn auch sonst, mein lieber Herr?!... Doch zu Dir hätte ich früher kommen müssen, seit ich hörte, dass Du zum Protestieren in den Königspalast eingedrungen bist. Deswegen bin ich gekommen; ich hatte versäumt, es Dir bei unserer ersten Begegnung zu erzählen; jetzt musste ich es schnell noch loswerden, bevor ich gehe. Wir sind gleich weg, ich will Dir keine Schwierigkeiten machen... Wahrscheinlich hast Du schon genug gelitten... Aber Du hast mich auch gern empfangen!... Hast Du gesehen, was in den Zeitungen steht?“ nun stellte er ihm doch die Frage, die er sich am Anfang noch verkniffen hatte.
„Da steht, dass ein Unbekannter einen anderen Unbekannten erschossen hat.“
„Mehr nicht?“
„Das ist leider alles, mehr konnte ich nicht erfahren. Ich dachte, es handelt sich um Sie.“
„Aha! – erwiderte er begeistert, als ob er das erwartet hätte; dann bohrte er weiter: War da keine genauere Beschreibung des Opfers?“
„Nein. Nur eine kurze Nachricht. In allen anderen Zeitungen auch so.“
„Wie viele hast Du gesehen?“
„Etwa vier. In einer stand gar nichts.“
„Sehr gut; das heißt, die haben ihr Wort gehalten!...“
„Wer?“
„Ach, es gibt ein paar Leute, die auch uns helfen, mehr kann ich Dir nicht sagen; deswegen wollte ich nicht mit Dir darüber sprechen, aber Du hast eine Art, das Vertrauen zu wecken!... Ich sagte schon, ich habe mein Gesicht verändert. So wie ein Räuber, wie ich heute aussehe, mit langen Haaren... Gab es da keine Foto, gar keine Einzelheiten?...“
„Nirgendwo; dieselbe Nachricht überall, bloß ein paar Zeilen.“

„Mehr war auch nicht nötig.“ - seine Verrücktheit schien zu wachsen, denn jetzt zitterte er erregt – „dann werden sie genau das auch Stalin berichten, dass sie mich umgebracht haben, so wie den Bajanov!... Du weißt nicht wer Bajanov ist, nicht wahr?... Ach, eine lange Geschichte!... Ihn haben sie im schnellsten Zug verfolg, den „*Train Bleu*“, nach Nizza; sie wollten ihn aus den Zug werfen. Aber er hat einen von denen weggeschubst!... Weißt Du, was die getan haben?... Selbst die Profi-Henker des GPU fürchten sich vor Stalins Vergeltung, also haben sie geschwiegen und behaupteten der Tote sei Bajanov gewesen!... So werden sie auch meinen Fall schließen; ich bin gerächt! Racheee!... Mensch, lass mich in Ruhe; ich bin ja gleich weg; warte nur, bis sich meine Aufregung legt. Nur eins möchte ich noch tun, so wie in meiner Jugend, als ich an diesem Punkt gelangte, wo der Elan mich trug: ich will das Rachegedicht meines damaligen Mentors aufsagen, Constantin Mille, der 1907 zum Verräter wurde!...In meinem Leben begegnete ich vielen Verrätern, aber ich gebe nicht auf!...“

Dann nahm er das Mädchen auf den Arm und sie gingen fort, beide glücklich und zufrieden, als ob sie miteinander in einer geheimen Sprache kommunizierten. Sein stürmisches Wesen beunruhigte das Kind keineswegs und so ertönten die Verse zugleich in seiner tiefen Tonlage und in der kindlichen, melodischen Stimme des Mädchens. Dies gefiel dem kleinen Paul, der begeistert applaudierte und bald steckte er auch seinen Vater mit seinem Enthusiasmus an. Wie aus einem Gewehr geschossen erklangen die Worte aus der Ferne:

...Ihr sagtet´s: gebraucht wird ein Stapel Verbrechen
Mit Tränen und Blut seit Jahrzehnten gefestigt,
Um unsere Auserwählten der Masse zu entnehmen
Die diese Menschheit zum fernen Ziel führen sollen.

Ihr sagtet´s: die Träumer humaner Gesetze
Verrückt und chaotisch das Volk rebellierend:
Der Sonne gleich wandern auf ewigen Pfaden
Auf Wege die gleichen dem menschlichen Fluss.

Ihr sagtet´s: ab morgen wird dies eure Rede
Selbst wenn auch wir, Narren gleich tönen wie ihr:

„Beherrscht wird die Welt durch den Stärksten von Allen”,
In Tränen ihr weinet, doch wir lachen drum!...

On Corneliu Leu's house wall.

LE ROMAN D'UNE AMOUREUSE REINE PAR CORNELIU LEU

Chapter 6. La femme même reine…

1

Passée de ces deux cinq, c'est-à-dire celui de l'âge, qui marqua sa moitié du siècle ainsi que celui qui lui additionna d'autres années, l'hôtesse à l'esprit vif du plus mondain salon parisien, consciente en même temps de l'autorité et de l'attraction exercées sur le monde des idées et des arts du deuxième Empire était, cependant, consciente aussi, de son âge ; une chose assez rare pour les femmes gâtées, même très intelligentes. A part le froissement de vêtements en soie très chère et l'ostentation de montrer son visage fardé avec insistance, acceptée pour l'épouse d'un peintre recherché pour décorer les constructions somptueuses, somptueuse elle aussi par ses manières et par la liberté des idées qu'elle n'hésitait pas à affirmer en public, elle savait souligner par ses opinions osées son rang intellectuel mais, en même temps, se garder, comme une dame arrivée à un certain âge et à des influences politiques. Elle ne dépassait jamais les limites, comme n'importe quelle française elle savait provoquer et accepter les compliments mis en valeur par son art de flirter, sans pour autant se permettre des coquetteries de mauvais goût, comme les petites vieilles vaniteuses et gourmandes qui oublient qu'elles ne sont plus des petites filles et se laissent pousser vers des espoirs d'amour dans ce Paris si prometteur qui, avec la grande science de la frivolité, est parvenu à lever les standards amoureux bien au-dessus des coutumes habituelles. Ce Paris-là, sans préjugés, offrant des midinettes voluptueuses pour les vieillards presque dingues, mais jouissant du terme italien de *gigolo* conféré aux beaux gosses qui ne se souciaient pas des peaux pendantes de celles qui, en dépits de leur âge, voulaient jouer encore les courtisanes.

C'était une vraie reine dans son salon bondé des grandes célébrités de l'époque et, en même temps, d'idées d'avant-garde qu'elles adoptaient, et n'hésitant pas à cultiver avec audace celles les plus révolutionnaires, ce qui lui avait donné la force de renoncer aux quatre millions de francs que, pour lui confirmer la réconciliation absolue, l'empereur Napoléon III les lui avait offerts. Certains disaient qu'ils étaient frère et sœur, sa mère à elle étant la nourrice de celui qui est arrivé empereur. D'autres en doutaient, la différence entre eux étant d'un peu plus d'un an. Une seule chose semblait claire : l'actuel empereur avait été désigné comme parrain lorsque la famille de Louis Bonaparte, le roi des Pays Bas, avait décidé de baptiser la fille de ses servants. De ce fait, voué dans son enfance à être son parrain, alors que sa mère donna son propre nom, Hortense, à la fille de la servante choisie d'être sa femme de chambre, il fut aidé dès son jeune âge par celle-ci et son époux, le peintre Cornu, dans la période pendant laquelle Louis Philippe l'avait condamné à la prison à vie, étant fâché sur elle, plus tard, lorsqu'elle s'était ralliée à ceux qui le huaient pour s'être autoproclamé Empereur, alors qu'il était Président de la République – pour lui confirmer donc la réconciliation par laquelle il l'avait attirée comme brillante dame de compagnie et soutien intellectuel à la Cour, Napoléon s'est offert de lui subventionner les dépenses de son élitiste salon. Puisque l'Empire aussi, acquérant l'importance européenne donnée par sa stabilité, détermina de nombreux révolutionnaires de 1848 de vouloir s'approcher à nouveau de leur ancien combattant qui se couronné en les trahissant mais, en même temps, Napoléon III avait des ambitions d'auteur, publiant son Traité sur l'artillerie, dont le langage a été corrigé par cette distinguée littéraire et, maintenant, il voulait écrire un livre sur Jules César, peut-être juste pour se comparer avec celui-là. Il avait donc besoin du talent d'écriture de Madame Hortense Cornu ou bien, peut-être, à travers celle-ci, même de celui d'autres bien plus grands écrivains, desquels il pourrait emprunter un style de génie ayant sa signature impériale et de combattre Victor Hugo qui, depuis son exil à Londres, ne voulait

pas le pardonner ni abandonner le sarcasme des pamphlets dans lesquelles il le nommait « Napoléon le petit ».
Hortense Cornu, née Delacroix de la servante de sa mère, la reine Hortense de Louis Bonaparte mis par Napoléon Ier sur le trône de Pays Bas, en héritant l'intelligence naturelle et la soif d'ascension de la famille très simple de laquelle elle provenait et, par-dessus tout, bénéficiant aussi de l'éducation aux côtés des enfants des familles princières, du talent littéraire et d'intelligence politique qu'elle avait déjà prouvés à elle-même, elle aurait pu lui être d'un grand usage. Comme une bonapartiste de deux génération au moins, les honneurs de la Cour ne lui étant pas indifférentes, elle avait accepté d'aider Napoléon à écrire son livre mais, moralement comme matériellement, elle avait calculé un bien plus grand gain que la somme offerte : une autorité politique de ses idées. Elle refusait donc celle-ci, en répondant à l'empereur avec une malicieuse persuasion : « Je veux être libre, Majesté, afin de pouvoir vous faire part des vérités dont vous avez si besoin »… Etant, à une époque, des enfants qui jouaient ensemble, ensuite des jeunes antiroyalistes au temps de la Restauration, puis des souteneurs des libertés de 1848, ils ont trouvé suffisamment d'éléments de réconciliation et l'Empereur, ainsi que celle qui lui devenait égérie, en remportant une prestance aux Tuileries et agrandir, de cette manière, la prestance de son propre salon littéraire.
Digne, intelligente, ayant un bien plus fort sens féminin de relations bien réglés que celui de coquetteries superficielles qui ne nous sied pas au-delà d'un certain âge, pouvant dire qu'elle est non seulement supérieure aux autres femmes, mais même que les hommes la sentaient beaucoup plus qu'une égale, elle savait s'impliquer dans les arrangements politiques, non comme une courtisane, mais comme un vrai tireur de ficelles, féminin juste par la délicatesse de ses gestes parfumés avec lesquelles elle traitait des affaires parfois compliquées, depuis les grandes commandes de peinture officielle pour son époux et tous les compères artistes, jusqu'à l'influence du deuxième Empire sur d'autres pays et maisons royales.
Dans un sens pareil, peut-être, elle dit à celui qui était assis sur le prétentieux fauteuil se trouvant devant elle, posé et détendu, sans agacement, mais aussi poli, sans le manque d'intérêt montré par

ces êtres nonchalants de salon qui savent exposer l'élégance bien plus que leurs bon sens :
- C'est bien !...C'est bien que je résous aussi le problème d'un pays comme le vôtre, mais en même temps résous pour ma chère petite Joséphine la situation des princes appauvris. Parce que le prince, son mari, Charles-Antoine, est pareil à son nom, tel deux morceaux de bois rigides ! Il est radin, peut-être dû au fait qu'il est issu d'une branche plus pauvre de sa famille ; il n'est pas si capable d'être un grand commandant ou d'arriver à nouveau Ministre ; il est obséquieux avec son cousin le roi Wilhelm, pour qu'il lui donne un petit gagne-pain comme celui de Düsseldorf, mais il n'hésite pas à piquer quelques sous de la vente des secrets à Napoléon; il essaie des affaires des voies ferrés, mais il a été trop peu de temps chef du Gouvernement pour pouvoir aboutir financièrement et il ne peut donc pas donner aux garçons un revenu digne de leur rang. C'est pour cette raison que Charles, de qui on parle, a pleuré sur mon épaule à cause d'Anna Murat qui s'est mariée au duc de Noailles, alors que la pauvre Joséphine, qui est une Beauharnais comme sa mère, Stéphanie, descendante de Joséphine du Napoléon le Grand, n'arrive pas à le guérir de son amour néfaste, dans lequel tombent les hommes sans imagination. Ceci est propre aux allemands et c'est pourquoi j'avais traduit « Les souffrances de jeune Werther » : il s'en lamente comme s' il n'existait pas une autre femme !...Mais Goethe était génial et a donné beaucoup de poésie au drame, en tant que ceux-ci, les banaux gourmands d'argent de Sigmaringen, l'on descendue au niveau d'affaires sournois : Charles, l'amoureux, a joué en bourse pour s'enrichir et il a perdu quelque cinquante-cinq mille francs ; Antoine, le père radin, a fait une crise et l'a consigné au domicile, avec un comptable veilleur en le forçant à produire de l'argent à partir de rien ; tout s'est réduit, comme leur âme sèche, à l'argent et aux affaires, avec aucune des hautes émotions de Goethe ! Des allemands stupides, mesquins et délurés... Ce jeune-homme-là a aussi eu peur de perdre de l'argent et n'a maintenant plus envie d'amour.
- Et celle qui soufre, est votre amie Joséphine de Hohenzollern – Sigmaringen.- préfigura Brătianu ces choses ou bien il eut l'intelligence d'offrir une excuse à sa partenaire de discussion.
- Bien sûr ; elle est bien une Beauharnais quoi !... Je pense qu'elle se mariée à l'allemand par nécessité et son ainé ressemble assez

bien à notre Empereur. Tu sais, entre cousins cela arrive parfois et cette famille de Bonaparte est mélangée, exactement comme cela, à des progénitures de Joséphine du Napoléon le Grand. Mais le roi Louis, le père du Napoléon III était le frère du Napoléon Ier mais, en même temps, c'était aussi son gendre, parce-que Hortense, ma marraine, était la fille du premier mariage de Joséphine, adoptée légalement par Napoléon Ier !...

- Ah ! –cria Brătianu cette interjection moins bien contrôlée et, se rendant compte, se corrigea rapidement : Au fond, je voulais dire, chère Madame, je commence à comprendre ces raisons impériales.

Puis elle, sans se montrer bouleversée, renonçant à son comportement contrôlé, demanda comme au marché :

- Quoi donc, ne croyez-vous pas que ceci est un avantage pour le soutien dont votre pays a besoin ?!

Chevalier parfait du jeu politique, Brătianu préféra se taire et lui faire un baisemain affectueux.

Sans lui déplaire, l'élégante dame se permit un geste vif et coquète, pointant son doigt vers le charmant homme, apparemment sanguin, au visage dédaigneux, qui se complète bien avec ses gestes de bon sens, d'un homme sûr de soi et expérimenté en relations. Elle précisa :

- Vous avez, donc, une double mission, Monsieur Brătianu, pour porter sur votre dos un roi pareil, qui vous sera reconnaissant !... Étant donné que vous allez également lui présenter les secrets de son nouveau pays mais aussi, peut-être, les secrets d'une femme qui parviendrait à le sortir de cette mélancolie piteuse de l'homme qui tombe au premier coup amoureux et pense qu'il n'existe plus une deuxième femme au monde… Qu'en dites-vous ?... Il serait impossible que vous ne trouviez pas une petite roumaine pétillante et pleine de vie; ça fera du bien à votre politique d'homme dédié au pays !

Brătianu répondit avec politesse, très équilibré dans ses mouvements sûrs et, ayant l'air de celui qui sait ce qu'il veut, tenta une résistance éloignée :

- Avec tout le respect, Madame, je vous informe que nous, depuis dix ans avons proposé un prince étranger, pour la simple raison de ne pas l'unir par mariage à une de nos propres familles et ainsi de rester objectif, comme souverain de tous les Roumains, sans préférences pour les uns ou pour les autres.

- Oh, que c'est beau, très beau comme réalisme politique ! – elle ne cacha pas du tout l'admiration, cette femme encore belle qui l'observa avec d'agréables et intéressants regards cet homme, plus jeune qu'elle – Et reformula sa tactique : Eh ! Nous allons trouver. Quoi, ne trouve-t-on pas de femmes dans ce monde ?!...Qu'il en soit capable ! – et, à nouveau, elle manifesta ses convictions ou ses expériences de parisienne méprisante envers les hommes gringalets : Qu'il ne soit pas trop allemand ! Vous savez, je pense qu'il est aussi rigide et enfermé que son père ; c'est bien le sort des hommes maladroits avec les femmes !... – Puis elle ajute vite : Mais, celui-ci ne peut pas être considéré comme défaut pour un prince souverain, mais tout le contraire! Vous allez apporter sur le trône un gérant sobre qui, étant aussi un chevalier, ouvre des portes vers d'autres maisons royales et cela, dans votre avantage. Pour tous ces détails, ne vous inquiétez pas, je m'en occupe avec Joséphine qui, comme je vous le disais : est une Beauharnais et compense l'insipide prussien. Sa mère, Stéphanie, a été la cousine de ma marraine adoptée par le grand Bonaparte…

Polit, l'homme aux regards droits et gestes réservés, sûr de lui, sans aucune inaptitude, au belles joues, saines, comme chez les enfants que t'as envie de baiser, se permettait, d'une manière très spécifique, celle de se démontrer à lui-même qu'il n'a pas peur de la sincérité de demander ce que, au fait, le torture depuis très longtemps.

- Dois-je comprendre, donc, Madame et distinguée protectrice, que, en parlant de Philippe de Flandre, les choses sont…

- C'est ne pas la peine. On lui avait dit qu'il est hors de question.

- « On » ?

- Oui, on lui avait dit.

- L'empereur ?

- Peut-être bien plus que l'empereur !

- Pourrait-il être question de ce qu'on dit sur le Loges ?

- Et que c'est qu'on dit sur les Loges ? – demandait-elle amusée, scrutant son visage d'homme robuste avec les mêmes agréables-intéressants regards.

- Qu'il est la seule tête couronnée ayant une influence aussi sur les Loges.

- Possible – répondit elle en démontrant qu'elle n'était pas contre une telle affirmation – possible que tous ces changements de

l'Europe puissent imposer une pareille chose. Mais il ne faut pas oublier ce rituel écossais ni le fait qu'il y a une maison royale qui est aussi à l'Écosse !
- Bon, mais…
Coquetant, peut-être d'une mise en branle innée, peut-être pour changer la discussion, faible mais révélatrice, elle lui toucha la main laissant le geste se prolonger comme si elle avait attendu de transmettre la chaleur de l'impulsion :
- Mon cher, sur ce thème, je ne sais rien de plus. Je suis une femme et, comme vous le savez, je n'ai pas accès au Loges. – Et elle fit un jeu de mots : C'est à peine maintenant que l'Europe découvre « les vertus de l'esprit féminin »… Je ne peux vous dire qu'une seule chose : Que le roi de la Belgique est apparenté à la maison d'Orléans, l'ennemie qu'on a éloignée du trône, en conséquence l'Empereur ne vous recommande pas son frère.
- Dès lors, il nous recommande quelqu'un provenant de la famille de Wilhelm de Prusse, avec lequel Napoléon a été et sera en conflit ?
- Mais pourquoi pensez-vous juste à l'insipide prince paternel qui, assez pingre, ne semble pas être indifférent à ce qu'il peut tirer de Napoléon contre certains services ? Pourquoi ne pensez-vous pas à Joséphine, à qui son sang crie « *Vive la France* » ?!... Ou, au mois, pensez au jeune prince, qui a fait une passion troublante pour la nièce de celui qui a été notre glorieux Murat et, s'il n'avait pas été stoppé, toujours par son même trouillard de père qui, lui a tout de suite annoncé qu'il n'a pas assez d'argent que pour vivre à Paris avec une femme du grand monde, il aurait été rapidement disposé à devenir citoyen Français.
- Vraiment ?
- Vraiment, *mon petit* ! – répondit gaiement la distinguée dame ne résistant plus à la tentation et lui caressant doucement, du bout des ongles, cette joue d'homme vigoureux, élevé comme les arbres des vergers ensoleillés. – Réalisez : le roi, qu'on veuille ou non les prendre en considération, ces rois, pour le choisir, il doit être une chance, et non un obstacle. Celui-là a été le favori de Napoléon, le fils d'Hortense, dont je porte le nom, une Beauharnais. Joséphine est aussi une Beauharnais, une sorte de cousine… En plus, je vous le disais : on dit que l'empereur, qui n'est certainement pas un saint… Allez, on va laisser cette histoire, je vais plutôt vous raconter une autre plus drôle, *mon*

petit : L'empereur, notre ancien de '48, dit toujours : « Je ne conquiers pas les femmes ; je m'en défends mais, parfois, je capitule ! »… Ha, ha ! Qu'en dites-vous ?...
- J'ai toujours apprécié l'esprit français ; je peux même dire même que je l'aime, c'est à mon goût ! – répondit l'homme, sans crainte de montrer une attitude coquette, comme il se doit d'aborder, humainement, les appréciations d'une dame très distinguée.
Alors, moyennant une habilité politique, il attaqua par tous ses moyens de franchise et sincérité :
- Ma bien distinguée protectrice, comme vous avez relaté cette réflexion osé de « qu'on veuille ou non les prendre en considération, ces rois», je ne vais pas vous cacher ce que vous connaissez depuis longtemps, que, depuis que j'ai conspiré au même endroit que votre époux, je suis, au plus profond de mon âme, un républicain.
- Je sais ; je ne le sais que trop bien, moi-même je n'en suis pas bien loin. C'est précisément pourquoi je me suis dit de vous : Voici ce beau républicain, qui cherche un roi pour son pays !
- Je suis aussi un pragmatique, Madame, et je connais la situation actuelle : étant donné que nous n'avons pas la détermination de faire de notre pays une République, à vrai dire de risquer comme chez vous, d'avoir quelqu'un qui met la main sur le vote et puis qui se déclare empereur et dictateur à vie. C'est plus sage de faire une monarchie constitutionnelle. J'ai le sentiment en ce moment, exactement le même que celui d'indignation lorsque votre République s'est métamorphosé en Empire. Je pense que cela m'a servi de leçon entre ce que veut l'homme et ce que est envisageable sur cette terre.
- Alors j'imagine que je vous ai trouvé exactement le personnage dont vous avez besoin : c'est-à-dire, allons parler entre nous, comme des républicains, un souverain à qui vous soumettre, mais au fond, qu'il obéisse à votre parti et aux idées élevées dont vous disposez.
- Êtes-vous persuadée ?
- Je connais bien la famille ; c'est la branche la plus déplorable des Hohenzollern et ils feraient n'importe que pour garder la tête haute.
- Quoi même, Madame, face à cet esprit prussien, même celui de la pauvreté opiniâtre, qui n'a pas de lien avec notre effervescence

latine, aussi fauchée, peut-être, mais de toute façon généreuse, chaude, enthousiaste dans l'esprit révolutionnaire – comparatif aux prussiens, je veux dire, non seulement la famille royale belge, mais la Belgique, en tant que telle, est beaucoup plus proche de nous ; est beaucoup plus proche de notre esprit ; son attestation nationale est un inédit exemple pour ce que nous voulons !

- Je serais désolée de vous laisser vous enflammer pour rien – elle tendit sa main avec son gant en mousseline de soie, comme si elle avait caressée sa chevelure sculptée qui lui accentuait son air de lion.

Mais il s'emporta :

- La Belgique, Madame, il y a seulement trente-cinq ans, a résolut la situation que nous voulons solutionnée maintenant. Elle a été sous la domination autrichienne, comme une partie d'entre nous le reste encore aujourd'hui. Quand ils se sont libérés, en 1830, on l'aurait fait aussi, puisque nous avons commencé la révolution depuis 1821 et les échos de la révolte de Paris vers Charles X sont arrivés jusqu'à nous. Mais nous n'avons pas aboutit, étant donné que les russes nous ont envahis et ils nous ont donnés un « Règlement organique » semblable à leur absolutisme et non à nos espérances libérales qui venaient de Paris, où la liberté de la presse était exigée !... Nous avons essayé à nouveau en 1848 cependant, vous, nos protecteurs, êtes devenus un Empire et les Turques ne nous ont plus laissé actionner. Un souverain qui a connu les ambitions de la Belgique, nous aidera beaucoup plus à passer ce hiatus qui dure depuis trois décennies, plutôt qu'un officier prussien, formé en ces régiments qui ont agenouillés la Révolution de 1848. Les Allemands ont cédé devant les Habsbourg et n'ont pas achevé leur rêve de devenir un état unitaire ; tandis que La Belgique l'est déjà, comme nous voulons l'être aussi !... Les miens, au pays, c'est certainement pour cette raison qu'ils se sont dépêchés de proclamer Philippe : Comme duc de Flandre il est plus qu'un bourgeon de gotha de Saxe-Cobourg tel que le reste le roi Léopold !

Elle ne fit qu'affiner son geste de tout à l'heure, en effleurant les boucles et le front du jeune homme pour le dorloter comme il le mérite:

- *Mon petit – grand révolutionnaire* !... Vous êtes véritablement fascinant, mais vous me rendez plus que navrée. Vous devez comprendre que c'est insensé : Le roi Léopold est non seulement de Saxe-Cobourg, il est également marié à Louise-Marie de Orléans, qui n'est autre que la fille de Louis Philippe, celui contre lequel Napoléon s'est révolté, qui a condamné Napoléon, celui que Napoléon a écarté ; c'est la famille la plus rivale de Bonaparte !

- Je comprends que c'est déraisonnable, Madame ; J'admets et je vous donne ma parole que je vais le respecter. Il y a autre chose que je n'en comprends pas et je vous avoue, à vous qui avez reconnu que vous n'avez pas le droit en tant que femme de vous impliquer dans les Loges, que vous avez le droit, en tant qu'esprit plus aigu que n'importe lequel homme, de disserter sur leur effondrement et sur les espoirs qui ont été apportés !

- L'effondrement ?

- Oui, l'effondrement. C'est un initié qui vous parle…

- Je sais : jusqu'au rang de maestro dans « La rose du parfait silence » !

- Je savais que vous êtes au courant : le contraire était inconcevable. Ce que vous ne savait pas, par contre, c'est que ce maestro commence à douter… - et, en soulevant soudain son front large, dévoila : La maçonnerie peut avoir des lois, mais pas des tyrans. Votre Napoléon « le petit », veut aussi s'imposer dans la maçonnerie qui l'a honoré avec ses hauts grades. Il a transmis à Philippe de Flandre l'ordre de nous refuser, en tant que maçon et non comme relations entre leurs maisons royales. C'est pour cela que le prince ne veut plus avoir à faire à nous !... Je suis indigné, ma chère Madame et, je vous prie d'être convaincue que j'ai enterré en moi cette indignation, mais devant vous je le reconnais : Il est inconcevable qu'une organisation qui a des lois, des grandes lois cherchant le renforcement de l'humanité, soit empiétée par le même homme qui a empiété la deuxième République en se proclamant empereur, précisément parce que les lois de la démocratie ne lui permettaient plus d'être candidat à la présidence… Je suis déçu, Madame, et je me pose des questions si, d'une certaine façon, nos lois initiatrices n'essaient pas d'être trahies en conséquence ! La maçonnerie est une grande idée, un chemin de perfectionnement humain ; mais si elle tombe dans les mains des tyrans qui lui changent le sens…

La femme resta perplexe ; même dans son ample intelligence, elle ne s'était pas attendue à ceci. Elle n'y a même jamais pensé qu'elle pouvait s'y attendre. Cet homme, d'une maturité intéressante, gardant son enthousiasme juvénile, se montra si averti, avec la fibre si intensément travaillée le long des décennies d'initiatives et persévérance révolutionnaire, qu'elle en était stupéfaite. Elle, l'amie de Victor Hugo le rival de génie d'Ernest Renan qui révolutionna les termes de la foi, des libres penseurs de la « Revue des deux mondes » et des plus originaux écrivains, depuis le vénérable Dumas jusqu'à la si innovatrice Georges Sand et au fascinant et jeune Gustave Flaubert, en ajoutant la série de plus nouveaux publicistes, passionnés d'idées novatrices, considéraient que la noblesse révolutionnaire et d'autant plus l'essor bonapartiste de devenir une famille sérénissime ne valaient plus un sou – elle, avec son intelligence libérale, était habituée à toutes les paroles protestataire de son salon où elle trôna. Par contre, ça ne lui a jamais effleuré l'esprit que le deuxième Empire se basait, en plus, sur les rênes maçonniques accaparés progressivement par ce Napoléon, qui se prouva être plus profondément dangereux, un combineur plus dissimulé, plus réfléchi, plus monopolisateur que l'habile aventurier qu'il avait été dans sa jeunesse, plus que l'autocrate sans scrupules qu'il est devenu après 1848. Elle regarda d'une certaine manière à Brătianu, caressa sans gêne son front élargi entre des grands tempes, éloignés, que seulement le reste des boucles coupés révolutionnaire couvraient, dans une suggestion de romantisme et chuchota désabusée, comme pour elle-même :

- Quel dommage ; quel dommage que cet esprit de grande politique, serve juste un petit pays !

- J'ai fait une bêtise ? – demanda-t-il plutôt en plaisantant, pour cacher sa flatterie.

Elle lui répondit tout à fait autre chose:

- Votre intuition en plus de la perfidie de dictateur qui, après avoir soumis sa République essaie de soumettre sa maçonnerie, a mis le doigt sur le point névralgique de notre libéralisme. Vous savez bien que je suis une républicaine ; vous savez bien que depuis 1848 jusqu'au 1856 je n'ai pas voulu avoir à faire à cet individu dont on raconte qu'il a tété le lait de ma mère. La comtesse Walewska m'a conduit au Tuileries et j'ai vu à nouveau le visage de Napoléon lorsqu'il est devenu plus humain, après avoir émoussé la terreur de la première partie de son absolutisme sanglant et penchait vers ce qu'on veut nommer aujourd'hui

« l'Empire libéral », comme je lui ai suggérée moi-même, pour échapper à l'accusation de tyran.
- Voulez-vous dire qu'il a adouci son absolutisme officiel, seulement parce qu'il a fortifié ses pouvoirs souterrains ?
- C'est vous qui dites cela. L'entendre de vous, je me suis expliquée quelques petites choses dont même les plus extrémistes de mon salon n'osent pas parler.
Brătianu la regarda en face et sans gêne de prendre ses épaules dans ses mains mais, au lieu de la tirer vers lui, il garda la distance de ses bras tendus, en révélant une chose grave, convaincu de lui faire cadeau son plus grand secret :
- Vous êtes la seule à qui j'ai fait cette unique révélation d'un fait que moi-même je voudrais essayer d'oublier : Cette maçonnerie française me fait beaucoup réfléchir car, au lieu de représenter les grands desiderata d'une société entière, se laisse dirigée par les intérêts d'une seule personne ; Encore moins si cette personne est l'empereur. La maçonnerie a des lois très strictes, justement pour satisfaire les engagements sociaux qu'elle s'est assumée afin d'assurer le progrès en aiguilletant l'être humain et en durcissant la solidarité du peuple. Il ne faut pas oublier que je me suis opposé à lui comme empereur.
- Vous vous êtes trouvé même parmi les conspirateurs, aux côtés de mon époux.
- A cette époque-là je n'ai été pas en droit. Sa trahison ne regardait que les Français. Maintenant, par contre : Qu'il essaie de profiter de hauts rangs de la maçonnerie… C'est ce qui en fait mon indignation et non pas le prince allemand.
- Que pensez-vous faire ?
Je ne sais pas ; j'ai le devoir de me consulter avec ceux de ma Loge ; mais oui, avant de prendre une décision. En tous les cas je serai loyal à l'ordre de mettre sur le trône le prince prussien, mais la décision négative en ce qui concerne le Duc de Flandre ne peut pas être mélangé aux lois maçonniques. Si nous acceptons ces faits, cela signifie qu'on sert d'autres intérêts. Et si on sert d'autres intérêts, personne ne peut nous demander de les respecter tout en ayant confiance, de croire en eux.
Se réjouissant néanmoins de cette embrassade distante, qui lui transmettait la chaleur des mains de l'homme obstiné par l'injustice faite à ses croyances, la délicate dame devint femme et

affirma en toute sincérité, non pas comme une allusion, mais plutôt émue sentimentalement, dans l'éco d'un infini regret :
- Quel dommage !... Quel dommage que je ne suis pas plus jeune, pour avoir le droit moral de tomber amoureuse de vous !... – Et le questionna soigneusement : Cela vous torture, n'est pas ? Vous sentez qu'on vous a fait une injustice.
- Je hais le totalitarisme, Madame ; je ne veux pas qu'on nous ordonne, ni que nous ordonnions, je veux que chacun obéisse au même statut.
- Oubliez le Duc de Flandre, comme moi-même j'oublierai l'instant interdit quand j'ai parlé d'amour.
- Il n'est pas interdit, Madame !... En ce qui concerne le Duc, rien ne me lie à lui. J'ai été indigné par le procédé autocrate à travers lequel on change les sens du carbonarisme que j'ai aimé autrefois. Cependant, me convainquant que votre préféré a la priorité, je tenterai de le servir aussi dans les desseins de mon pays.
- Il n'est pas nécessairement mon préféré. Il est la meilleure solution pour vous, croyez-moi. Si vous voulez une tête couronné, vous avez besoin d'un homme agréé à de nombreuses Cours. – En changeant le ton de sa voix, elle redevint la parisienne malicieuse : Moi, en parlant de Prussiens, j'ai une mauvaise perception concernant les hommes, et non les princes ; je l'agrée pour le trône, non pour le lit !
- Vous avez raison ; il est important d'être bien vu par Napoléon.
- Tandis que vous, comme la personne qui a conspiré contre lui, jamais vous n'allez trouver la porte ouverte chez Napoléon ! – précisa-t-elle bien calculée – Pensez-y à cela : je veux être sincère, justement parce que vous ne m'êtes pas indifférent. Manié avec habileté, Charles peut être un tampon entre vous et les rancunes de l'empereur… Et répéta : Je vous ai dit que vous ne m'êtes pas indifférent.
En se libérant de tout ce qui lui avait réveillé le frémissement outré de son éloignement d'un engagement qu'il considéra ferme, mais en même temps encouragé par le fait qu'elle se répétait l'intime révélation, Brǎtianu redevint galant :
- Chère Madame, ma gentille dame, puisque vous m'avez fait l'honneur d'une grande sincérité concernant les têtes couronnés, je vais vous répondre à ce que vous m'aviez dit plus tôt de la boutade de l'empereur relatif à la capitulation envers les

femmes : Pour des dames si belles que vous-même, je capitulerais aussi !
La coquinerie marcha, l'atmosphère d'intimité s'accentua ; la femme raffinée trouva la modalité élégante d'apostropher sans un sentiment de rejet et l'humilia juste assez que pour l'encourager :
- Vous vous y connaissez. J'ai vu comme vous appréciiez ma soubrette quand on nous a servi le thé. Vous ne pensez pas qu'un révolutionnaire tenace comme vous, connu, homme d'action tant évident en gestes, s'il échappe un seul regard de plus de ses yeux fougueux, il bouleverse la vie de ces malheureuses filles ?!
- Je suis naïf, Madame – dit-il tendrement – ne m'attribuez pas tant de…
- C'est la vie qui vous les a attribués… et l'expérience. Vous, ces hommes qui commencez à grisonner après avoir vécu une jeunesse tumultueuse et plaine de volonté…
- Nous méritons d'avoir le droit à un peu de complaisance, n'est pas ?
- Vous savez la prendre tous seuls !... Vous savez la provoquer d'ailleurs, ou bien cela fait partie de votre instinct – affirma-t-elle en matière de connaisseuse comme femme et comme écrivaine très attentive de retourner au plus vite à son sujet: Il aura quoi apprendre de vous ce prussien qui est bien plus sans imagination que sans argent, de la même manière qu'il a hérité les complexes de son père ; aussi, il est bien plus pleurnichard que sentimental, ce qui peut le rendre introverti, au point qu'il devient brutal.
Brătianu fit un geste de courtoisie en lui baisant la main et avouant :
- Je vous suis si reconnaissant que vous me partagez vos raffinées observations dignes d'une vraie écrivaine ! – et c'est seulement après qu'il dévoila son but, en insistant : - La finesse d'une pareille constatation psychologique peut énormément aider un politicien rudimentaire que je suis. Je vous prie…
Cependant elle se révéla maîtresse de la conversation et lui souligna la faveur :
- Écoutez, pour qu'on ne dise pas que je parle dans le dos de gens, je vais vous donner un exemple devenu publique : Vous connaissez bien Frantz Joseph, l'empereur qui semble maintenant équilibré, être sur le trône depuis un certain temps déjà, choisi par les siens en 1848 et non révolutionnant puis renversant la révolution, comme l'a fait Napoléon.

- Nous le savons tous trop bien.
- Puisqu'il règne depuis dix-huit ans. Juste pour cela. Qui est-il, comment est-il, personne ne le sait !... Le monde ne se rappelle plus qu'il a été un immature quand sa mère l'a mis sur le trône en promettant une autre constitution aux révolutionnaires. Qu'elle a donnée, qu'elle leur a aussitôt reprise, mais pas brutalement, comme l'a fait Napoléon. Néanmoins, contrairement à Napoléon, Frantz Joseph est un guignol. S'il n'y avait pas eu le scandale avec la folie de sa femme, l'impératrice Élisabeth, Sissi de son diminutif, de qui on raconte qu'elle a des accès délirantes, mais qu'on a promu comme la vedette de l'Europe, celle qu'on retrouve dans tous les journaux comme la beauté de toutes les beautés royales et impériales et celle qui, avec toutes ses toilettes, lance la mode dans le monde entier, s'il n'y avait pas eu toute cette loufoquerie, on n'en aurait rien su. Cependant, en déclenchant le scandale, cette vérité concernant la stupidité de ces zigues de nobles allemands a éclaté : car la femme qu'on suppose heureuse et que l'on retrouve dans tous les journaux lançant la mode, est folle. Elle est devenue instable psychiquement à cause de cet abruti de Frantz Joseph qui l'a violée quand elle n'avait que quatorze ans, en ignorant la manière de caresser une fille. Sa mère l'a poussé à s'unir à une autre, mais lui, le balourd, en se sachant empereur qui commande, a sauté sur celle-là et lui a ordonné de lui faire amour. C'est tout ce qu'il a eu dans la tête, alors que sa mère l'avait mis sur le trône ; ou bien c'est justement cette raison qui l'a persuadé que tout s'obtient en donnant des ordres. Il avait abusé d'elle et, pour dissimuler le scandale, ils ont vite célébré leurs noces. De plus, ils ont eu aussi des enfants !... Dès lors, on pourrait dire de cette fille qu'elle a eue le bonheur d'arriver impératrice, tous les peintres se dépêchant davantage de lui faire le portrait en la déclarant la beauté du monde. Mais voila qu'aujourd'hui, lorsqu'elle este devenue célèbre par sa splendeur et vedette de tous les journaux, la petite fille violé a culbuté ; elle manifeste ouvertement sa folie et n'a pas un délice plus grand que celui de se moquer des frivolités impériaux de son violateur. Qui, l'abruti, en tant qu'empereur, s'il avait su la caresser, il l'aurait eu à vie. Seulement voila que cet imbécile grandi à la caserne, a cru qu'il est empereur et qu'il peut commander. Et il l'a brisée pour la vie. C'est ce qui arrive quand on ne sait pas se conduire avec les femmes !... Vous avez compris ?

- J'ai compris ; j'ai compris cette parabole, ma chère dame ; vous pouvez en être sure.
- La femme, vous pouvez la rendre reine, vous pouvez la rendre impératrice ; si vous ne la rendez pas heureuse, en vain ! Qu'en dites-vous ? Pour un homme expérimenté et sanguin, comme vous-même, - dit-elle avec un soupçon d'allusion, de subtilité avertie – ce serait une chance de donner des leçons d'hardiesse à ce monarque que vous allez avoir. Hardiesse dans le sens de la découverte des secrets de la virilité, car lui aussi monte sur le trône en étant célibataire. Vous allez épargner ce jeune homme de sa godiche envers les femmes et il vous serra reconnaissant à jamais.
En lui baisant avec acharnement les mains qui consentaient ce fait, Brătianu répliqua croquignolet, dans la libertine et parisienne manière:
- Il va falloir, sans doute, répéter ensemble, très chère Madame !
Mais, tel que le voulaient les bonnes manières, elle lui donna une petite gifle surtout encourageante et, pour interrompe pour le moment la ruse :
- Sage, *mon petit* !... Êtes-vous convaincu que je souhaite vous conseiller, vous aider ?!
- Convaincu est peu dire ! Je suis votre vassal, Madame !
Elle le regarda dans les yeux en prenant soin de lui attirer l'attention et levant son doigt en signe d'admonestation sans pour autant s'empêcher de lui montrer le cadeau qu'elle lui faisait, en omettant par contre de lui dire ce qu'aurait du être la récompense :
- Ces comportements, soi-disant sentimentaux qui, au fond sont sexuels, en disent beaucoup des hommes, Monsieur Brătianu ! Dans mon salon, des célébrités académiques ont commencé à développer cette théorie qui, je suis certaine, deviendra dans le futur une science essentielle concernant le comportement est les besoins humains… Mais oui, c'est pour cette raison que je me suis décidée : je vais vous révéler un secret, chose que je ne devrais point faire. Seulement, c'est une habitude entre les conspirateurs et moi j'ai l'excuse que nous conspirons une belle chose pour votre pays… Et, au fond, pourquoi ne le dire-je pas ?!... Même pour vos ambitions de révolutionnaire aux belles pensées…

A ce moment-la, elle se leva en faisant ressortir son allure élégante de femme qui sait ce qu'elle doit mettre en valeur et alla vers une écritoire jetant un œil sur un tas de lettres, sans pour autant cacher sa curiosité d'épier son regard afin de vérifier s'il la contemplait avec les mêmes critères d'égard associés aux mouvements de la soubrette.
- Vous êtes bien plus distinguée que dans le portrait réalisé par votre époux ! – lui dit Brătianu comme si, par cet à-propos il lui aurait démontré qu'il comprenait tout ce jeu habile.
Malgré cela elle était devenue attentive à la partie grave de choses :
- J'espère ne pas avoir à regretter ce secret qui restera le notre. Peu importe le moule, si nous deux le sculpterons à notre manière, le roi ne pourrait que parfait !... Lisez-moi cela et vous verrez que c'est à vous de lui donner une part de cette fibre volontaire et vigoureuse qui est la vôtre !
La lettre était datée d'il y a plus de deux ans, plus précisément du 2 décembre 1863 :

« *Ma chère et tendre Hortense,*
Revenu depuis peu à Berlin, je me dépêche de vous exprimer mes plus sincères remerciements pour la grande amabilité que vous avez eue envers moi le dernier jour de mon séjour à Paris. Il est merveilleux pour moi le souvenir d'avoir été reçu avec tant de bienveillance par ma chère Hortense. Ce dernier jour, ces dernières heures à Paris, ont été décisifs. Vous connaissez bien le proverbe allemand : Les dés ont été lancés... »

- Celui-là, ou bien il souffre d'orgueil gotique, ou bien il ne s'est pas documenté sur ce qui se dit du Rubicon- s'amusa Brătianu mais, en agitant une autre lettre, elle lui fit signe de continuer :
- Lisez, en partant de chez moi il s'est rendu chez Anna Murat, mais il a été incapable de se conduire en homme. Ehe, voici la raison pour laquelle les yeux des allemandes pétillent en pensant aux hommes ! Il va finalement se convoler avec l'une de celles-ci et va annoncer de manière protocolaire, avec deux semaines d'avance, qu'il a programmé une partie de sex. C'est comme ça qu'on se moque, Joséphine et moi, de son père.

« Après vous avoir abandonnée, je me suis rendu, comme vous le savez, avenue Montaigne, afin de faire mes adieux. La pensée de devoir quitter Paris m'était pénible à supporter. Je vous ai relaté, chère Hortense, la manière avec laquelle la princesse Anna s'est séparée de moi, en me bouleversant tellement, au point qu'il fut arrivé un moment où je me suis retrouvé tout à fait renversé. Elle a serré ma main en me disant : J'espère que nous nous reverrons bientôt, n'est pas ? Vous allez revenir prochainement – et elle a eu du mal à me laisser partir... »

- Écoutez cela : elle a eu du mal à le laisser partir et lui... - s'amusaient-ils ensemble trouvant un moyen de plus grande intimité dans cet amusement.

« M'en allant, je pansais la revoir bientôt afin de s'unir à elle à jamais. J'ai été très heureux de pouvoir demeurer un jour à Düsseldorf chez mes parents, auxquels j'ai tout dit : ma mère est ravie et mon père, il semble ne pas s'y opposer... Maintenant, il faut faire les démarches. Si nous attendons trop longtemps, la princesse Anna va penser qu'elle ne m'a fait aucune impression, d'autant plus que j'ai été assez réservé devant elle à la Compiègne... Je vous ai dit, chère Hortense, je l'aime de tout mon cœur et elle est la seule qui peut me rendre heureux. »

- Qu'en dites-vous ? : Anna va le rendre heureux, mais elle n'en sait rien. Parce que, au lieu d'avoir le courage de le lui dire à elle, le pauvre garçon sot, me le dit à moi, en tant qu'amie de sa mère ; avez-vous saisi !? – demanda-t-elle approchant de lui son parfum et changeant les papiers se trouvant dans sa main – et regardez ici comme le prince-père ne s'y oppose pas, ce prussien bien calculé. Encore, je suis sincère, je te les montre tels qu'ils sont : Le fils est un timide, complexé sentimentalement davantage à cause de son obtus esprit et s'avérant être sans personnalité. Ce que, soyez attentif, Monsieur Brătianu, ce n'est pas plus mal pour un monarque constitutionnel dirigé par un politicien si malin comme vous l'êtes !... Aussi, le père est un paria de la grande famille, qui cherche à décrocher le gros lot mieux que son fils afin de débourser l'argent en compagnie d'une parisienne prétentieuse ; puisque ces princes d'aujourd'hui ne doivent pas être perdus dans ces grandes capitales où l'on dépense des sous, mais doivent devenir une bonne affaire pour leurs familles ; ne voyez-vous pas qu'on les vend, aux divers pays qui s'émancipent, comme on vend les chevaux de race ?!... De cette façon devraient être regardées toutes ces choses par les politiciens réalistes ; ce que, de nouveau, pourrait vous être convenable à vous, les hommes, qui voulez un avenir pour votre pays.

« Je me fais même quelques reproches d'avoir écouté Charles » - *écrivait Charles Antoine à Madame Cornu. « La jeune personne (Anna Murat), habituée à vivre au centre du luxe et du monde le plus brillant, pourrait-elle se contenter avec ce que Charles peut lui offrir, qui est un tempérament pur germanique et, plus que tout, allemand ?... Saurait-elle apprécier ce que nous tenons le plus au cœur, la vie de famille ? Voudra-t-elle demeurer presque toute la vie à la campagne, pour créer là-bas un petit centre d'occupations subordonnées ?...*
Charles ne peut disposer que de 50 000 francs de revenu annuel, que moi-même je ne peux pas accroître à cause des autres enfants et des impôts élevés que je dois supporter... On dit que la princesse est très riche et dotée, mais sa fortune n'a rien à voir à ce que mon orgueil me dicte, que l'épouse doit vivre de revenus de son mari... La rente de Charles jamais ne permettra une pareille chose ; elle ne lui permettra même pas de vivre marié à Berlin ou dans une autre grande ville, il ne pourrait vivre qu'à la campagne, exceptant les voyages et les visites... »

- « Un tempérament pur germanique et, plus que tout, allemand » - cita Brătianu en s'amusant et faisant rire la dame à qui il avait à nouveau commencé à lui baiser les mains d'une manière encore plus intime.
- Ha, ha, ha !... Madame, ma chère dame Hortense, votre allégation est géniale ! Mais oui, ils sont ainsi : Ils se marient pour annoncer à leurs épouses que, en vertu des engagements conjugaux, dans deux semaines, à une certaine heure, ils vont faire un peu d'amour…
- Vous aimez cela, n'est pas ? – caressa-t-elle ses joues, en se laissant bercée dans tout l'amusement qui les rendait heureux et les rapprochait. Pour s'arrêter tout à coup, attentive à ce qu'elle avait de plus urgent à fialiser: Allons, donc, mettre les choses au point, étant donné que Bălăceanu est sur le point d'arriver et nous

devons l'envoyer chez Napoléon, avec la leçon apprise par cœur !...

- Nous l'enverrons ; nous l'enverrons aussi vite que possible – l'assura Brătianu en saisissant la gaieté de ses pensées et en souriant avec complicité.

II

De là où il fut déposé par la chaise de poste, prés des auberges de l'Evêché, la rue de l'Académie se trouvait assez prés, dès lors Brătianu pris un bagage léger, abandonnant les autres au chef de la poste afin qu'il les lui envoie à Piteşti et commença à marcher tout en respirant insatiable l'air de Bucarest avec des jardins noyés dans la nuit et des sifflements de gendarmes dialoguant au clair de lune à intervalles fixes. Cela, de même que la rotation des lanternes des tours marquait l'ordre nocturne de la ville, tandis que l'odeur des fleurs de cerisiers ou de pommiers et l'autre dialogue, celui des chiens au-dessus des taudis, avait des ondes chaotiques, tantôt discrètes, tantôt intempestives, répondant peut-être à certains signaux des étoiles qui clignotaient par-dessus la ville au ciel bas, de campagne, en restant fixes seulement quand, de plus prés, du pont de Mogoşoaia qu'on sentait au dessous de petites ruelles délimitées par des clôtures au végétations bourgeonnantes, on distinguait les voix des passants, des portes des estaminets ou encore le son des sabots des chevaux attelés aux calèches qui portaient les premiers fêtards à la maison ainsi que les pétulants vers des endroits encore plus obscures que ceux dans lesquels ils avaient festoyé jusqu'alors.

Malgré son arrivée hâtive et précipitée, en marchant sur ces pavés il paraissait nager dans la familiarité de l'atmosphère qui était la sienne ainsi qu'à sa ville. Seulement la sienne et à cette ville dans laquelle il avait fait des affaires et des soirées et des choses politiques et des révolutions, avait tenu des discours graves sur la liberté, avait accompli des fonctions d'une grande responsabilité et attention, avait encaissé des injures, des accusations voire même des arrestations ou encore il s'était amusé avec ses confrères en sortant joyeux des soirées et en provocant les cochers qui restaient en file, la nuit, pour gagner un sou de plus :

- Cocher, êtes-vous libre ?
- Oui, m'sieur.
- Vive la liberté !

Parce que chez eux tout gravitait autour de l'idée de liberté et même les blagues ne pouvaient faire oublier le desideratum vital et, pour cette raison, ils avaient légèrement modifié la plaisanterie habituelle de Mitici (n.b. personnages caricaturaux de I.L. Caragiale) :

- Cocher, êtes-vous vide ?... Retournez à la maison vous remplir !

Il revenait chez lui, c'est-à-dire dans l'insolite atmosphère de Dâmboviţa et, même dans la hâte qui l'emmenait, il était heureux de gouter de la nuit de ce « chez lui » : plus lente, moins spectaculaire, mais certainement pas plus inferieure en tant que grouillement des gens, plaisirs et intérêts que celle parisienne. Alors, il ne manqua pas d'aplomb en frappant à la porte de Rosetti à une heure qu'on pouvait considérer comme « trop… », mais pas plus que « trop », parce que elle pouvait tout aussi bien être plus tardive que « au petit matin ». Il savait que dans les ateliers côté rue, les typographes travaillaient plus activement que la journée, pour pouvoir sortir le journal et que l'heure du réveil n'était pas bien loin ni pour le patron, qui veillait comme un cerbère les mouvements politiques de la ville, toujours déçu par ceux qui étaient alliés pour la "cause" et toujours certain de cette cause qui semblait être unique ; constamment sans indulgence envers les adversaires et les fougueux, mais toujours dévoué à ceux qu'il représentait génériquement sous le nom de « cause ».

Comme s'il avait été là en permanence et n'avait pas été absent pendant tout l'hiver et une partie du printemps, il fit un signe négatif au travailleurs qui, durant leur temps libre, ils lui vendaient son propre vin apporté de Drăgăşani et Ştefăneşti ; signe vers les fenêtres d'en haut, du fond de la cour, pour ne pas réveiller le maître. Et il commença à lire les galées, voire même, à l'envers, les titres de plomb se trouvant sur la matrice, pour matérialiser l'image de la ville qui l'avait reçu en cachant ses mouvements dans la nuit. Que lui-même les connaissait, les devinait, il avait l'esprit de trouver en eux la vérité ; il voulait juste mieux les déchiffrer pour les buts qui l'avaient emmené en grande hâte.

Parce que, du jour où, à Paris, on avait entendu de l'inclinaison des sept pouvoirs garants de donner aux turcs le droit de déchirer et de séparer à nouveau les principautés pour ne plus admettre qu'un souverain de souche, c'est-à-dire de recommencer la zizanie, il était dans tous ses états. Il avait fait tous les cabinets parisiens où il avait accès en essayant de trouver des alliés pour éviter une telle chose. Il avait communiqué, tant que le télégraphe le lui a permis, avec ceux d'ici, dont seul Rosetti lui avait répondu ferme, franchement entre eux deux, et même si le langage était codé, il devait comprendre la nécessité d'une solution radicale et, instigué de ce « il fait froid comme en janvier '59, quand seulement nous et grâce à nous… », ce que, dans la métaphore conspirative du langage de Rosetti, voulait dire qu'ont émergé tant d'oppositions qu'il fallait agir comme au 24 janvier 1859 quand, en feintant toutes les restrictions, ils ont procédé comme personne n 's'attendait, ils ont choisi Cuza également à Bucarest, en mettant tous les ennemis face au fait accompli. Ils se sont confirmés l'un l'autre de cette façon que des situations assez graves se préfiguraient au point qu'ils devaient actionner en s'imposant et en mettant, à nouveau, l'ennemi devant le fait accompli, uniquement à travers eux-mêmes et lui, fuyant à nouveau en Allemagne pour voir le jeune prince qui, une semaine auparavant, lui avait confirmé ravi, et même impatient, la reconnaissance pour l'offre qu'on lui faisait :

****

On Corneliu Leu's house wall.

Corneliu Leu

Chapter 7. ON THE ALTAR OF THE REVOLUTION

The journal of an Expat Journalist
A Novel

Front cover reproduction: CIGOLI (Ludovico Cardi 1559-1613)
"The Sacrifice of Isaac" – Palatine Gallery, Florence

Front cover design: Tudor Leu and Veronica Ionescu
Editor: Veronica Ionescu

ISBN: 978-973-9025-79-9

English Translation by Georgeta Bostean

THE REALITY

126 Dacia Blvd.
Bucharest, Romania
Phone: 031-104-5047
034-411-6730
Email: leuc@upcmail.ro

ON THE ALTAR OF THE REVOLUTION

is, in the chronological reading order, the first out of the twelve books that form the novelistic series entitled:

1000 PAGES of HEROIC ACTS of some civilians during THE CENTURY OF THE WORLD WARS, or what POWER means.

In order of publication it is the last, closing in the series which comprises the other eleven books:

1. DEVIL'S EYE, OR WHAT POWER MEANS
2. THE INCOGNITO BESERK
3. NIGHT AND NOVEMBER
4. THE BULLET AND THE THOUGHT
5. SQUARE HEAD OT THE MEDAL'S OBVERSE
6. THE POWER
7. THE POLITICS BEGIN
8. THE SENTIMENTAL LIFE
9. THE TIMEOF FREE SPEECH
10. POLITICAL LOBBIEST
11. THE WOUNDS OF THE VICTORS

CHAPTER 1

The Mission of the Superpowers

At the end of winter, Bucharest is usually quite an ugly sight. Its urban skyline, with frontispieces and the nicely decorated roofs sparkling joyfully in the sun like shiny white petals of snowdrops, or the raw green of the leaves that look like stems. But as the flowers pierce through the snow, their roots are engulfed in mud - a mixture of melted ice, street running water, and dirt.

On Calea Victoriei boulevard the ladies are dressed up, wearing elegant fur coats with shinny hair, but their legs up to the ankle that they do not yet reveal, are enveloped by cheap galoshes, so that they may tip-toe in the muddy potholes; the men, with their tall, sturdy hats or warm astrakhan hats, dressed in black suits accentuated by a white scarf, splash their pants when their galoshes fill up with water, flooding the inside of their shoes. Their walking cane penetrates the dirty snow. The ice clinging on the laced wrought iron adorning the balconies is melting and dripping on the passers-by; the Parisian walls of the buildings, with their caryatids and ice-shaped adornments start to reveal their cavities, crying for repairs; the coffee shops windows are still foggy from the steam created by difference in temperature but they can't be cleaned yet, insinuating an undefined humans cape inside, like and aquarium filled with smoke; ice needles are still hanging on the eaves of the inns, making the walk by those buildings a risky adventure; vagabonds, street florists and other ambulant merchants take refuge in those spaces; the horse-drawn wagons, the royal carriages and every now and then the automobiles with thin wheels, are splashing the passers-by. And only the brick walls of the churches, with their arched byzantine contour and their colored niches from which the saints watch the street, show a pleasant age, like the rosy cheeks of some handsome older people.

The traces of snow are grayish or cooper-like, testimony to the fact that the snow only covers the dust of Bărăgan plains, the salt thrown on sidewalks in front of their shops by the owners becoming a sandy mud, like the fur of the stray dogs or like the shawl that wraps up the women selling stuff in the corner of the streets out of their baskets; the leafless trees extend their weird skeletons; the merchandise is still frozen in the shops' windows, while the abundantly decorated roofs and the upper levels windows enjoy the warmth of the Spring much more than the street buzz; white line of smoke raises up from the chimneys, unabated by the wind, almost like destined to frame the sky between the cross- and bell-adorned church towers that stick out throughout the city's skyline, to the horizon.

So, it is more pleasant to watch the people, the street with its vibrant pulse and colors, from an upper story window in the comfort and coziness of a warm room, rather than strolling the streets; and to watch the distant outskirts of the city with its medley of gardens, churches, towers, storages, or windmills with their tall roofs between the water towers, and flocks of crows taking off, disturbing the serenity of the sky with their flight that foretells the last snowfall, of the season, the "snow of the lambs".

That's what I was doing during my short breaks – enjoying a few moments of calmness in the tiny room upstairs, in the attic that housed the telegraph of the typography, having only a pick-a-boo view of the Sarindari church tower. If I turned my head a little obliquely, my eyes would travel past this church's tower and reach as far as the Academiei Street, landing further on another rising tower – that of Enei church. Or, if I was looking down toward Capșa, I would have had the best perspective of the liveliest corner of the capital of the kingdom, the place where the best of the day's fashionable events *de bon ton* happened.

No matter how narrow and difficult to access through the winding stairwell, this tiny room in the attic, where all the wiring from the telegraph and later from the telephone switchboard are intertwined, is a special place, filled with the morning sunlight, and for that reason I was immensely thankful to my boss, the owner of the typography, for having moved me away from the lead vapor-filled workshop where, as an apprentice typographer, I had gotten sick with saturnism, a lead poisoning condition, specific for our profession. Moreover, the owner allowed us – me and a few fellow workers– to share a close-by sleeping quarters as long as we monitored continuously the telegraph and the switchboard, decoded the telegraph messages and forwarded the urgent ones to the editor via a network of tubular pipes that traversed all floors, spitting the papers directly on his desk.

He was a real entrepreneur, the boss, with a progressive outlook, standing testimony of it being the fact that he was able to build a modern Press Palace in Bucharest, a replica of the "Figaro" in Paris; his Press Palace was second only to the one housing Cazzavilan's "Universul" newspaper. As for me, I was not only deeply thankful to him for having helped me become a telegrapher and thus saving me from the professional illness that plagues the workers in a typography; I sincerely admired him and, whenever there was a party of the industry, I would recite his poems, poems that our boss had written in his younger years, when he was a revolutionary, like the revolutionaries that were trying to recruit us with crafted, alluring speeches at the meetings of the "Romania muncitoare" club.

So, I did the same thing recently, the third day of Christmas when, as usual, the boss summoned us to work on a shorter edition of the newspaper with a two, three columns of preface and including the New Year's calendar; generous as he always was, the owner, Constantin Mille, had reduced our work hours to allow everyone to attend the holiday party has was throwing; with food and drinks galore for everyone gathered in the Art Nouveau hall or in the Jugendstil rooms, or between the walls covered by the green Meissen tiles and colorful prints of modern typography mounted in the modern architecture, even in all other halls and rooms of the enterprise - secretary's office, documentation room, sales room, up to the lunch room – all lighted by modern lamps with green shades. He wanted everyone to enjoy the party, from the supervisors and writers to the typographers, from the super stars of the industry to the last employee of his prized, modern typography, of which he was so proud – and rightly so.

The beginning of that century had brought to Bucharest not only the new wave of a modern architecture that used revolutionary, technically advanced materials, but also a change in the civic behavior by the adoption of a more vocal attitude by the members of the more or less socialist circles that promoted either a generous emancipation or, boldly, anarchy. New voices were promoted within these circles, voices that often shifted their political views, advancing their careers by protesting in an yet romantic fashion the Malthusian predictions that called for certain restrictions among the population at large which was proliferating at a demographically exploding pace. This triggered the government intervention. The poems that I had learned some time ago had pathos; either because they were literary exquisite or just because I had an unconditional admiration for Mille, they sounded perfectly fitted for our new aspirations, in spite of the fact that, for unknown reasons, or maybe because of his peers' envy, our boss had been excluded from the socialist leadership, and he broke his ties with the movement afterward. Paradoxically, in his younger years he was thrown out of university for belonging to the socialist movement. However, judging by the way he treated his employees, as a team, the politics played no role in the management of his business. The former poet of the revolutionaries, today's great patron that had taken over from Beldiman the anti-Hohenzollern dynasty newspaper that had on its front page the logo "Beware of the foreign nail on the wall of your house, Romania!", he, Mille, hugged me when I recited the verses that he published in, oh, 1881!

Meanwhile he had become another person, both in regards to his wealth and social status, and as a writer, rounding up that year an entire voluminous literary work comprised of a novel, several short stories and two volumes of his "Letopiseți"; but he did not recant his earlier literary volume written in his younger years, whose title was "Caietul Roșu" no less!

You said: your right was
The heavy law of nature,
And those led by Malthus
Are standing hereby near.

In life's struggle to be
At happiness' table,
Our children lack the glee -
No place for them at the table.

You said: the strong prevails,

The first is the all-mighty,
The fight for progress ails,
Your dreams will shatter surely.

The ceiling of the hall was two floors high, on the left side reaching the height of the rotary machine, while on the right it was lowered to the mezzanine level of the arcades, where the offices were lined up ingenuously, as if the architect had played with an infinite repetition of the windows. It was in those offices that famous and feared signatures would write their articles. The hall vibrated with my voice which sprang vivaciously from my chest; it was an older habit of mine to wear my shirt unbuttoned, exposing my bare chest - that gave me a revolutionary allure, the allure of a young lad with the hair flying under the wind's blows.

My voice resonated in sync with the equally revolutionary resonance of the verses, while the successful, handsome man that was the owner, continuing the legacy of that *fin de siècle* which rendered his middle age a certain elegance, raised his glass and toasted with everyone across the nicely designed paper decorations. He then came to me and my foreman, who pushed me in front with that undeniable mark of authority that defines a leader:

- You guys don't give up, do you? You recruited these youngsters too, Axinte!..

- I didn't recruit them; they are joining voluntarily – said proudly Axinte, as if he would lecture the owner. - Look, even this youth, my relative; he took me by surprise when he showed up there, being introduced by someone else!

- They are young; you may still be able to deceive them a little bit.

Then Axinte, while raising his glass to toast, mumbled, as if he wanted to reassure Mille:

- Were you not young yourself, boss, when you wrote those poems?

- Yes, I was young and deeply honest in my beliefs, you know that, you are older than I am; I really believed, from the bottom of my heart.

- If you hadn't left, if you had stayed with us, you would probably still believe!

- May be. You are clean and you have your own needs that I still attend to, Axinte; you know that.

- How can I not know? Who is picking your articles, who can decipher your handwriting?

- These young men, as young as we were ourselves once upon a time, they can read not only my calligraphy – said Mille, teasing Axinte, obviously in the name of their old friendship, because he would immediately sugar it up: - Never mind, buddy, I know they learned from you! You are the one who can always decipher my handwriting!

But the other one wouldn't give up:

- By necessity… If Eminescu were still alive, today I would be working at "Timpul" rather than deciphering your hieroglyphs among lines and little flowers! Oh, God, what a wonderful handwriting he had! Clear as a teardrop; smooth as the birds' flight… those that fly confidently, dominating the sky – he added after sipping from his glass, as if he wanted to put out a fire. – You guys shake your wings with such speed that that the letters are coming out like unreadable hieroglyphs!

- You are a poet, Axinte; I told you that.

- No, I am not. If I was, they would have excluded me as they did you and Mortun… I am a simple worker and I have my needs, and I have nowhere else to go. Let those go who ……. … you know better!

- In a way, I should thank them for that – said Mille cynically. I owe it to them to…

- To be "generous", isn't it?

- Even more: to be the first among the generous! Just think about it: Mortun, who was part of our group where we started to speak out the truth in 1895, stayed with thc movement another four years before he did what he did. You are older than we are, Axinte, you should have realized what was going on before we did!...

- I am 52; you are 46, Mortun 47… But your kind, the intellectuals, you have a lot of doubts; we, the workers, we have needs… I am not behind you; I fight for my people's needs.

- And did I not respect your fight?

- Yes, you did respect it, I can't deny that. Even though you broke ties with those in the leadership, for me, Cristescu and Frimu, you were close to us.

- Why do you speak in past tense?

- You ARE, boss, you ARE! – thundered Axinte, raising his glass and toasting as the leader that he was: - For the boss! If all the owners would be like him, you wouldn't have to elect me as your union leader!...

And he forced the boss into having a drink, to the joy of everyone present, even though Mille had one other problem on his chest, so he said:

- I can't stop seeing things in perspective; I see no need for German theories that don't relate to our pains, or for those coming from Russia, bringing anarchy along, boy! We must think Romanian; and for us, the first and foremost painful spot is the peasants; and this is a big one!

- You, the intellectuals, have more doubts; we have needs… - repeated Axinte while toasting again.

- We have more questions and seek more answers. We don't want to just take someone else's theory and run with it, as they would like us to do. The doubts surface when we start noticing those underground games that some are playing.

- You mean you yourself are clean and not playing those games? - the other insinuated, forcing Mille to admit.

- I do sometimes play it too. But I admit, cross my heart, that I do it for my own benefit. I don't pretend to be an idealist politician so that I may deceive you, guys. I think about the problems the peasants face, and other people, and these problems are yet to be solved. You, the workers, are only a few compared to a big country like ours and, for better or for worse, you are organized in a manner that I admired and continue to admire so long as it does not become cosmopolite but remains genuinely national. I don't trust the internationalist theoretical speculations of Marx and Engels for reasons twofold: I smell some foreign interest in those theories, and in addition they don't provide solutions for the Romanian peasants. Romania is a big village, Axinte, and you are just a few, thus unable to solve its problems. What is that young man, Cristescu's opinion? He seems to be a smart guy.

- The young blanket-maker? This old typographer's opinion is the same as mine, what do you expect? We each think about our own needs.

- So long as only those needs are considered, it's ok, Axinte. But did you notice the employment agency that recently opened at Athénée Palace, run by an Austrian guy who brings laborers from abroad? Whenever I bring new machines for my business I send you guys abroad to learn how to operate those machines, rather than bringing in foreign workers. Who is then the patriot?

- Who is the better patriot? – laughed imperceptibly the old typographer with many and rich life-long experiences. Well, it is the one who makes more money!

- You surely are right! I don't deny that I do business with foreigners, but you guys get a share of what I make. For the millions of peasants I can't do anything yet, and that's what makes me sad. And in the teachings that are being sent to you guys from abroad I did not find any solutions either. By the way: Were you not scared last year by what was coming from Russia?

- Over there they have the tsarist police; there is a dictatorship over there…

- Yes, but also a wide spread anarchy; Gherea is hiding this from you; he doesn't want you to know. Axinte, you know quite well that I smell whenever there is provocation or anarchy. Look, even Nadejde, the last of the socialists that knew the theory, left the ranks!...

- See, that's exactly why we cannot leave; we have a responsibility toward those who elected us.

- That's right, you do. However, I believe in the Romanian working class' self-esteem. You worked for me in the past at the ""Drepturile Omului", at "Munca", and at Panu's "Lupta"…

- You even hired me here, even though we were not sharing the same political views anymore; I admit.

- Axinte, I suspect they want to continue to suck the wealth of our country. Look, I got fresh statistics from London: until 1877, in almost 500 years, the Turks squeezed 400 tons of gold; since 1687, in 200 years that is, the Austrians squeezed from Transylvania, Banat and Bucovina, even from Oltenia, 800 tons.

- Did you count how much it fell through your fingers? - said unforgiving the smart typographer, only to quickly switch gears and show the other more affectionate feelings: - At least you deserve it!... You are a great editor that brings to light this kind of real data, for the whole world to know!...

2.

I was eavesdropping to their conversations and gluing it all to my head, because I liked it so much!...Although I had turned twenty one some time ago, an age appropriate to enroll in the military, I didn't quite understand how did the relationship between the two men worked; evidently their lives intertwined up to the point where each defined his own place in society, reaching an experienced maturity. On one side - my relative from my village, Axinte, who, welcoming me upon my arrival in Bucharest, told me straight: "well, lad, I'm going to send you to work and, if you work, you could do pretty well". On the other side – it was that tumultuous poet, our boss. As a young man that crossed the mountains, by himself in this new world, the serendipity sent the two men my way and they hired me, and trained me to become a typographer, whereas I would have taken any job among the flocks of ambulant salesmen that took a load of newspapers underarm and trotted the city selling them. Later I learned to respect the two for their ideas. Each had their time-tested convictions about the purpose of life and about the people among which they lived, and their problems; the only thing that confused me was the fact that I couldn't understand whether their discussions were confrontational or if they were confessing to each other.

I was fond of my foreman, Axinte, for his Ardeleanian patience meticulously displayed in the public life of the workers' meetings, but I also liked Mille, whose comradeship-like authority I admired. Moreover, I somehow had become his ally in his efforts when he poetically had written an article on the mission of his newspaper that proclaimed: " anyone in this country, who has a complaint of any nature, knows that, when all other hope is gone, there is still one more, that of a sound of alarm which resonates far, of "Adevarul"... I also liked his poetry; he was sometimes an iconoclast bard, sometimes a humanitarian, disgusted by the hypocrisy of the corrupted. So, it was no small thing to work for this undoubtedly successful man in the ever modernizing world of Bucharest, a man that commanded, if not always admiration, at least curiosity. A totally different type of owner from the one I had in Ardeal, the German craftsman who, with his few lead letters that would make you sick of saturnism, used helpers like me to print small newspapers and prayer books.

Because, after the death of Alexandru Beldiman, Mille had purchased Beldiman's newspaper, probably as a result of his reversal of the radical ideas that he had adhered to in his younger years; some people criticized him behind his back for having given up his older motto: "Beware, Romanians, of the alien nail in the wall of your house!". But he couldn't care less because, he said, even their revolutionary author, the renowned Alexandri, had become a Royal Court poet. And he affirmed that, deeply in the philosophical foundation of things, from "Dacia Viitoare" whose publishing house he and Mortun had moved from Paris to Brussels, where they were working on their doctoral degrees, to Rosetti's "Romanul" and Panu's "Lupta" where he had been a helper and started publishing when he came back in the country, then to "Drepturile Omului", Munca", and ""Lumea noua" that he had founded himself thus becoming the owner of this newspaper publishing house, his radical intellectual spirit didn't deny his revolutionary label for which he had been excluded from Iasi University in his freshman year. But his disapproval of some conspiratorial inclinations that were manipulating the workers' unions for goals foreign to the country's interests, alienated him from his envious peers in the smaller publishing houses, the ones with demagogical language and limited socialist interests, while his newspaper that, in time, became newspapers, in plural, with increasing number of issues and increasing revenue, allowing him to build that Press Palace and typography with elegantly, artistically decorated hall and with the latest modern typographical technology that attracted the best professional workers, no matter the efforts of some to channel the workers toward extremist behavior. "Adệvărul", in whose spelling he preserved the old fashion "ệ" with a hat as a way to underscore overtly the Latin roots of the vocal originating from "veritas", a newspaper that was of late being published in several issues a day; then, the "Dimineața" appeared, with its women and children issues, that gathered almost all delivery carriages from downtown that were loaded with newspapers to be dropped off at Gara de Nord, lined up in multitudes according to the schedule of the trains that would deliver the papers throughout the country; same way as the "journalists" of the capital, which is to say the boys with stacks of folded newspapers held by the belt around their neck, were suddenly emerging from the other end of the expedition, like a rotating flock of birds that poured over the streets, yelling frenetically the name of the newspapers and the headlines announced by the posters.

Animated by his wide ideas – which combined the combativeness of tens of pens having the know-how of the daily news with the handling of popular interest columns of yet other tens – and managed by the iron fist of Sache Petreanu, with whom he had brought the nucleus of the old location on Karagheorghevici street near Lipscani, the business was as prosperous as the palace raising up in the heart of Bucharest; to the envy of his former comrades, the socialists, which were only talking speculatively about the poor whom they could only instigate. Because he was offering to all, laborers and intellectuals alike, modern working conditions and higher incomes, a cafeteria and elegant halls for activities, sales events, exhibitions, orders, for the services provided by the magazines for their readers, and even for some parties like this one. This fact gave the prestigious man, with his whirling moustache, the satisfaction of telling those that had to swallow bitterly because, driven by revenge, were theorizing a sort of fetish of the poverty that should be politicized rather than resolved, that in spite of them banishing him from their circle, they had not succeeded at changing his visions about the role of the written word vis-à-vis the people it was addressed to. His pen was writing in the old fashion, as he had learned in the old days from the real socialists. No matter how much they gossiped about him, he did more for the workers than they did, who in their mean, perverse way, only knew how to instigate to revolt, to advance foreign propaganda and, instead of bringing some relief for the population, managed only to keep the unrest growing in the country. He, Constantin Mile, was a smart fighter at that fulfilled age of accomplishments which, those called "reds" during the time of not-so-distant Paris Commune, proclaimed these accomplishments as being the fruit of the concept of "do-it-yourself", especially as a pragmatic sentiment of a European Latin spirit, a concept that Bratianu imported in Romania, thus invigorating the entrepreneurial spirit. And he found in it a better solution than the lamenting of the socialist circles where, along with the genuinely unhappy guys, there were those comfortable failures, the gossipers who were looking for scapegoats and even some that were paid by who-knows-whom from abroad. Reason for which, even though sometimes he and his old collaborators were in disagreement, most of the time they admitted he was right. Like my foreman, Axinte, who kept his adherence to the labor movement to which he was genuinely dedicated and did not consider doing anything else; but in his job as a typographer working for a good newspaper maker, he did not actually part from his employer, but followed him from "Romanul" to "Drepturile Omului", to "Munca" and, for many, many years now, right here…

Here, at the "Adevarul", that was no longer just a newspaper. It was a well-defined place and a palace in the prosperous downtown Bucharest of that beginning of the century which nurtured the pride and the foundation of some European national states; as well as defining them as appurtenant to the tentative alliances resulting from the provocations of the big empires. A castle of free ideas which, even though were debated in the biased circles of various political parties, were ultimately flowing free toward the public at large, without being subjugated by the interpretations of one or another. Just as Beldiman had envisioned it when he entrusted Mille with the publishing house "… to ensure the future of this newspaper… because I do not wish it to become either conservative or national-liberal"… And Mille was proud of not having left the newspaper fall under the influence of other political inclinations either, keeping his compass in such a way as to be able to criticize the social injustices more firmly, less subjectively and in a more patriotic approach than the socialists who started to disappoint many of those who, in the century past, would have been on their side.

It was a palace where, for many years now, they had enjoyed teasing each other at those fiestas, where the large hall embraces everyone in joy. It is a majestic hall, with thick rugs and a few portrait frescoes, illuminated and ornamented in a festive style, its walls covered with posters and portraits of some collaborators and artists, reproductions of works done in its own studios by its own designers and painters, with its grand staircase leading to the rich libraries accessible to anyone needing documentation, to the golden Byzantine chapel, to the meeting rooms and the chief editors' rooms, with big tables, to others' offices, to the different sections of the typography, to the machine rooms with their paper storage above and the pulleys lifting the rolls of paper as high into the dryness of the attic as possible, all the way up to those corners where the wiring of the Bucharest telegraphic space reached, and from where I monitored the switchboard.

Me, the youth who keeps wondering if my superiors - one the worker and the other the poet - were really confronting each other or merely confessed to each other... Were they enjoying teasing each other or were they contradicting each other?... Were they setting limits by marking their differences or, conversely, were they recognizing each other as the poles of a natural social binome, and even from the point of view of the nature of all things which fixed antipodes for all dimensions?...

When he brought me here, Axinte taught me what he himself had done for twenty years: deciphering the fleas, the lace and the hieroglyphs that were inlaid meticulously and perseveringly in our boss' penmanship; which, at that time, was exactly what formed the tandem between the writer and the editor, thus ensuring a speedy publication process. Due to this position, the foreman and I were the first readers of the most combatant articles that the master signed and which by now started being collected in the "Letopiset" volumes. And, whenever he met us while he was making his rounds about the sections of the typography, Mille used to raise his chin inquisitively while his wrinkles between his eyebrows, above his eyeglasses, became deeper, thus showing his willingness to listen to the first opinion, just by insinuating with this facial expression, the question: "Well, what do you think?!"…

Axinte would tell him. He would not spare the other's feelings since they knew each other for such a long time, and more often than not the master would agree with him and make the revisions by cutting, modifying, etc. Once in a while – and then only with a subtle smile indicating that he recognized the source of Axinte's ideas – he would cut him short:

- Tell this to your comrades at the "Romania muncitoare!"

- I will, don't you worry – would Axinte reply, as a stubborn Ardelean he was – and if I don't, again, don't you worry because someone else will!

- I am worried, Axinte, - one could detect the amiable sting –'cause if others will talk about it, the ones that mispronounce "cadaver" and "putrefaction" in translating what Marx says about capitalism elsewhere, then we won't ever succeed at teaching our children either Romanian language or what we think about our needs!... And he didn't hesitate to throw Axinte back in his apprentices' hands: "Toni, I know this uncle of yours takes you there instead of taking you in his quarters where you could learn better things; but make sure you don't lose your accents from that Ardeleanian School!...

At that time I, Celaru Anton, nicknamed Toni, was about sixteen, seventeen years of age and I was timid in front of our master but, even though I didn't verbally make any remarks, I did show him my findings on the still-wet proof by underlining with the indelible pencil some inadvertencies or even some extravagant idea. And that wouldn't upset him; on the contrary, he would tap me on the shoulder and make the correction. But as far as those blamed for their broken Romanian accent, I couldn't help but agree with him, as I had heard them myself.

Therefore, I earnestly questioned if the master and the foreman were disagreeing with each other by using those stinging remarks; or if they were confessing to each other, knowing that neither was hundred percent right, or just being unwilling to overtly admit some of their failures?... And I had many such questions but I didn't dare to ask. I was trying to understand by myself and, whenever I heard a new word, I went to the library and looked it up in dictionaries, something that I really enjoyed doing. But I still wanted to ask the question, I wanted the talk to someone that would be eager to debate over those things. So, I felt at ease talking to Cristescu. The mattress maker had served in the military, and he even had his own shop where he hired some of his relatives from Giurgiu, taking advantage of the fact that they could sleep right there in the shop, on the mattresses they made. He was both resourceful and smart; everyone present at the conferences and debates considered him a leader of youth kind of; and from doctor Racovski, who descended from an anti-

Ottoman Bulgarian family that defected north of Danube, but who was schooled in Occident, the mattress maker had learned quite a bit about political parties and about democracy, outdoing the fanatics that had brought in the narodnic theories, thus sowing the anarchy that Mille so overtly condemned and warned Axinte that this anarchy was triggered by other interests, with disguised motifs .

This is exactly how the mattress maker answered my questions, revealing that he knew what went wrong within the socialist movement circles, when they forced Mille out first, then Mortun, who had been active in Iasi, becoming a very important pawn, and lately Iosif Nadejde himself, the one that had found "Contemporanul" and the Moldavian circle where the first socialist line of thought had been nurtured. The unhappiness triggered by the way things were going with the party that used to be called "Socialist Party of the Workers" was noticeable to both those who jumped ship and those who were still part of the movement, which explained their comments and their relationships. And this kind of contradictory points of view permeated throughout the entire press industry, regardless of the fact that Mille's newspapers were powerful… But Cristescu, the smart guy with sparkling eyes, speaking persuasively, was assuring him that the workers must vote and choose to rebuild a stronger and closer-to-the-membership party, to which some of the older members may adhere; especially because doctor Racovski was now coming from Geneva. Doctor Racovski, whose father, one by the name of Stancev, owned land in Mangalia, but he, Racovski, had kept his revolutionary grandfather's name, the one that some time ago had defected in their town, in Giurgiu; he was friends with Plehanov and Maxim Gorki but chose to get a job as a military doctor in the 9th regiment cavalry, working with Frimu and Bujor and printing the publications of "Romania muncitoare" in order to rebuild a Romanian social-democratic party. Therefore the talks, even though heated as they seem to always be in the politics, could have led to the foundation of a party that would be acceptable to most, provided each would make concessions or agreements. A party that the workers needed – would Cristescu convincingly declaim, he, an energetic young man that quickly glued in his head important things, especially those about democracy, that he then explained to the students who, while better educated than him, did nevertheless come and listen to him…

Then, all of a sudden those news that turned everything upside down, broke through.

3.

Because I had been an apprentice in typographies for a long time and I knew I didn't have enough education, I started being very alert and was doing my best to learn as much as I could and as fast as I could while I was working on my assignments. And when, as an ambitious Transylvanian, I sometimes proved to be able to do more than I was supposed to do, I was lucky that my employer appreciated it. Thus, I was promoted from a telephone operator and a telegrapher position to that of an editor, because I was able to transcribe some information coming in Morse or in the telephone headset, and which usually the others would forward to their supervisors, directly in the form of news articles.. A fact that Mille, being himself a smart guy, knowledgeable, with hands-on experience and flair to recognize others' efforts, noticed. And so, one day, reading the fresh newspaper, I, Toni, the telegrapher, noticed that my name, Anton Celaru, was the signatory of a bunch of news that the owner found out that I had put together in a rush in order to save the paper's column which was lacking news. Intimidated, I thought it might be a farce of those in the typography but, inquiring with them, I found out that, when approving the issue, the master noticed, asked how that article showed up at the last minute and signed my name on the paper himself, ordering a monetary penalty for the journalist who did not do his job. When, from the attic where I was working, I came down to the sumptuous first floor to thank him, the elegant man, although on his way out to some important meetings, found the time for a comradeship gesture, pulling my hat, which was fashionable to wear at night under the spotlight of the incandescent bulbs, over my nose, and showing that he remembered me he said:

- You are the one who asked my permission to read in the journalists' library, aren't you?

- I thank you for that too, Mister Director, but especially for that signature…

- One draws the other. The more you read, the better you write. When I was your age, in Iasi, I was excluded from the university and someone helped me to sign up with a newspaper. It might be that I have rewarded that guy, not you! Journalism must be done with generosity. The readers are easily detecting the mean guys, the frauds!...

And, tapping me on the shoulder, he left, leaving behind that generous scent of his open character, of a confident man who doesn't hide the fact that he enjoys his success. Moreover, I could say that he left in my heart an even more intense, more vibrant sentiment, as if his success was mine. As if I shared with this handsome man the successes for which he was envied, I was living, indeed, the happiness of having been able, me, the child of some poor Transylvanians, to live in this bustling city full of Romanians from beyond the mountains, the brothers that the people in my village missed so much but are happy for them, knowing that they were enjoying the freedom in the country that helped them become prosperous. Because, as it was the case with this Constantin Mille, there were hundreds of successful Bucharesters; and there was enough room for hundreds more if they made the effort, as he did.

Consequently, devouring the books in that library, where I was spending more time than the editors to whom, in the modern spirit of the press enterprise, it was dedicated, I was reading those big encyclopedias and the incredible collection of newspapers from all over the world, and I got energized even in the work I was doing in the attic, no longer content with being just a telegrapher. Sometimes, weighing what the agencies would say, I would share some information with the correspondents and I would then entice them to look for new developments in those directions, thus provoking fresh news – *that* being the soul of journalism: to know how to set things in motion with the people at the other end of the wire. This way I was bringing to life Mille's desire to have his newspaper stand out by that thing that seems to be easy to learn, yet in reality is very complicated: a press bombshell; because all his effort of buying machinery and using new technology was indeed the modern secret of the gazette-makers in the large typographies. Secret and talent that he used here, in the effervescent and ambitious Bucharest, to satisfy the appetite of his readers that were bragging about being up-to-date with the world's events, with the latest fashion, considering themselves in a better position and even wealthier when they were commenting the latest news… And this was *the* secret of success of the modern press.

Even if we never met in person, I became familiar with all the correspondents that were calling from different places; moreover, some vendors or acquaintances of the master, noticing that I made a faithful effort to connect them with the owner when they called and he wasn't in the office, they started trusting me and were now leaving messages for the boss with me. So, to have a boss that noticed that and encouraged me, it was serendipity. But Constantin Mille was more than that, he was a boss who, from the hundreds of employees, knew me personally, me, a solitary boy that came here by himself from afar. It was my extraordinary luck, which awoke in me the sense of responsibility and the desire to climb on the social ladder, to reach perfection in this ambitious craft that is the newspaper-making. Which craft may be learned by watching the others do it, by stealing their secrets, living in the midst of its turmoil, knowing whom to admire and who to imitate from among the well-defined, brilliant personalities that gather around a publication whose owner is not as much the boss as he is a motivator. And that's what Mille was: the soul of his human intelligence-based enterprise, knowing how to appreciate this intelligence even in my person, despite the fact that I was but a child when he transferred me from the typography to the telegraph; and later he had the flair to notice that he could use me even better, as a transcribing editor, and he encouraged me to do that. I may have acquired good working habits from the education I got from back home, as all children that work around their parents from an young age do, or, as it may be the case, being among strangers, I have to admit that I became aware of these traits only after the owner noticed them and brought them to my attention; so my admiration for that generous man, as all talented people are, became a sort of gratitude when, after the Italian's departure, he promoted me to that guy's position as master over the heavy, wooden piece of furniture full of shiny couplings in which the connecting terminals penetrated quickly like bullets tied together with a myriad of wires, with commands from the metallic bells and rotating ebonite buttons marked with levels of variable condensers, frames within which the level of electricity oscillated, and the myriad of rotating keys, switches, plugs connecting and switching, through the networks of wires made of ductile materials, wrapped according to the imagination of the likes of Marconi, Edison, Bell and Howell, who seemed to carve, model and isolate the metals with Bakelite that would not permit the signals to leak, thus preserving the quality of these materials of allowing the signals to travel flawlessly the long distances of the modern communication, announcing the arrival of new message by bells situated at the extraordinarily far distances and bringing in from those distant places the voices that were only a tiny bit altered by the vibration of the membranes at the bottom of the little trumpet that sucked your words and amplified those you were listening to.

In addition to my daily routine, I learned from that Italian guy to write down everything, transcribe the messages on those pieces of papers specially cut to have them handy, then roll them to make sure they would slide through the tubes three floors down – this proved to be a welcome addition to the cutting edge technology of the new telephone switchboard which, by interchanging those terminals that made various connections, looked like being hitched to the entire world. There were only a few field correspondents who were still transmitting news from far away, less modernized places or from distant foreign countries through the patient rattling of the old "Morse" telegraph. Indeed, this entire toy that we operated – we, the guys upstairs and the guys from the almighty office of the editor on the third floor – as well as the quick answers we were expected to give simultaneously with taking and forwarding the correspondences to the editors' desks, correspondences loaded with news that were flying to the lead of the lettering proofs and were multiplied in an immense number of issues spit by the rotating mechanism; all this influx of information was giving me a feeling of frenzy. And it made me admire the owner even more. Because that man who always knew how to diplomatically show how well informed he was and how promptly the world news reached him, made a passion from updating his business equipment with all the cutting edge technology of that beginning of the twentieth century, when new technologies were exploding and the pace of modernization was ever so valued. And, even though some were questioning the blurry methods he used to bring in those machines, and some of his adversaries were joking or insinuating about his nickname “Milu”, calling him “Milu-stilu”, “Milu-copilu” or “Milu-crocodilu”, I found much joy in reading Mille’s writing in which he was publicly debating the acute problems of the day and being proud to disseminate the breaking news gathered by means of the most modern technology, without having to worry about the cost. Choosing between his open mind and his entrepreneurial spirit, and his competitors’ spiteful, shabby way of doing business - like at “Romania muncitoare” where unsold journals were laying on the floor and on the staircase around the hall - was an easy task for me. Even from a rational point of view, meaning without the enthusiasm of having found my own aspirations, I was inclined toward the man worth of admiration.

If anything, my inclination as a poor boy was toward the ideas insinuated by my foreman, Axinte, in a traditional Ardelean spirit of revolt, or expressed more vehemently and more precipitously in an imperial style by Cristescu, that would allow me to hope, sentimentally, that one day they will reconcile and Mille would come back to the movement and would lend everyone a share of his aura… My mind, that of a child raised among patient teachers and used to the sad Ardelean songs, was secretly longing to see these impulsive Romanians from this free country south-of-the-mountains, a country of which many of my kin were dreaming of, to see them more tolerant. That’s why I was oscillating between the meetings where we were told about the needs in our lives, about things that could have triggered a revolt, and Mille’s publishing house, where we worked according to other standards: those of tougher yet more successful businesses, those businesses where there is less talk; and I , who was thinking about my needs, was realizing, that I could become an accomplished person, raising above my destitute status that was the object of mockery for my people across the mountains, just by working hard at Mille’s enterprise.

And I was making progress toward my goal, commensurate with my needs which at the time were not many. Even at the beginning, shortly after I became familiar with the building and what was going on inside, when I timidly waited in the antechamber to ask his permission to use the editors' library, with its huge encyclopedias and lexicons, the boss noticed my shyness and encouraged me, saying:

- Do you really like the library?

- I like it, sir, because you were so generous when you allowed us to sleep in the attic so that we can take turns in relieving mister Disgraziato, that now I don't have to get out of the house but I can stay here, among the books…

Scrutinizing me, the boss only repeated, significantly:

- "Among the books!…" Look, I give you permission to use the other one, my private library where you may find rare books which others don't know how to handle. You only need to make sure you put them back in order; and before you do, dust them off!

I was now having another duty beyond assisting Disgraziato, the Friulan-Tirolean who, when drunk, was speaking in broken Romanian dialect, an old womanizer who labored in German and Italian publishing houses in different towns where he built ephemeral nests. As his permanent residence, he said he had a German Catholic wife that he couldn't get a divorce from, somewhere upstream Danube; because until he specialized in this newspaper-making business, which gave him reason to request that we call him "counter master", he was a telegrapher's apprentice in the Marine, on the river boats, in riparian ports-of-call where "the slaves were carrying the earth's burden", as he was saying, reciting revolutionary poems, the kind our boss liked. He was reigning over the switchboard that I later took over, monitoring it throughout the day, coordinating with the editor's office, with whom he needed to cooperate and make prompt, on the spot decisions. Reason for him to dress comfortably, with light sandals and striped T-shirts, the type the marines are wearing when they are working on the deck; sometimes he was singing, some other times swearing, all the time talking, a lot of talking and chatting with everyone that called, from the chief editor on the first floor, who was giving him orders though the same tubes that I used to throw the messages transcribed on those pieces of paper especially cut to have them handy and folded, to correspondents in the four corners of the country, or, whenever he had a break, talking to us, the lads around him, we, who admired his versatility in maneuvering the muffles, the bananas and the buttons in the middle of which he looked like a warlock who was harnessing the whole world with those ties.

He was like a temperamental talkative marine who was laboring skillfully on the suspended deck of this building in Sarindari. But, whenever he felt like being fashionable, he would put on his gala uniform. He had a marine jacket, with shiny metal buttons he used to wear when he went to the community balls, where he would try to hook up with lowly women, and as a result he would, more often than not, end up being beaten by their mates. Mille had hired him to handle the telegraph station designed especially for newspapers and assembled in Zürich, with the modern accessories that ensured the simultaneous transmission of the influx of information from agencies and correspondents, the conversations with other people that called in, and other places that were sending telegraphic messages; with tubes, as I said, like gutters, for the folded papers with articles sliding down to the editor's office; and with telephone wires reaching the supervisors' offices. It was a marvel at the time, and the Helvetian-Tyrolean with an Italian accent worked in tandem with Simionescu, the albino sub-secretary of the editing department who, hidden under the hat covering his eyes, was working on the papers sent in by the correspondents, formatting them for publication. They worked well together, coordinating with each other, like two machines; one handling buttons, plugs and rolls of papers thrown down the tube directly to the editors, as well as the telephone communications branched out directly to the stenographers; the other – the penmanship, the grammar, measuring quadrants and the couriers' itinerary; together they formed that which was the pride and joy of the owner – the spine of a modern publication.

The only drawback was that the Tyrolean-Friulan who found a nest for himself in Bucharest, the city with pretty women who spoke a language very much like his, was a sort of a drunkard; and that touched a nerve with the abstinent Simionescu, who was able to sit down for hours at a time, frozen at the huge desk at the end of the hallway on the first floor, moving only his wrist when correcting papers, writing specifications on pages, or throwing papers at the couriers and pointing suggestively with the fingers from the other hand the direction where they had to deliver them urgently. An efficiently running motor that I, as a young new comer, was watching curiously ever since I had been working in the typography because our bedroom, the bedroom in the attic where the apprentices were allowed to sleep so that we may relieve the telegrapher during the calmer moments, was just next door. Moreover, the first bed, separated from the others' by a wardrobe, was reserved for the counter master, for the days when he was thrown out by one of his lovers, as it often happened. Those nights he would stay with us, would send us to buy him drinks, and, for those of us who were interested, he would teach us some Italian words and we, in turn, would teach him the correct pronunciation of those words in Romanian; given my inclination toward learning and my desire to fill in my educational gaps, this thing fitted me perfectly.

And that made the counter master to like me and, even in the first year, when I worked in the typography, and would come up here only to sleep, he was giving me his ration of milk, as a supplement, to heal me, or at least to prevent me from developing saturnism. Because at the time, saturnism was one of the job-related illnesses under much scrutiny and monitoring by the social-democrats and the labor unions and, to prove that they were representing the workers, they were accusing the business owners of being responsible those job-related illness. And counter master Disgraziato, who considered himself a "condotierre de la societa" – a fighter for a myriad of causes, praising the owner for his modern approach to business, for providing milk for the employees, a measure seen at the time only in the typographies in France and Germany, every time he had an opportunity, at the ball organized by Constantin Mille who, as a generous man, would treat everyone with beer, Disgraziato would, in his colorful Romanian-Italian language, toast to the owner's health, wishing him to open his heart more and offer the workers a ration of hard liquor too, since "questa bevatura cures even more illnesses than the milk does!... It cures even the albinism, not only the saturnism" – he was saying, alluding at his human tandem with whom he was in permanent contact through three floors due to all those wires and tubes, ensuring the spinal transmission of the breaking news, which made the owner proud of having the best, latest information and, by its dissemination, becoming the all-powerful master over the politics and the influence of the public opinion.

"To your palazzo, boss! – would Disgraziato toast at such occasions, vocalizing the sound of the broken words with an Italian accent, knowing that it pleased our boss – To your palazzo which, here, next door to the palazzo reale, leads, in Romania, the kingdom of news!"… And thus, pretending and addressing the other in a loud voice, he'd say: "What; don't you want to toast to our boss' honor?", he would convince even the abstinent Simionescu to have a drink. The one who, whenever he would lose his patience with Disgraziato, and sensing over the three floors between the switchboard and the attic and his sumptuous desk on the first floor, that "mister" counter master had lubricated too much his communication tools, would yell out loud through the tubes through which the rolls of papers were sliding: "Disgraziato, refrain yourself, you drunkard, we still have two hours to go until the printing is over!!!"… But the other wasn't the shy type and would retort also through the vibrations emanating from the tubes across the floors: "Non ti preocupare, abstinento!... I have the good boy that agiuta me!"...

The good boy was me, Toni, who, in the same way that I had learned some German from the guy I had worked for in Transylvania, was catching up with the counter master's Friulan-Italian. Fact that made him like me; he would sometimes pay the cover charge for me at those community balls, frequented by those lowly women carrying their shoes in their hands so that they won't damage them while stepping onto potholes; and at the entrance the women would pull their skirts up and wash and rub their heels till they became pink and tempting, before putting on their shoes and enter the ballroom as if they were high class ladies.

And then once inside, after having shown at the fountain their knees and thighs by lifting their skirts to avoid getting wet, undulating their round butts when bending to wash their feet, they would become sober and would hide their ankles under their skirts. Because the tacit game at this sort of balls, where one could pick up a date, was that the women would wait in a corner, shyly, to be invited to dance, and would even accept candy treats if they became more intimate with the cavaliers. My counter master was teaching me that the steps were not difficult, that I could even jump around like in a "Sîrba", a circle dance familiar with the villagers, because the quarters where the girls were coming form were not too far from the village. And he also was teaching me how to recognize those girls that "were making things easier", 'cause you could ask them out for a date in Cismigiu, or you could adventure with them to the end of the railroad and beyond, at the outskirts of town, where they lived. And that's exactly what the counter master used to do: he would hang on to one woman, would keep talking to her over and over, and of course he wouldn't let her go. He would send me home while he offered to accompany her to her home; and that ended up badly at times, when he would return beaten up, his bones softened by the local gangs which, in spite of women's protests, had their own rules of not accepting intruders.

One time, however, he took me somewhere near the Old Court, by Hanul lui Manuc, to a bog hall, where several speakers went up the stage, speaking broken Romanian with heavy foreign accents just like the counter master, some with a hoarse German accent, others with a sobering sobbing, whimpering Slavic accent, anyhow sounding like a twisted Romanian. Just as I heard sometimes the boss humiliating those foreign speakers in front of Axinte who, I admit, had moral principles and was living up to them. He never pushed me or tempted me to go there, but he rejoiced when he saw me at the meetings. Disgraziato was well known and even applauded by the participants; they nicknamed him "the garibaldist", while he, proudly ballooning his chest, spoke of "mundo operai" and "vittoria finale", fact that set him apart from those who would go around the bushes and, pretending to philosophize, talked about one Malthus, whose theory was well known at that time, or about one Marx, about whom I didn't find much in the lexicons at the publishing house where I always tried to find answers to my many questions sprung from my lack of education.

So one day I met my foreman Axinte at one of those meetings; as a more balanced, serious man, he usually gave me different sorts of advice, more Transylvanian-like than the temperamental exclamations of that Italian with a musical tone in his voice. Next day at work he said to me:

- If you went over there with the garibaldist, it's ok, son; I stayed aside because this is the agreement with our boss: to respect each other but not to influence each other.

And I had the guts to ask him something that I didn't dare ask the counter master:

- Do you think the boss will get upset if he knew we went over there?

- He has no reason to get upset, son, because he spent time over there too in his younger years; he even tells us himself that workers need a party… The only thing is that, in his opinion, the workers are not the most important class in this country because the pauperism is much wider, and he considers himself a tribune of many sorts of poor people… And he is right, son, I am not saying he isn't. Because look, we the Transylvanians, have certain type of injustices to fight; others have different ones… He makes this newspaper for all. On top of it, why not think out loud, he may have realized that he profits from everyone. That's his business, son, because there are many needs in the world and, whatever resources are available are not enough for all… Some have more, others don't but wished they did, and still others are happy with less.

- Everyone with their own burden… Look, he's rich and that's why he is not agreeing with the guys that claim they are making newspapers only for us… Me, as a worker, I understand, but others…

- Does this mean our boss is better?

- He wants to prove, and he did it successfully, that people working for him are earning a better and more stable salary – said wisely the Transylvanian – and I want you to know, my son, that I didn't see him getting angry because I work part time at the other guys' journals in order to supplement my income. Therefore, I am not asking myself other questions, but by the same token I don't want to have anything to do with their parties because I don't have the kind of money they have. I told you: in this world there isn't enough for all, because we are not all alike either: and people like Mille are gathering wealth right and left, while those that didn't want him to be one of them anymore, they, well, they either disappeared, or never succeeded as he did!...

- Then he is better– I was insisting, happily. – Master, you were the one who had me learn his poetry.

- Well, son, - the foreman said, emphasizing that paternal sense – you are some sort of relative to me and also work with me, so I am telling you what and how I see things: We have no other option; he is, but he also understands why we get together over there. And sometimes he even writes in a tougher language than the way the other guys are doing, which I don't like, and neither does he. But that doesn't mean this is not my party!... This life is a two-way street, damn it, son!... Mille knows that I am not joining his party, although I wish one like him would join the party I am in with the others that are not up to his stature, especially because he is more Romanian and more of our own… This life is a two-way street, I told you!

Corneliu Leu and his wife Rodica at home, 2013.

4.

The counter master, however, talked to me in a different way. Considering himself a heroic garibaldist, his tumultuous, anarchist spirit needed to become theatrical and have an audience whenever he was drinking; he was not spelling out the issues, like the prudent foreman Axinte did. He always exaggerated, ranted, instigated, exploited the Latin roots commonality concept, compared himself uselessly to inappropriate circumstances from France and Italy, confused between the royal dynasties and imperial dynasties, mumbling about those more recently proclaimed that were of less noble ancestry, getting as far as the Mexican revolution where a German emperor was shot, but mistaking Oliver Cromwell who decapitated a British king and Abraham Lincoln's assassin whose last words were a quote from a drama that talked about tyrants.

- Ragazzo boy – he started boasting while handling the muffles and sockets from his desk, dressed with his stripped matelote T-shirt carried in his luggage, a reminder of his real or unreal maritime life he was bragging about – I am a descendent of outlaws; my people are those brigands that are strangling the miser Tyroleans… For me freedom is everything and I turn vicious if I don't get it. I became an anarchist against the commandment that wanted to enroll me in the imperial army, and also against the church, which wants me to be, my entire life, the slave of one single woman, and, on top of that, she is an ugly German!

He seemed nice because he was telling us unusual stories, to us, the apprentices with whom he shared the bedroom in the attic and to whom he gave life lessons; he told us stories from his life as a marine, or stories with outlaws, where he always found a role for himself as a revolutionary or a revolted guy, as he liked playing, stretching his exaggeration so much as to affirm that he reached America with Garibaldi. Actually he was just re-counting events heavily speculated by the European newspapers. He was bragging about a cousin, a republican anarchist who stayed in Italy after Garibaldi, who killed Franz Joseph's empress in Geneva, shouting that he wanted to kill the tyranny, later crying when he learned that the unlucky victim, whom he killed to take revenge on Vienna throne, was herself a revolutionary and hated the tyrannical emperor that was her husband. But, most importantly, he said he liked Romania because people like to party and have a good time, women here are not like the German ones, and the king, no matter how German he was, was unsuccessful in his endeavor to change the apathy and the corruption of the policemen, since in Romania the dictatorship doesn't fly. And he'd go on and on with more stories, his mouth always finding words and sounds that made him coherent in Romanian, thus satisfying his desire to stand out of the crowd by his emphatic gestures that softened his aggressive penchant from which, indeed, sprung his speeches.

Doctor Racovski and Dobrogeanu Gherea used him whenever there was a need to agitate the people in that big hall at "Romania muncitoare", and Disgraziato would bring us, the lads in the attic- turned-bedroom, to those meetings, introducing us to the bosses as the future generation of "carbonari" he was mentoring. Moreover, one day, when he installed in doctor Racovski's house a wire connecting him directly with Bulgaria, the counter master took me with him and introduced me to the doctor as his helper. That day, without me understanding why, I became the focus of doctor Racovski's attention, not only medically –because he noticed that I had an initial stage of saturnism – but also as an example in his speeches when he was talking about the exploitation of the young workers and about the employers' indifference toward the job-related illnesses to which they are exposing us. Axinte then told him how I was transferred to work the telegraph specifically in order to take me away from working with the lead, but the doctor continued to consult me, to monitor me, and to give me special medical treatment and advice on how to take care of myself.

- Come over to these meetings, if you are interested in our discussions, we are doing it especially for you – told me sharply the doctor - but always come whenever I am here, so that I can check the progress of your illness. It's a job-related illness, it comes from the work you are forced to do, and we must be careful, must unveil and eradicate all the putrefaction of the bourgeoisie.

It was impressive to see this man who looked bitter when he was on the podium speaking about revolutions, suddenly changing once he put on his white medical robe and started to consult right there and then, for free, at no charge, the poor that were seeking him out. As far as I was concerned, he persisted. He requested the City Hall to register my job-related illness, he wrote to newspapers and abroad until he received from Paris a paper with the latest scientific research on saturnism. Only then did he do a complete examination on me, gave me a prescription and a recommendation for a free treatment at the Military Hospital, and recommended that, in order to boost my immune system, I walk outdoors, rain or shine, without a hat on my head, and wearing an unbuttoned shirt, exposing my bare chest – a modern theory that speculated on the ability of the body to fight and adjust to the fluctuation of the ambient temperature. Simultaneously, he gave interviews related to my case while checking up on me with a caring authority, which, I admit, I appreciated since I felt protected by this man also. And only when I noticed that my boss, Mille, didn't really like it, did I start asking myself, with sadness, why in the world is it that exactly the men I admired the most, or the ones that I was grateful to, in my heart, were on different sides of the fence.

Because, seeing what was happening, Mille, the owner, couldn't but notice how the doctor politicized my case.

- You are a celebrity, Anton Celaru; you are in the socialist newspaper – he said ironically – The worker I exploit, as Marx says, is treated of the job-related illness discovered by his Marx's follower, doctor Racovski… And thus the medical field enters the fight between social classes!

- But sir – I was saying apologetically, showing that I learned by now what the press is all about – I asked to have it specified in the article, and it is clearly written, that I already had this illness when I came from Ardeal, that I got it over there, at the old typography, and that I am thankful to you for not letting me continue to work with lead.

- You brought from Ardeal even less humor that we have over here, Toni. I was joking about the way Engels taught those guys at the "Internationala" to promote themselves. Never mind this; just tell me how you feel since you started to take walks like this, hair-in-the-wind and bare chest.

Hair-in-the-wind and bare chest. Yes, that's precisely how I was walking and I was truly feeling great! I had gone through and fought the winter and was proud of myself.

- I feel good, sir – I answered, showing off what else I had learned at "Romania muncitoare", other than the treatment prescribed by doctor Racovski – I feel brave when I walk hair-in-the-wind and bare chest, fighting the cold and… the prejudices!

- Good! Keep doing it! - Mille encouraged me maliciously, unforgiving toward those that had excluded him some time ago from their ranks. – And be careful about their prejudices, 'cause they have many! – then, becoming softer, more conceding: I have bigger fish to fry; I respect the doctor because he is educated, molded in the West, not by the Russian nihilism. Moreover, - he let himself loose with the fantasy of a foamy comment characteristic to his articles as well – although he is a stubborn Bulgarian, I could say he totally became an Oltenian here, in Romania; he looks at things more liberally, more jokingly, more matter-of-factly that Gherea, who still wants to preach dangerous esthetics. Racovski, no; but Gherea treats everything with gravity, evolving around the importance of his personality and of some theories that he caught *en route* from Cernisevski, through the more rudimentary brain of Plehanov. He would have been better off catching up with our language, so that he may pronounce it correctly; with "I" being "I" and "a" being "a"!

-I don't particularly like Mr. Gherea either – I answered, encouraged by Mille.

- Why, Tony boy?

- Well… he is… hmmmm… more military style!

- Military style? Bravo! You just put your finger on the problem!... said Mille, not missing the opportunity – Not only does he speak a broken Romanian, but he also asserts leadership position and wants to give orders! – And Mille, confident on the subject matter of his polemics, would become the orator that captivated us: Look, boys, learn the ins and outs of that nihilism, anarchism, and even the unions that seem to be peace-loving, and when you will realize that they are being manipulated by some very mysterious forces, you will also realize that nowadays the large European movement is not about the international social-democracy but about the need of common sense, of the emancipation of the nations. The social motor of our times is the pragmatism of a national conscientiousness that demolishes empires and facilitates the countries in their normal borders, where people are managing themselves according to their own needs, ensuring the wellbeing and progress of the many, not only of a handful of them!

I liked the fact that the owner was sticking to his practical principles, for which he was applauded by both his own peers, the guys in the publishing house whom he was passionately coagulating, as well as by the audience in those big meetings where he would bring his acclaimed journals. Yet he was relaxed; not threatening, like the other leaders that were calling for revolt; instead he was joking and understanding, even though he was doing this within the limits of his polemic with the social-democrats. And more often than not he would amuse himself making fun of Disgraziato blaming him for everything that went wrong with the nihilists of which he had purposely severed his ties with. Having lived in that world and not trying to avoid it, but rather making an effort to show it some consideration, the same way he didn't forsake his poetry of his youth, the owner Constantin Mille was unforgiving, as I said, with both the foreign accents exhibited by some of the socialists he broke ties with, and with the way others from that group mutilated the language that was so dear to him. While rebutting their fundamental statements, he was also taunting their precarious way of speaking: "See, the crooked way of speaking mirrors the crooked way of thinking – these are the fruits of the internationalist propaganda." So, he was amused by the Friulian sonorities that the counter master had when he spoke in his broken Romanian. He tolerated the drunkard because he appreciated the guy's work at that sophisticated machinery which was the pride of his enterprise, and he would admonish the guy only when this one would go overboard by shouting apocalyptic threats about a revolution that will destroy everything. Something that, in his rational judgment, he could not agree with. While, in the same time, he proved his highly intellectual persona and his solid information system that made him so proud, and he cut short the Friulian's exaggeration:

- Hey you, German macaronian, those things were written by Plehov in a clearer style and yet he was mocked by the real philosophers. The philosophy searches the creation not the destruction; it opens people's minds, does not blacken it with nihilism!...

- I am nihilisto because I want to break my chains! – would proclaim Disgraziato theatrically.

- And what are you beginning with?... Be aware, I asked this question to people wiser than you! – would the owner show off his popularity by openly discussing those things.

- What am I beginning with? With the Church!... With the Catholics that don't allow me to get a divorce! – would admit the counter master – If they did, I would have gotten me a pretty wife from here!

- See, Disgraziato, see?... You want to turn the world upside down just because of those who beat you up because they won't let you, a married man, get close to their daughters or sisters. Heck, you macaronian, it's time to learn that the gossipmongers have an elevated sense of family pride!!... Just admit it: how many times did you wish they would let go if you shouted that you would marry their girl?

- Gossipmongers, little bourgeoisie full of prejudices!... – the anarchist in him would wake up – The unjust world makes us become nihilists!... the world that must be destroyed!

- Well then, start with Racovski's estate and with Gherea's restaurant! – would the owner reply in a way that made him understood by others too – I was not a worker, therefore I had no business being in your political party; and Mortun was even more wealthy than I was, so nobody can accuse him of being a traitor; well then, why is it that others, that are not workers, are leading you according to interests foreign from your own?!

- Ask them about that; I am a garibaldist, not a nihilist! – would the Italian proudly rebound, ready to make concessions: Look, I am debating with you in a friendly manner, you, my own employer…

- You are a rare phenomenon, body – would the owner caress him, putting the finger on the problem – You are a Latin nihilist; not a Slavic one, like the others!... Had you had some schooling, you could have become a Cartesian; but the others are not capable, they are hunted by other ghosts; their philosophy is different; it is strange and crooked for us, just like the sectarian religions of those coming from deep inside Siberia, bringing all kinds of mutilations!...

He was pleasant, the owner, when you caught him in one of those moments, and he had that ability, common among the smart lawyers, to explain everything in detail, always bringing new information, more updated than the adversary's, the same way he did things in his journalistic writings. And he found his virtue in presenting himself as a modern pragmatic. The workers as well as the editors were fighting to get hired by him, given the solid, sure wages and the modernizations that provided the means for him to offer higher wages than what these guys could have otherwise gotten from those with union claims where, on top of everything, they were taxed by their leaders who pretended to be leftists. I started to understand this after I had seen the rigorous rules that the manager, Sache Petreanu, was implementing on behalf of the owner; not in the least laudative but instead pointing out that "whenever the gazette is good and sells well, you are only doing your job!"... Indeed, some time ago the owner had made copies of the photo of one Zaharia Carcalechi and displayed them throughout the publishing house as a memento of what must not be done; this guy was a bankrupt journalist that gained celebrity the last century for publishing intermittently, every now and then for twenty years, an issue of "Vestitorul romanesc". Not on a fixed day, not following the news of the day, not even taking out the old news but leaving them in the new issue. Doing the same thing over and over again, publishing whenever he felt like or had enough money to buy the paper, but wondering "why" each time he had to file bankruptcy.

A modern owner, bringing in top of the line machinery and saving money to buy the adjacent property from some sacs manufacturers where he could expand our workshops, Mille showed the same consideration to all his employees; he was demanding yet fair with us; even friendly, paying attention to our problems whenever he had time to chat. That's how I knew him ever since I arrived there as a new comer that was growing up with them; and also how the capricious Disgraziato, who insisted that we call him by that strange name of "counter master", knew him. Both of us – me, who left my parents to go into the unknown, he, running away from the wife, maybe knowingly coming back beaten up by the prejudices of those whose women he was pestering – we admitted that we were adopted by Mille's prosperous enterprise and, due to his entrepreneurial spirit, we knew, as many others did, that, for better or for worse, we had our daily existence ensured as no other workers from other business had. We confessed that to each other once, feeling the need to analyze the situation, and, in spite of our age difference, we felt we were friends.

But one day, misfortune struck and Disgraziato did not return at all, not even beaten up. Rumor had it that, after they beat him up, the gossipmongers threw him onto a cereal train wagon going to Giurgiu “pouring” him into the grain barge together with the grains. Other rumors, though, held that the police may have been involved since they were on alert due to the Russian revolutions, and they were trying to get rid of the agitators; especially those that couldn’t document their identity - they could be caught, as it was the case with the counter master.

Before any of those rumors transpired, the entire editorial panicked because, exactly at the pick hour when the circulation of messages, letters, news by telephone and by the cylinders that were ensuring that flux of liaison between the attic and the central switchboard, the leadership from the first floor with the big table where Simionescu was glued, and the offices, the news assembling room, the pagination room from other floors, exactly in those moments Disgraziato did not appear. No matter how much of a drunk or womanizer he was, no matter how many bitter coffees with freshly squeezed lemons the boys from the adjacent bedroom would give him, at those hours, dressed in either clean or wrinkled outfits, he would always show up and did not fail when he was handling those buttons, therefore the albino from that huge table in the hallway would only mumble in discontent in the first few minutes; later on, once he noticed that things were set in motion, only his ordinary commands would be heard.

This time, however, Simionescu was shouting madly, cursing the drunkard with uncensored words because he did not realize that the man may not have been there, present at his job, thus the motor may not have run, may not have started, may not have functioned at all, therefore the whole machinery may have succumbed. The chief editorial secretary appeared by the big, massive desk, having left his own sumptuous chair that had previously belonged to the former owner, Beldiman, and one could peak inside the room through the widely open door of this office that was three steps higher than the rest, allowing him to monitor all the activity on the hallway as he pleased, over his assistant's, Simionescu head. The other secretaries were coming too, portfolios in their hands so that the gazette could be printed – portfolios of articles from the editorial, of freshly gathered material, of proof-read articles off the desks of the proofreaders, material off the desks of editors, of formatting and pagination desks, portfolios shaved, shaken, re-dimensioned, improvised quickly on their laps, so that the typographic process wouldn't stop, all while Simionescu, with the telephone over his ear yet still yelling in the funnel that ended over his head, was making verbally the same efforts to start the motor that others were making by either forcing it, praying, molesting it, begging it… And the motor suddenly started, without anybody realizing it in the midst of that turmoil, the rolls of paper started to slide noisily through the tubes, the first batches glowing under the spotlight, Simionescu's pen, detaching from the verbal orders of his commanding voice, was now jotting formatting and pagination instructions on the corners of the sheets, while one could hear the phones ringing in the offices whose doors were left open by those who flocked around the assistant chief secretary's desk, who exclaimed:

- Yes, yes… dam you, drunkard!...

I heard him all right but I didn't say anything and I kept going. I couldn't do anything else because, in desperation that Disgraziato didn't show up, I had secretly started the mechanism and I couldn't stop it. Only when I got upstairs, after the bulk of materials went into printing and they could now blame the drunkard for the scare he put them through, did they realize that, sitting in front of that board full of buttons, like little light bulbs, plugs, wires, the frame full of marks for the plugs, and the whole amalgam of branched and de-branched connections, was not the one wearing the stripped undershirt, or still having his coat - decorated with Marine's buttons – on, as he used to when he came to work last minute, or having a hang-over, or just barely awake, it was not Disgraziato, the bad-lack angel of consciousness, exemplary character, at the commanding desk in the hallway.

Instead, with perspiration running all over my face and body but not giving up, muttering an order in Italian here and there as if I was riding a traction animal used to respond to commands made in that language, with my hair raised and uncombed, with my shirt unbuttoned, it was me, Toni, admitting, as if guilty, that I was the one who didn't let the machinery of the influx of the news collapse. It was my forth year at "Adevărul" and the owner promoted me on the spot to Disgraziato's position, without asking me how many more times had I done the same thing, camouflaging my foreman's absence, whose drinking habit did not affect his ability to perform.

Unfortunately, it couldn't be proven that I had substituted my foreman in the past since Disgraziato vanished, being missed and liked by many as he was - with his good and bad habits. His contradictory personality left a vacuum, although most of the time he was acting in a cold and egocentric manner, satisfying his exhibitionism with which he attracted the attention of both young and old fans. This magnetic attraction marked youngsters like me who, with the characteristic superficiality of our age, took him as a role model of well-defined personality whose tricks of success one is tempted to imitate, as well as older people who couldn't help but notice him. So, probably because I was considered a follower of Disgraziato, one day dr. Racovski himself asked me, while we were there, at "Romania Muncitoare":

- Toni, does anybody have any news of that Tyrolian-Helvetic, garibaldist, Italian guy?...

Thus, about four years after I had considered myself a Bucharester and loved this lively city as much as I liked my childhood's hilly orchards, I had inherited the bed separated by a wardrobe which in the past formed that private bedroom so well deserved by my foreman. And now, two more years passed since I took over his operating board with all its installations that I learned to operate efficiently and passionately, way up here, on the top floor where the switchboard was, on the exterior wall of which - a brick façade facing the tower of the church -, anchored on the isolating porcelain like freezing white birds, there were tens of wires crossing the sky of Bucharest bringing news from the world. It was through this communication medium that I received that late night message, during the break when the wires were cooling off, after the start of the printing of the night edition, and while the big rotary machine underneath was making the walls vibrate, I was opening the window to breath in the fresh winter night air before I went to bed, listening to the snoring of the horses harnessed to carriages lined up around the church, waiting for packages to be thrown in from the storage room and loaded then delivered to the messenger wagon of the night train. It was a brief moment of pleasure as I was otherwise left with no more than four hours of sleep before the thin tongues of the ring bells started buzzing, asking for contacts with those that were competing to deliver the morning news as early as possible. So, I was getting ready to close the window when the telephone rang again insistently until I was able to reach it and answer:

- Hello, Toni, is it you?... I am from Cernauți. I'm Pitaru… First, write down some names I am gonna give you, then I'll tell you what's all about… ok: Eidingher, spelled E-I-D-I-N-G-E-R; got it?... Now another one: general Fischer; spelled F-I-S-C-H-E-R… all right; one more: Mochi Fisher; spelled also FISHER but without the "c"… You wrote it down, didn't you? Now listen carefully, I am calling you at this hour so that I can tell you verbally, because nobody can hear us; I'm not putting anything in writing through the telegraph 'cause the gendarmerie may intercept it… The first Fischer, the general, is their boss; make a note of it too… OK, now listen what's all about; At what time does the owner come in? Don't call him at home, wait till he comes in, then go and see him immediately!... Only if you see that he's late you may call him; but don't tell him anything over the phone, 'cause in the morning it's different; got it?... Just ask him when is he coming to work or see of you need to go meet him somewhere else; do you understand, Anton?

5.

The owner arrived though, early in the morning; so I, having the sleeves of my shirt chocked by the rubber circles, waited for him to finish with those that were customarily the first in line - the chief editorial secretary and the management with the financial papers - so that I may slip through ahead of the editors that slowly gathered for the "big operative".

- Did something happen to you? – Mille asked me, because usually he was the one who called me when he was getting ready to leave, to give me instructions on how to handle the messages that came in during his absence.

- Not to me; Pitaru from Cernauti… Actually him neither… He asked me to tell you that something very bad is in the works… by General Fischer of the Austrian Gendarmerie, but also by another Fisher, one Mochi from Botosani who reached Austria. And another one, by the name of Eidinger; I think he's the one that calls you sometimes and I transfer him to you when he does… That's what I think; the one who advertises from Athénée Palace; Pitaru didn't give me this guy's other name, and I didn't tell him that I knew the guy, just so that I can tell you first.

- Ok, ok, I got it, these are the guys; got it. And what says Pitaru that they do?

- He says that they train spies; that the Austrian Gendarmerie at Cernauți is looking for Romanians, or persons that speak Romanian, and they train them, and afterwards they sign a four year contract. But in the first year they must mandatorily go to work here in the kingdom or in Banat; he didn't tell me if they were sent in other parts of our country. He only told me that he has seen the people waiting in line at the recruiting center and that he also has seen, with his own eyes, such a contract which promises that, after one year of work in Romania, they'll be dispatched as gendarmes in other parts of the empire, or they'll be assigned as acquisition managers for crops from our own farmers here in Romania to be sent to the Austrian army; but first, they must be field workers; to sow, to plow, to pick; to be agricultural laborers, wherever they'll be assigned to go work; even old people are accepted, so long as they had worked in the Romanian villages and they have friends and acquaintances over there. And Pitaru kindly asks you to have the matter investigated among the farms where those guys have been sent; because he telegraphed me the list, look, here it is, I transcribed it. The rest he told me over the phone and asked me not to write it down but to tell you privately so that only you know, 'cause over the phone nobody could eavesdrop and at the telegraph there are only names of farms, estates, or farm brokers that nobody knows what they are all about… And he also told me that this Mochi wrote and published an article in one of the local newspapers that he doesn't want to sign anything with the farmers and the peasants because this is a good year for the crops and he has other plans; in other words he may use those laborers, hired over there, whom he would pay after the work is done, rather than giving tithe to the farmers… But he said he didn't understand clearly 'cause that newspaper is controlled by the other Fischer, the general, and one cannot trust it; therefore Pitaru asks you to look into it… That's what he said, please forgive me for shooting it out so fast but I was worried not to forget something, 'Cause he called just when I was going to bed, and when he told me about Eidinger I thought this might be the one who calls you over here…

I think my nervousness made me tell him the whole story in one breath, since the owner was trying to calm me down:

- OK, Toni, ok, boy… Now sit here and write down what you told me, and leave the paper on my desk until I finish the operative.

- Do you want me to wait for you?

- No; you may go upstairs. Just turn the paper upside down so that nobody entering the room may see what it's written on it.

- And to Pitaru, if he calls?

- Tell him that it will be published… to continue to inform us of whatever else he finds out… And, speaking about the Germans: If one Günter will call for me, put him through; if not, just remind me around noon, after the paper is out, so that we can call him ourselves…

- OK, I got it – and I sat at the small table where sometimes the owner would dictate to the stenographers, trying on the fountain pen, while Mille, predisposed to notice everything around him, to get as much information as he could and to show off that he is informed, remembered to ask one more question:

- Pitaru didn't mention anything about his travel expenses, did he?

- Well… yes, he did, sir – I guiltily admitted - but he said to ask you later 'cause right now this other matter is important…

- OK – the owner, flattered that his unsurpassed attention was once again validated, said – tell him that, look, right now, in the upcoming meeting I will ask the management to solve that…

In the noon edition, under a wide title that implied many things without actually saying much, a piece of breaking news appeared, of which I rushed to inform the correspondent in Cernauti, in the same time telling him the good news about the owner's promptness regarding the administrative measure… The guy thanked me saying, as if I had known everything he and the owner discussed:

- Ok; now I can have the means to follow them, if they start going places…

And only two days later, when he probably got the newspaper, did he ask me if the rest of the information that he had asked me to tell the boss will be published.

But I didn't dare troubling the owner with such a question. Especially that I was so busy up there, in the attic, managing the telegraph strip, the notes I was taking over the headset, juggling the wires of the switchboard, connecting and disconnecting them while changing their direction, as they were amassing around my window through which I was contemplating the city skyline and the shivering sparrows that were waiting for spring too. I couldn't interrupt what I was doing but I also couldn't bother the boss, seeing how busy he was and how he was running around; even more, unusual for his otherwise balanced temperament, one day I even heard him screaming during a conversation with that Gunter that I had not forgotten to connect him to.

After I connected him directly to Vienna and to that office at Athénée Palace where that Eidinger was answering with a military tone: "Ja wohl…", it seemed to me that they were bargaining or even arguing over something. But me, inheriting my family's moral cleanliness and the Ardelean pride, I was consciously fulfilling my duty of not listening to the conversations that I was connecting people to, as Sache Petreanu, the manager that had hired me here to replace Disgraziato, had instructed me the first day of my employment. However, I couldn't avoid hearing bits of beginning and end of conversations when I made the connections or reconnections, if the connection was lost. Consequently, I had to understand some momentous nervousness, as I understood the frenzy among the correspondents when they were rushing to transmit breaking news.

However, when I found a little break for my own pleasure – that of slipping into the editors' documentary library and indulging myself and read from those large and rich encyclopedias which the editors were only quickly leafing through to clarify some terms – I went straight to the newspaper collection and I carefully read that article that appeared with a wide title, at the last minute, about news from the un-annexed provinces. I re-read and I realized: from all the information I passed on to the owner, even writing it down as he ordered me, the published news didn't say anything about the Austrian spying, emphasizing instead the forecast about the good crop:

"According to news published in The Morning Leaf of Czernovitz, the agricultural broker that represents some large farms in Botosani and Piatra, the renowned Mochi Fisher, forecasts a very rich crop this year. For this reason, the businessman intends to bring daily workers to work on the farms and pay them after the work is done rather than giving the tithe to the locals, to the villagers, thus ensuring a bigger slice of the pie for him, a bigger profit from the bigger crop, if it will grow bigger."... And he added something that was not in Pitaru's message: "We fear that the peasants, who are disgruntled and already armed themselves with scythe and forks and took the justice in their hands, may revolt once they learn about this plan of one of the most powerful brokerage family in Moldova. Storages are empty, and the specter of famine takes the peasants to action; the danger grows bigger and bigger."...

6.

A few days later, as proof that he had received the money and he was now able to travel, Pitaru was transmitting via the telegraph from Burdujeni train station, where the train wagons were switched from the Austro-Hungarian Railways to the Romanian Railways, on the old tracks that were coming from beyond the border. The Customs Offices were housed there too, in that imposing, grandiose building brightly lit, ornate in that defiant imperial architectural style. The old tracks, though, continued for several more kilometers, reaching the Moldavian train stations with small platforms guarded by colorful lanterns and the water pump that was lifting its trunk between them, designed in a modest and utilitarian style when the new network of railways of the kingdom was planned. A network of railways the construction of which made the German entrepreneurs rich; at the time the newspapers were even claiming that that was why Carol I of Hohenzollern had been crowned: with the mission to award concession rights for all Romanian public works – streets, bridges, railroads – to German construction companies, which meant eliminating the Austrian and English competitors that had profited in the past, and to funnel thru the banks of emperor Wilhelm's Berlin a bigger piece of the market pie than the banks of emperor Franz-Joseph's Vienna for the financing of the fledgling industries that were founded around these railroads…

With such statements was Pitaru starting his reporting in order to demonstrate that the Austro-Hungarian Customs and Transportation officials were claiming their ownership of the railway tracks on the Romanian territory by driving their passenger and freight wagons deep into the country, to train stations that did not belong to them. And once arrived in those stations, the passengers were unloaded - groups of people that were either waiting for other trains or were forming a file and started to march along the railroad, splitting at the crossroads and taking different routes that led to the villages of the northern Moldova. Short lines of people, like an army in dispatch, some even wearing similar outfits as if they had been dressed in a Uniform store; moreover, even the rucksacks of those that were not carrying their clothes in a bag were looking much like the ones the imperial army was equipped with, and that gave a sense of social movement to this insinuated advancement by groups dispersed in different directions, it was bringing, along with the spring winds of March's Babele, some sort of a rumor of flying the flag with eagles and the abbreviation "A.E.I.O.U" *(Austriae est imperare orbi universum – Austria must lead the entire world).*

As it could be noted, however, since 1848 Austria's emperor, old Franz Joseph, with the strong support of his military-police-like organization, was reigning unchallenged in this core part of Europe; Pitaru was describing even the way this army kept splitting itself, rarefying throughout the Moldavian hills and infiltrating its presence within villages, where the foreign instigators mingled with the locals and part-took in their problems. And the problem was that the powerful broker Mochi Fisher left and went to his kin or namesake in Cernauti, the general, without signing the leases with the peasants, and the time to start plowing was approaching, but without the leases they didn't have the land on which to start working with their bulls, which meant that, instead of having a good, rich harvest, as it was forecast, they could face a year of poverty, with no food on the table. This way the concern was growing, the dissatisfaction was spreading so much so that the villagers didn't know any more if it was coming from them or from the foreigners among them, who were stirring the spirits making the people even more unhappy and revengeful and making believe that they were even madder than the locals, as Pitaru was saying. And thus the sparks started spreading; the Northern Moldavia was boiling with unrest movements instigated by those aliens, and the newspapers in Cernauti, those morning or afternoon German leaflets, the "Morgenblat" or "Tagenblat" that had correspondents who were transmitting, as Pitaru was, ballooning the news, agitating the spirits by the way they were conveying their fears, thus making the uprising bigger in the newspapers than it was in reality. Those journalists from the German newspapers justified Mochi Fisher's departure from Flaminzi as based on his fear of the people that were left without work because he hadn't signed their leases; but they were silent about those foreigners that, under the pretext of looking for a job on the farms, were mingling with the locals urging them to take to arms, as Pitaru himself had seen with his own eyes. These were people who claimed they had been sent by the employment agencies in Cernauți but they had a certain military manner of speaking when teaching villagers how to get organized. And it wasn't just one or two, but groups after groups which, as our journalist personally verified, were going deeper and deeper into the Lower Moldavia while new groups were entering through Burdujeni and Mihaileni; they were agitating the people to such degree that, said Pitaru, some peasants had to jump and appease others who went crazy and allowed themselves to be under the command of some who were not their peers but who bought them drinks and seeded the spark… A thing that a

Romanian just doesn't do; but the newspapers in Cernauti, sponsored by General Fischer, started writing and sending telegrams, forwarded afterwards to the agencies in Vienna and broadcast throughout the world.

7.

After the publication of this article, combed and trimmed in some places, especially those that were signaling that some imperial army units were stationed at the border for an intervention in Romania, the article having been revised by the owner himself, additional articles started coming in from correspondents that previously had announced some civil unrest movements in the middle part of the country, but now even those correspondents started noticing the foreigners who were instigating the locals, were speaking on their behalf, and even set fire to country villas. All while the complaints and petitions reported by some prefectures had, interestingly, the same writing style and expressions, in spite of their provenance from different villages. As if they were written by the same hand and only copied by those who rushed to come to the villagers offering them their help, thus igniting the uprising. Without noticing this fact, the socialist newspapers published them out of their desire to side with the fighting peasants whose claims they supported. Either alerted or requested to inform his own people, the next morning, after having finished the pagination, when only the helpers were left in the typography to undo the forms, and the machinists started printing the newspaper, foreman Axinte came up to my place. I could not hide any work-related secrets from him since he had recommended me to the owner for the job, and to Sache Petreanu who had trained me regarding professional discretion. Therefore, while I was on the phone, I pointed to him the stack of messages received that, sooner or later, would have ended up on his desk anyhow for screening. I knew that the foreman enjoyed the owner's unconditional trust, even though life looked more complicated in the relationship of the two men. Those were human relations, much more serious than the "class fight" which was the topic at "Romania muncitoare"; and me, I still couldn't understand everything Cristescu said.

The foreman was leafing through the papers puffing and huffing while I was on the phone with Pitaru who was back to Burdujeni railroad station telegraphing something from over there. Because, he would insinuate, he couldn't tell me everything by phone from the station, where there were many ears nearby – imperial customs guys, border patrol policemen: "Got it, Toni"!"... So, the conversation was lasting longer, his efforts to imply something by repeating often: "... tell the director that mister count, my boss at the Foreign Affair Minister ordered all these, got it, Antoane?"... "I got it, I got it, look, master Axinte sends his regards too!"... And the guy took advantage and jumped in: "Give him my best and tell him that I will send someone... I'll send someone with details with the first train; the person will be there tomorrow or after tomorrow"... And in between he'd quickly slip: "But tell the boss to publish! Why doesn't he publish everything I send him?!"... Or, after several small talks" "I write one thing and I read something else... Don't let him take stuff from others, or else... Who did you say was greeting me? Axinte? Pass the phone to him, let me talk to him, we are old friends!... And don't forget: I am sending you a messenger"...

- So, you are old friends? I thought he was much younger, more of my age – I told Axinte while I was taking the headset he used to talk to Pitaru off his head.

- No, son; he is my age... or closer to our owner's – he said hesitantly, only to hesitate again: We acted together at... you know, at the beginning... He, like Mille, wasn't too happy. Because he's a patriot; he had come to Bucharest with big dreams. Later he returned to Cernauți, saying it would be better if he fought for the Romanians over there... He got settled in Cernauți. He didn't make it big but he is doing well. He took himself a wife, she is a teacher, and he made her four daughters. I think they are all beautiful, well-built Bucovineans that stand out from the German and Ukrainian blonds who turn fat right after they get married, yes; he once showed me a picture! – the foreman seemed to be in the mood to talk, to tell stories, as he usually was after the exhaustion of a night's work. – Watch out, he is sending you one, so he told me over the phone: That we need to convince the owner and, to be sure, he is sending his own daughter as a messenger with the documents!... Make sure you wait for her, buddy, 'cause I will leave word at the gate to send her up here to you when she comes… OK, I am leaving, I'm going to try to see the boss 'cause Pitaru may be right; the war will be at our door if we allow ourselves to be manipulated!...

- Why, master, why isn't everything published? Why some things are being mixed with others? Or, who gets involved in some…

- Whoever gets involved, doesn't get involved only here; that's why I wanted to see what kind of news reached your desk – answered confidently the foreman – I am watching what the other guys are doing; they too avoid publishing those news about the preparations for occupation taking place in the empire. This is to say, they too are lying! – he said, as if he was swearing – They are no better, and Mille is right when he says that they don't particularly care about the peasants!... Although, now the peasants' hands are starting the fore of the unrest. It's not true that there will be famine. That's just a rumor some are spreading. I even told Frimu not to write anything like that, he is an old socialist and it's a shame to lie. The years are good for crops; there is no famine; but someone instigates!

- Pitaru says it is not the peasants doing it, it's someone else. That's what I am wondering: why does the owner cut his texts!

- Well, I am asking myself the same thing. I just wanted to verify first.

It was the time for the people in the offices to start working, and bells kept ringing loudly, bringing simultaneously several calls at once. One was from the minister Pherekide who didn't even ask for the owner but left word with his cabinet secretary that he was on his way; others were from correspondents that were saying that the civil unrest was spreading toward Bacau and Vaslui, and whoever called from the Royal Palace was transferred directly to the owner. The telegraph was tapping news from other correspondents; there were secret reports from the prefectures coming in, sent by our illicitly paid informers from over there or from the ministries, who made copies for us. After the foreman left, trying to get a meeting with the boss, I went down too. I was fumbling around pretending I was busy with my messages, trying to get to the boss myself, but I soon realized it was almost impossible, just by looking at the sumptuous coats under the tall, hard hats hung on the richly decorated coat-hanger, even before crossing path with the couriers-valets. So, I took the opposite route, toward the open door of the editor-in-chief's office at the other end of the corridor, from where he monitored the entire activity on the floor. The guy assumed the secret or the circuit of the papers received either from the inside or from outside, monitored with a vigilant eye the discreet coming and going of the personalities in the elegant space that he had the duty to maintain intimate but all the while functional for the precipitous activities of the publishing house, activities that had different norms and relationships than the ministerial offices, due to a more comradeship-like collaboration between those involved in the secrets of journalism, irrespective of their status. And it was only during those moments of high tension when the high profile personalities would come to the publishing house, that both doors of his office were widely open giving him an unobstructed view that dominated the action, over the bold head of that albino, Simionescu, who worked in a sort of antechamber, himself dominating his own mountain of papers that were dropped on his desk, at the same time supervising the courier-valets used either as security guards, or for personal matters, or for immediate help in printing business.

- Did you see my foreman, Axinte? Was he here? – I was pretending asking while putting the papers on that huge desk draped in cheap vinyl spotted by ink, the work station of the very person who now was my supervisor-in-fact, after I replaced Disgraziato, and who worked meticulously and had a sharp distributive attention. And Simionescu, being also subject to the same communication customs as all these guys that were wearing hats with visor so that the light wouldn't fall on their eyes but on their papers, and having their sleeves rolled up and tightened with elastic, to allow them the flexibility of movements, a custom that had become kind of a uniform in the industry, he would cut me short:

- Com' on, drop it!... It doesn't fly with me today!.. It's fucking tough, so go back to your place where the bells ring, don't rely on the helpers!... Why do you think you have the funnels to drop the messages in, directly to me or to the editors?!

And he was pointing to the opening of the that nicely tailored tube that was crossing with its ramifications all the floors, going to proof reading, to typography, up to my switchboard, designed by the heirs of Graham Bell, from which I was spitting on that huge desk different papers with notes, transcriptions or Morse signals.

Actually, that vulgar expression “fucking tough” spoken in that environment, in the sumptuous hall with elegant coats hanging on the fine coat-hangers and watched by the couriers now converted to valets, could only be excused by the journalistic jargon; it proved to be very appropriate though when I got back to my place and put my headset on my head and my trumpet-like speaker over my mouth. Because, as a reaction to the news that general Averescu was assigned to certain military position in charge with dispatching military troops, miscellaneous types of information and calls started flooding in… And later that afternoon, after much bustling and hustling, when one of the owner’s phone calls was interrupted and I had to re-establish connection, no matter how rapidly I joggled the plugs and wires, I still heard the boss going ballistic into the phone, yelling at the guy who was answering only with “Ja, wohl, ja wohl!”:

- And just what are your superiors and Aerenthal thinking, Günter? That they can pay only with three linotypes and a few spare parts for the rotary machine?!... This is expensive stuff, yeah, expensive!... Tell them I won’t do anything unless…

- Ja wohl, we’ll communicate this immediately, ja wohl!...

The metallic membrane that Graham Bell placed over two tiny electromagnets, just as much as to place the hard carcass on the ear in the most modern conditions, was bringing some sounds from those big cabinets that were hiding powerful installations wrapped and connected to large batteries, through the flexible cable that allowed one to move around freely with the chair, getting closer to or farther from the trumpet-like microphones that were stuck in the elegantly made wooden supports. That voice with the desire to appease but coming out in an army-style subordinating attitude, resonated in my ears for a long time:

- Ja wohl, ja wohl; we will communicate immediately and will get back to you, herr Direktor!...

And again, with vehemence, the boss responded:

- Remember, I have twice as much distribution with my newspaper than "Universul" and "Epoca" combined! If you don't pay fairly…

8.

The next article that Pitaru sent – although it did not bring any new information relative to the long rows of people infiltrated from abroad to incite the peasants, but only informed us that he had seen a concentration of Romanian troops at the border, consequently the danger of infiltrated spies was confirmed as real and it would even be demonstrated if the Romanian authorities would hold and identify some of those persons – was balsam on my young soul raised in the conscience that we, the Ardeleanians, needed to be united with the country; it seemed to me that his article was that in some other parts of the land too, not only in the villages I was from, people's hardships brought about these kind of feelings.

The Bucovinean was no longer writing as a journalist who just conveyed information, facts, but transformed his penmanship into that of a tribune who talked about his people's hardships, whose only desire – that to unite with those from the Romanian kingdom – was like a thorn in the Habsburg Empire's throat whose army's only mission was to protect Franz Joseph's domineering power over the countries in that part of the world for almost sixty years, countries whose right to determine their own destiny, their appurtenance he did not recognize, as it was supposed to happen according to the basic principles of the 1848 revolution; however, having reached Vienna, the revolution turned belly up by the enthroning of the emperor and by the strengthening of the police power in the empire. Therefore he, Eftimie Pitaru, was alerting his readers from the Romanian kingdom that, by instigating peasants to uprising, the imperial army may indeed target the occupation of those villages. Being a well-informed journalist, he was praising the Romanian king for having sent those troops, as Pitaru had seen himself, along the border lines from Suceava to Mihaileni, in order to protect the kingdom from the empire's provocations. This was breaking news that no other publication from Bucharest or any press release of the conservative government of Gheorghe Cantacuzino or of general Averescu, freshly nominated in that powerful position - had broadcast. But Pitaru, guided by his patriotic Romanian Bucovinean sentiment, realized that the official discretion manifested could be explained by the inherent diplomacy of the king's Germanic ancestry which dictated a subservient attitude toward the two Germanic empires' relationship, and congratulated the king for the Romanian nature of his decision to protect the country's borders, hoping that, in this way, even the provocateurs that had been previously infiltrated inside the country and which, as he had heard from the Viennese agencies, had been able to spread the uprising and the arsons as deep in the country as Facliu, Tutova, Tecuci, Covurlui, Putna and even Rimnicu Sarat, would be chased away. He made fun of the equivocal order issued by the prime minister Cantacuzino, nicknamed "the Nabab", who ordered the reprimand of the uprising "with the utmost firmness and kindness", and he was confident that general Averescu would be able to keep the country under the control of its own army; he thus rejected the imperial newspapers' statements which, driven by their implicit interests, implied that the situation is out of control and calls for foreign intervention like appealing to that "manu military" of the Austro-Hungarian troops, specifically meant to destabilize the country that represented the hope of those Romanians beyond the borders who were longing to unite with the kingdom.

Such a possible scenario couldn't but touch a chord and leave an imprint in the sentiments of a youth like me, whom the six years working in Bucharest only reinforced the hope inherited from my family. I was following the consecutive editions of the newspapers, driven by both my own interest and also by the desire to let him know, the author whose soul I now felt closer to mine. And I was very disappointed when, the following morning, I didn't find anything in either "Adevărul" or "Dimineața", other than long, deceiving titles about the way the peasants were fighting; moreover, about the way their bands were confronting the army, who was trying to keep the order. And there was more and more information about the dead, citing figures in the hundreds, which the foreign papers converted to thousands.

These figures were counting those who had died in confrontations, others in arsons and house invasions, yet others that had died by shot by the artillery which was shooting from a distance, insinuating that there was a war between the bands of fighting peasants and the other peasants, the ones that were forming the army troops, thing that didn't make sense to a rational mind. Screening the communiqués from the foreign press relative to the advancement of the uprising into Muntenia, Romania was on the verge of a civil war; and based on the Viennese press which, allegedly, alerted the local state security, the empire didn't have to wait until it was called to intervene, because the Romanian army wasn't able to stop the peasants. More and more allusions and direct references to the need of having the Austro-Hungarian army intervene, sounded as if they were made to defend the Romanian king. These were the topics, but nothing was mentioned about the other bands, the bands of provocateurs against which and for the discovery of which the army's actions were targeted, as Pitaru was demonstrating by citing general Averescu; 'cause the army didn't have such absurd commanding officers that would order brothers to fight against each other.

I searched the whole day, pretending I had business to do even in that typography whose every corner I knew, since I had worked there at the beginning. But a suspicion that grew bigger and sadder in my mind started to trouble me, as I could find nothing either in the titles that were ready for printing or inside the articles waiting for revisions; nothing, other than the peasant's anger and their confrontations with the army, a situation that was becoming more dangerous and resulted in more and more victims. I could find nothing that I was hoping to find, as much for my own knowledge or something to tell Pitaru. And that night, when I heard the carriages that were delivering the last batch of freshly printed journals leaving the building, I was struck by a suspicion that someone, a cynical influence maneuvered from the shadows, had a vested interested in talking more and more about victims, arsons, dangers, rather than talk about the provocateurs that Pitaru was pointing out. It was painful and I was even ashamed because I knew that, in the morning, Pitaru would call and ask me that question to which I had no answer: "Why?!"...

Saddened and resolved I resumed my work, because the news were flowing in about the government changes, the summoning of Take Ionescu, Marghiloman and the liberals at the royal palace, the summoning of the parliament. I was either forwarding or transcribing whatever needed to be transcribed and then throwing the papers into the mouth of that big pipe that looked like a devourer of news, stirring toward either right or left, wherever the news were to be analyzed, as it was the case, according to their provenience, and where they were corroborated with other news coming from some agencies directly to the editors; or throwing into the middle pipe the ones that I was specifically instructed to deliver on the overloaded desk of editor-in-chief. Everything was happening precipitously; gone were those relaxing days when we all were working in camaraderie, when sometimes I was even able to see the owner himself with some special deliveries … I couldn't even go past the courier-valets to give the owner that anonymous protest, indeed more of an accusation, which was alleging that the minister Pherekide was the paid informer of the Habsburg cabinets and, alluding to the kinship between king Carol of Romania and emperor Wilhelm of Germany, was perfidiously insinuating the hope that, one day, the Hohenzollerns would distance themselves from the Habsburgs. I had to put the protest on that big desk, under the pretext that I had come down at that late night hour only to get the latest newspaper. And I started reading that newspaper under the scrutiny of Simionescu and I continued to read while going up the stairs, my eyes glued on the newly published article written by the owner himself, which was the very reason the paper was printed late… And thus I'd seen with my own eyes how Mille himself was urging the peasants to revolt and to more vehement actions.

He was calling to tough actions, backing up this prompting with facts from different localities and showing that, wherever the uprising was manifested properly, the landowners conceded. And he was stating that this was the only way the revolted ones could demonstrate their might, and that landowners had already began to sign the leases as a result; that this was the only way the authorities could be determined to seal those leases, thus acknowledging the success of the revolt; and that the power of the revolt must be exercised and stimulated further. That meant that the entire country should revolt and confront the landowners, the authorities, even the soldiers that had been ordered to shoot. Unequivocally and without hesitation, the entire article was feeding the fire of the uprising.

Such an overt attitude, which disregarded all the information Pitaru was sending, was troubling me profoundly and generated all kinds of questions in my mind and, moreover, made me wish that Pitaru would not call me, nor would my relatives from Ardeal that might ask me what was my sincere opinion about what was going on in the country. I was feeling that the hope instilled in me in my childhood by my family and my teachers, who were telling us stories about the king that people on the other side of the Carpathians had brought themselves, the hope that one day their king would free us too, was vanishing, and that made me so enraged, I had the urge to hit the walls. I was grabbing the ends of my shirt - which I always wore open in front, as doctor Racovski recommended me in order to help strengthen my body in its fight with the cold weather – as if trying to avoid being suffocated by the indignation that was growing inside me. I was capable of anything in those moments; if someone would have given me a pistol and showed me the person that was behind all these things, I would have shot without hesitation.

And most of all, I was wishing I didn't have to handle the headset; to be the one who answered Pitaru's calls; to stretch the time so that the newspaper gets to Pitaru later so that the Bucovinean might live those feelings by himself, without me giving him the news, me, who'd rather shoot someone. And it seemed to me that I was now understanding why Axinte, tied to this work place his entire life, was reserving the right to frequent the other place, if he wanted to really help solve the workers' problems, problems that are different and only they, the workers, may relate to – as my foreman was saying without a shade of malice but firm in his determination.

And when the door of my attic quarters opened and the young blonde wearing a traditional Bucovinean mink vest asked about "mister Anton" and told me she was Pitaru's daughter, I got moonstruck and precipitously invited her in, saying, more as a wondrous exclamation than a remark: "You are the girl, then;

Eftimie Pitaru's daughter!" – I surprised myself hugging her, in a way you would when seeing a dear relative.

Afterwards, clumsily, I realized that I needed to explain myself and I did that in a defensive manner, talking nonsense in an effort to hide my shame:

- I want you to know that I, too, am not from the kingdom; I am from Ardeal!

The girl, though, didn't seem to have been affected by such familiarity.

- Father told me; he told me that you are his friend over here – she said, openly scrutinizing my face; moreover, she seemed to be interested in my bare chest, my cheeks, my forehead, in the way I was looking at her, as if she wanted to say: "so, that's how you look like"!... And, in her childish way, she abruptly admitted: "I was just wondering, while I was riding the train, how you would look like. I thought you were much older!...

9.

The girl with brown braids wrapped around her head like a wreath, and then turning to the back of her head just to be tied with the bow whose ribbon was falling on her shoulders, came to me confidently, a confidence that she was displaying overtly, as if she was dealing with the very guy she had been seeking. The sincerity in her hazel eyes was confusing me.

- So your father told you that I am his friend over here, didn't he?... If that's the case, then what is the owner to him? They go back together a long time.

- Well, the thing with the owner is different; an owner is an owner, my dad is also an owner, a smaller one over there, in our town, where things are different; because the Romanians are looking for jobs at other Romanian business owners, and thus they are united and they are considering my dad not only a business owner but also a leader for their rights, as well as a Sunday school teacher for their children… Things are different back home – she said, repeating for the third time the word "different", which could have been her opinion, formed while crossing Bucharest from the train station – you know this as well if you say you are from Ardeal… I learned some things since I started helping my father at the Sunday school; yes, I copy some of his articles from his notebook, when he sends them through the mail, and now I came myself…

- But how old are you, that you can do all these things?

- Well, I am … almost sixteen; and you? How old are you?

- Twenty two. If I was there, back home, I would have been in the army now!... I came here when I was sixteen; but I worked over there, in Ardeal, too, therefore I can relate to what you are saying… I mean… I understand – I answered nonsensically and laughing stupidly because I could not find anything else to say.

And she laughed gaily, with sparkling teeth, the kind you imagine shining when biting in an apple. My foreman Axinte was right when he compared her with Pitaru's wife, whose beauty he had seen; the girl had a healthy honesty and a simple beauty that irradiated the joy that it was me the one that she was sent to, that I was younger and closer to her than she had imagined, that I wasn't looking too shabby either, as she evaluated me openly, with the straight looks of an innocent girl who is not hiding her feelings. And the intimacy that she was not trying to hide intimidated me.

- I hope you understand me, she said; and you are not even much older than me, so I wasn't that wrong when I called you by name. Forgive me; it just came to me, just like that, when I noticed that you were not the "mister Anton" that I had imagined when they told me to come up here.

- You know how to get things done!

- I do. I do because I like helping my dad; and I love my dad.

Her statement reminded me of my earlier sad thoughts that were now coming back. And I was realizing that, no matter how hard I would try, I couldn't share them with this girl, who was taking everything so lightly and naturally. I feared that she would ask me, any moment now, or that she would ask me to call Pitaru; and I would have been happy to find any escape from being forced to talk about that article. So, I preferred to switch gears, and said:

- Look, I am trying to find him where I usually do at this hour – I told her while I was maneuvering the wires – so that you may tell him that you arrived ok; I am going downstairs to find out when the owner could see you… Go ahead and talk as if you were an employee; I know the feeling, I came here when I was your age!...

When I came back, it was as if we had been friends forever; and, happy that this time I managed to get off the hook, I decided to use this time off for another plan that sprung in my mind:

- You said you copy his articles, didn't you?

- My dad's; yes.

- The article that you brought, does it have many pages?

- About four; but it also has a letter with explanations for mister Mille.

- OK. Have a seat here and start copying it. The owner is not in his office now, and God knows when he will return in the afternoon. They are saying that he went to the Parliament for an important meeting; also a royal message is expected… You arrived in Bucharest at such a busy time. Let me know when you are hungry; I will take you to the cantina; we have a cantina on the premises, right here… This is a big palace and many things are happening here… Nowadays I notice things. This is because, whenever I have spare time, I spend it mostly in the library. Do you go to the library?

- Yes. At school, because we have a Romanian library, although it's not too large; my dad has many books but he said that he would donate the books to the school after we grow up, because my mom are lending them out anyhow…

- So you grew up around books; this is…

- How is it?

- It's good, I'd say; not too many people were that fortunate…

- I am also going to the metropolitan palace library. They have many books; old books, like the leather bound ones…

- Over here they have encyclopedias… Big, thick and heavy, you can barely carry them!... I jump on those and leaf through them, even though I don't know the language, but they have all kinds of wonders inside… All the wonders of the world are inside these encyclopedias. Also, with the little German I managed to learn from my past employer, a typographer of German origin, I began to understand some… The German ones are called lexicons. I speak Hungarian too because I learned it in my childhood, but I wasn't schooled enough, so I am now trying to catch up and learn as much as I can – I felt the impulse to confess, humbly, like a child, without knowing why. And I added: here, in this job, I learned shorthand and some stenography, and that helps me a lot; but those subjects that one learns in high school, with discipline, those are my sore spots…

- I know German too; and I just started to learn French. That's what I'd like to be: A French language teacher, and I could translate daddy's articles, 'cause he says the French people are closer to us and understand us… Yes, it's a nice language and I learned a good deal of poetry.

- I too learned poetry; but I did not learn some other stuff, because I only went to school to fifth grade; in the sixth grade I dropped out of school and went to work for a German employer, so instead of school I learned some German. But now I am trying to catch up. I told you: there are two libraries here. One is for the editors, and it has those encyclopedias and many manuals; but the other, mister Mille's own library, has rare books, because he is a poet and collects them. He allows me in his library too, because he noticed that I like the books, I take care of them and put them back on the racks in order- I even do that after the others, who leave the books on the tables - then I dust them, sometimes I glue their ripped edges… I think that, in his special way, the owner likes me – again I realized that I felt the need to confess, as if I was clarifying things for myself; because the girl's inquisitive looks and her obvious joy of sharing with me some small details of her life, as if she was talking to someone familiar, created that warm feeling of a familiar, intimate ambiance that encouraged me to tell her thing which were coming to me in flashes, from who-knows-what subconscious mind, like: The owner likes me, even though there are things I still don't understand, or barely start to understand… - And, by idea association, jumping from one thought to another, I asked her: What is your dad saying? What's his opinion about things?...

And thus, telling me with delighted confidence about her father's opinions but also about his activist deeds in organizing the Romanians in Bucovina, as if she was spoiling me, I suddenly realized that I was watching how the lines of her beautiful face were becoming even more attractive while she was talking, in a serious manner, about those things, making her appear like someone between a smart child and a wise woman… I was looking at her, and as I was listening to her absent-mindedly, I surprised myself telling her that she is beautiful.

The girl was startled and stopped talking, or maybe she lost her train of thought. She had big eyes, as if they were inlaid in oak, borrowing golden sparkles. And her large forehead, even very large, uncovered by the crown of braids above, was lending those eyes a depth that went beyond her age, no matter how naively she asked:

- What do you mean by that?

- I mean that you are beautiful; I am looking at you and you are beautiful, like the girls in my village; they are also wearing vests, like you do… But made of black fur, of sheep, not of mink, like yours – I added, scrutinizing her more intensely – The mink, on you, is like blending in with your brown braids and your hazel eyes; you look like you just descended from a painting… How did they come up with your name, Roxana? – Then I told her straight, with more confidence: I would call you Roxolana and I would spoil you in more ways than one!...

The girl did not back up; either she had the courage to listen to those words that made her cheeks blush, or she had the instinctual pleasure to be spoiled; no matter what her motif was, she did not reject my compliments; if anything, she would change the topic to show off her knowledge:

- Roxolana is something else, the Roxolans were fighting with the Dacians over there, in our land; but father, who is good friends with mister Hurmuzaki, says that the free Dacians are our ancestors. Yes, the Dacians had this kind of brown hair, and even today we are different from the others, the blonde people that came from distant lands. The Roxolans, I don't know how they looked like, but they were living among the free Dacians… the Roxolans and the Iazigis… I learned this in the history class…

- You are an educated girl; you learned many things; I only told you that just because I asked you about Roxana and we were talking about you hazel eyes, not the free Dacians', of which I know nothing 'cause I didn't go to school…

- The free Dacians are the ones left beyond the borders that the Romans built. The Romans had dark hair, they were brunets; that is why we have brown hair; It's from a study of a German guy, father borrowed it from mister Hurmuzaki…

- So, your nice eyes that I…

- Please, stop… - she grabbed my hand.

- Why stop? Just now, when I finally got the courage to tell you?

- To tell me what?

- For example that I didn't think that your beautiful eyes are coming from Dacians – I said jokingly. I didn't read the German's study…

- Mister Hurmuzaki gets the latest collections and publications… - I sensed that she, too, was happy to talk about something else, a subject that would not intimidate her.

- Tell me what its title is, so that I may look for it in the owner's library. I told you that I know some German…

- You told me; yes, you did. You told me too many things… - And, honestly, she lowered her eyes: Please… please don't tell me anymore!

- Not tell you?... Why not?!

Short of stature as she was, she came unashamed close to my tall body which, due to my long hair, had the appearance of a windblown tree, and she said, laying her hand on my arm:

- Because this evening I will be gone. And…

- And?

- And… - she said, slowly caressing my arm – I wouldn't want to long for this place; I wouldn't want to…

She stopped, silently raising her hazel eyes with golden threads in their iris, as if defeating, or may be acknowledging, her adolescent dreams.

On Corneliu Leu's house wall, 2013.

10.

When I took her to the owner, I had a better understanding of Pitaru's point of view. And I congratulated myself for having insisted to obtain that appointment with the owner for the girl. Because Simionescu, a fixture in the editorial office, was feverishly working, almost going berserk at the number of news coming in, the type of news, the type of articles written or withdrawn, and the corrections transmitted; he would not let me in to see the owner, instead he was asking me to bring the girl the next day, although I was telling him that she had to leave later that night.

But I insisted and, when that call from the Athénée Palace switchboard came in, from that Eidinger whom the boss had yelled at, and he hurryingly asked to be connected and, when I informed the boss of the incoming call and he immediately answered, I took advantage and, before the other could interrupt us, I rapidly asked the owner: "may I bring in Pitaru's daughter?... Pi-ta-ru"… Thus I obtained an appointment with him within a decent timeframe: "Not now; in about half an hour, or three quarters of an hour."!

After reading silently through the letter accompanying the article, the boss, his nose dug into the paper, started to read it aloud asking the girl for details:

- Look, it says here that you will tell me more about the count Aerenthal than he writes in this paper.

- Yes, because father said that this is what he wants to explain to you, that there are things unnoticeable from here, from Bucharest, but if he would write about them, he could be sued in our land… May I talk now?

- Of course; look, Anton – and the boss pointed toward me, as I was seated at the table that always had pen and paper ready for stenographers – will take notes, as he always does whenever your father calls him; he is a reliable guy, this Toni, don't pay attention to the fact that he is as young as you are. Our craft is learned by watching the older guys doing it, by just doing it, as Pitaru and I did a long time ago. Let's go, if we work efficiently, the article will be half done – he was displaying his pleasure at teaming with the youth, something that he considered imperative for that effervescent and hectic profession. Are you ready, Anton? – he used my entire name again, as if he wanted to show to me, in front of the girl, that I was important.

Meticulously, the girl pulled out a notebook in which she was looking for the ideas she needed to expand on; fascinated by the way she did that, I found myself admiring her childish determination to repeat eagerly what she learned from the adults' language, and taking notes with a childish patience and attention to detail as I saw her do rather than listening to what she said.

Count Aerenthal was the author of the politics of expansion "Austriae est imperare orbi universum"; Pitaru always received information from a few fellow Viennese journalists as well as from the French liaison officers crossing en route to the tsarist army, coming from the Polish lands. These connections he had were secret, therefore the news were conveyed only and directly to him, about the sources he was collaborating with and about the false rumors disseminated expressly to provoke war. Because all those news relative to uprisings, fights, dangerous situations and conflicts that were igniting in the bordering countries, news that were disseminated through press releases from Vienna, were exacerbated in order to justify the preparations within the imperial army for marching beyond the borders and expand the imperial occupation. That is evident by the way they now encircle Serbia, while they bring troops toward Romania too, in Brasov and Cernauti... The Viennese sources say that the intention is to repeat the story of the insinuated invasion of Bosnia and Herzegovina, when the Turks could not intervene because an uprising was instigated in Creta isle. As for Russia, the uprisings there were also provoked by Vienna in order to make sure that the tsar could not defend Serbia anymore... That the whole thing started way back in 1905 when they provoked uprisings in some Polish lands and in Russia, which was weakened by the war with the Japanese. And the French liaison officers, who gathered additional information from the French merchants from the Danube ports, observed that, while they were provoking uprisings in the tsarist empire, Alois Aerenthal's men opened that employment agency in Bucharest and were sending workers to work for those agricultural brokers, on the Romanian owner's lands, many of which had relatives in the empire, and they were enticing these brokers by contracting their crops for the Austro-Hungarian army. So, the dangers for Romania are coming through in two ways: one is through those provocateurs infiltrated among the peasants to determine them to take to arms, and the other is through those wealthy that are shouting, when ordered, that they are the victims of the revolution, that the Romanian army is unable to protect them, and ask the help of the imperial army which, thus, can cross the border. The stand-by units in Brașov and Bucovina can't wait to respond to the victimized brokers' appeal. And in Vienna rumor says it that king Carol of Romania changed the conservators because they had paid men that were doing just that, as it was common knowledge that minister Pheredike was Aerenthal's paid informer; while Günter, who is the chief spy in Aerenthal's network, is bragging that the newspapers are writing what he wants, and they exaggerate the facts proportionally with the amount of money he is paying them, to make the events appear much more dangerous than they are in reality; and all that for the purpose of making the revolt, which actually was triggered by the newspapers, to lead to the need to have military help from Austro-Hungarian empire, which will thus extend its occupation, as it did in Bosnia and Herzegovina; and the war thus provoked, to lead to the victory of

A.E.I.O.U and to the emperor who will celebrate sixty years of reign. Pitaru included some of the facts in his article, to make himself useful. But some others he doesn't want to write about but instead chooses to transmit them this way, with his daughter. Because if it was ever revealed that this news came from him, he could be sued, arrested, or, at any rate, prohibited to continue his fight on the other front: that of protecting the Romanians over there, in his land. Because they, the Romanians beyond the borders, feel they are stronger if they are backed up by the kingdom, and any weakness resulting from the uprising in Romania, is strengthening the empire which is keeping them hostage. This is the situation; and not only with the Romanians, but also with those Serbian and Italian lands, which the empire is holding tight on because it wants access to the Mediterranean through the Trieste harbor; likewise, it would target the Danube's mouth to gain access to the Black Sea. And who suffers most? Those occupied by the empire, those who lose their hope.

Writing these things at my little table, hurrying to handle the pen so that I may keep up with the rhythm of the girl's story, I was watching her recite those words with both the confidence gained by the fact that they were her father's words, and also with the childish, scholarly ambition to show that she learned everything, glancing only every now and then in her note book; I swear I felt like I was involved deeper and deeper in Pitaru's pleading. And, because she stopped, I put my dot on the paper and couldn't refrain to talk: I recorded everything Pitaru had said, especially this last part, which triggered in me the old Ardeleanian sentiments. So I couldn't refrain and exclaimed:

- It's true!... – Only to repeat in a low pitch voice, as if excusing myself for having had that uncontrolled outburst in a different tone, the tone of the boy who, even though I hadn't learned it, I knew how to be polite and aware of my position: Me too, I feel the same way, mister director!... Forgive me if I am wrong!

But I didn't dare, as I wanted to, really wanted to, go to the girl and hug her. I realized that my role as well as hers, was to be there to find out what the boss was thinking and to listen to what he had to say.

- I am glad you feel that way – said Constantin Mille – I didn't doubt that, as a good Ardeleanian, you would feel that way; but be aware that Pitaru doesn't want to have some of the news leaked either, because that would put him in jeopardy. So make sure you don't make any comment over there, at "Romania muncitoare"...

- But I go there to learn, mister director, not to spread rumors; and you allow us to, don't you?

- I am ok with you guys going over there because I worked my whole life with workers; but I learned that the anarchy doesn't do any good to them but to others. And I am teaching you this.

- I understand; I know it works against us, but I am not listening to the nihilists, mister director – I answered as if I felt guilty for my doubts of late.

And the owner didn't back up but rather seemed to confirm that he expected some people to doubt him, therefore he was determined to counter those doubts by using the weapon that was always handy for him: the latest and most reliable information, which gave him the upper hand.

- Very well then; I trust you and Axinte; but doctor Racovski is too much of an internationalist to care about Romanians; stick this to your head, I am telling you this in front of this girl: both Pitaru and I left that movement before doctor Racovski came to us, but others showed up, claiming that the nihilism that I was demonstrating didn't work for the laborers… Now the doctor associates with Kolarov from Bulgaria to build a Balcanic organization. Well, what is this? Isn't this an empire as well, as in Turkey, or as in Vienna?... Tell this to your father, I was just planning to transmit that information to him – he addressed to the girl, pointing to her notebook with that confident gesture that always underscored the fact that he was up to date with the events.

- I will tell him – the girl showed that she knew her duty by taking notes of what she needed to transmit, but, meticulously, as a good apprentice she was, she asked: And shall I tell him when will the article be published?

- It will be published… - Mille answered evasively – Whenever we will find the right moment it will be published.

You just assure him that, published or not, I will transmit everything to the Government, to the Palace… Where they can take action; he has seen himself what happened on the border!... Even Pheredike, the minister, who is the Habsburg's ears, came here at that time, alarmed; but I told Averescu, that young general who was just appointed minister. These are complicated politics but we are dealing with them accordingly; that's what I want you to tell him: Maybe some of the things are not published, but I am communicating them to the government, and that's what is important!...

And, as a generous nobleman he was, he pulled out of his wallet a big, very big bill and put it in my hand:

- You do have some apprentices upstairs, don't you? … Go and give the girl a tour of the city; take her to a bakery, better yet, take her first to the cinema, then buy her a nice souvenir for herself and a bottle of French cognac and a box of luxury cigars for her father, who is an old friend of mine; then bring her back because I will ask Sache to send her to the train station with the first carriage that leaves the building to deliver the paper…

Corneliu Leu (left), his wife Rodica (right) and Michael Dediu, at Leu's home, in 2013

11.

Obviously the administrator - who was personally going to go to the train station because there was only one carriage - coordinating the loading of the papers on some wide platforms that were seated on big, heavy wheels drawn by those large horses, with big hooves and thick ankles, he understood why, after having brought the girl near the carriage, I didn't move and didn't want to leave my spot near that lamp with sparkling mirror, lit to light the way for the driver of the carriage.

- Do you want to go to the train station to see her away?.... Well, jump right in; you will return with me afterwards, I may need your help anyhow!...

And I didn't hesitate to jump on the little bench in front of the couch and take the luggage from the girl's lap, holding it tightly in my arms, as if I were holding her.

I was feeling such an overwhelming joy that, sensing in her the same timidity that made both of us silent during the ride under the scrutiny of the austere administrator, once we were on the platform, I didn't know what to say to her. We were standing there, staring in each other's eyes, our breaths mixing, me holding her sack between us, as if something had frightened us. Or as if we were ashamed of all the small talk we had had, joyous and superficial, during our stroll through Bucharest… I had taken her to Cișmigiu, to the cinema on the Boulevard, to the Luna Park behind Batiștei Street where the donuts were raising in the hot oil of the metal barrels and the chestnuts were popping on the fire and where the closets from the Mosi were stored during the winter. I had bought her, from Academiei Street, a nice purse that would have looked sharp with matching hat and umbrella, but at her age she was happy with just a nicely laced scarf; and for her father, the cognac and, to go with it, the box of expensive cigars from Macedonia, from the passage full of exquisite shops that took us back to Calea Victoriei, where we stormed into the "Continental" bakery and liberally indulged in its big cakes. Afterwards I took her to the royal palace, to see the change of guards, but that did not impress her, since she had seen the more impressive uniforms of the imperial army; instead, she was struck by the massive colonnades supporting the dome of the Romanian

Athénée, and then at Athénée Palace, she insisted to go inside, in the hallway, to see it with her own eyes, so that she may tell her father, where that Eidinger had his office and from where he was tempting those landowners and brokers with Austrian money. I took her there, not knowing that I would meet that Eidinger that very evening, somewhere else. Then I took her to the White Church where, on the porch lit by the gas flames, I recited to her those poems I had learned in the elementary school about Mihai Viteazul; we crossed the street so that I may show her Momolo Theater, and only the early darkness that covers the earth in the days before the Equinox prevented us from going to the Șosea, so we went back on Calea Victoriei to the National Theater Place, whose posters began to be hit by a sharp hail. That prompted us to take refuge at the café Terasa Oteteleșteanu, where we warmed our hands on the glasses filled with hot drinks, eye to eye, as if we both needed to discover each other more… and more…

This was the place she had liked best, the crowded café where people were finding refuge in winter; not only because we warmed up both our bodies and the relationship between us, allowing ourselves to sit as close to each other as we could and timidly touching our hands; but also because of the frenzy that spread among the audience when, on what was the stage in summer and now used as dancing floor, performed that older but vivacious couple that animated the public with their songs, dances with exaggerated moves, duets, old jokes delivered with Parisian humor. Watching the show intensely, the desire to happily share impressions about it, joining in the cheerfulness of the patrons, made us hold hands all the time, lest when we felt we needed to applaud. Only to quickly reach for each other and feverishly braid our fingers together, freed of feeling reluctant or shy.

It was a famous couple with names sounding too cosmopolite not to be pseudonyms of some local talented entertainers who, even if they hadn't come from world renowned cabarets, they surely had seen those shows before coming back here, to their adoring audience, an audience that would spoil them no matter what, even if hidden under that heavy make-up. And they were singing, my God were they singing, and dancing and making the show lively with pantomime!... And what a funny pantomime!... I even exclaimed to Roxana: "You see? Just as in

Paris!", when the artists turned the piano all the way around, while the pianist was still playing, undisturbed… And how they sung, how much fun they had, mingling with the public!... But what Roxana liked the best, as did the rest of the cheering patrons that were singing along and clapping, was the dancing song that the lady artist danced on, a dance with modern choreography that did justice to her exquisitely exposed legs while the man made a very funny pantomime around her; and, accompanied by the pianist, the couple announced the new song of the season as being "launched simultaneously in Paris and here, tonight, especially translated for our honorable audience in Bucharest". Pretending he was just reading the score for the first time, the pianist started first slowly, then joyfully, to play in concert with the two:

Iffff hairy Mary-Pegs
Didn't have such stylish legs,
Her mother and her faaaather
Wouldn't even bother!

We danced in our seats, as everyone else, and sung along, and enjoyed the moment, expressing our joy by hugging each other, cheek to cheek, without being ashamed of it anymore, even laughing jokingly; and at one moment I asked her:

- Hey, Roxana-Roxolana, aren't you afraid that we will fall in love with each other?

- What do you mean? – she said childishly.

- I mean, we will no longer be two children; I mean you will no longer be a child; and we will make love… and…

But she defied and, due to her open and sincere way of being, the thought of becoming a woman, of loving and letting herself be loved, the fact that all those changes were bound to happen in the normal course of life and she needed to talk about it, all those things didn't make her uncomfortable, so she perplexed me by saying:

- If it passes to be… if we are to be man and woman, then maybe it is meant to be!

- If? – I asked, stupidly.

And she joyfully answered with:

- "*If hairy Mary…*"

We left the place humming and holding hands, as if those verses with a banal humor encouraged our frivolity" *If hairy Mary-Pegs/didn't have such stylish legs*"... We were imitating the artists - from whom we took leave only because of the train schedule - by happily dancing on the sidewalk, falling in each other's arms every now and then. And we didn't realize that we were gazing at each other longer and longer and closer and closer, until we almost got scared of what was about to happen when we kissed. And we started running, hand in hand, our cheeks red, until we arrived at the carriage where the administrator, coughing in a reproachful way, was waiting for us.

On the platform, however, our looks, while intertwined, had a different expression, as if looking for something lost or about to be lost. And I surprised myself pouring all those sentiments of an alienated child, one who had lived away from home for a long time, by saying:

- Ever since I came to Bucharest I had no one close to me to see away at the train station, to be able to experience the feeling of separation!

And she answered somehow more joyfully, with a big smile that revealed her shiny teeth:

- But I am luckier than you to have you see me away at my first trip!... Even to have you spoil me!...

- How do I spoil you? – I was now spoiling myself.

- Roxana-Roxolana! – she murmured, as if she had told me a secret; and only after that, reaching the moment of truth and anxiety, did her expression changed, and, with childish fear, she asked me, as if she had asked the destiny: I am wondering what will become of it?!

- It must; it must happen!... – I alarmingly answered, as if I didn't want to let her go away – It must, you are my Roxana-Roxolana!...

But, somehow more realistic, more natural, more conscious of the implacable insinuated by the huffing and puffing of the locomotive which was ready to leave, the childish girl came close to me, gave me a kiss, caressing my forehead, as if she was the one older and smarter between the two of us, the one to bring peace and calmness:

- God willing, we will see each other again! If not, we will still have the memory.

- What memory?

Then she got closer to me, slowly, slowly, lovingly, humming:

If hairy Mary-Pegs
Didn't have such stylish legs...

"Her mother and her father/Wouldn't even bother?" – I continued, holding her in my arms, this time unable to imitate that frivolous style of the entertainers. Instead, holding her, sad and daydreaming, because I felt the need to resist: "God willing"?!.. He must be willing! – I said sharply, as if I wanted to protest, without realizing that I was holding the crude beauty of that slender, warm body that I first thought was still unripe, but now I felt it whole, shaking, touching my chest through the unbuttoned shirt.

I realized all that and was exhilarated it had happened, only after the train left the station, taking with it in faraway lands, the portrait in the frame of the window, of the girl with brown braids tied like a crown above the wide forehead and the hazel eyes that were flooded with her girlish tears.

That portrait was inlaid forever in my heart; so much so that sometimes it overshadowed my other preoccupations

For that reason I didn't react impulsively, as I would have had in the past, instead I was even impersonal when, crossing the railroad to get to the station's message center, I found the newspaper's administrator filling out and signing some documents in front of the customs patrol and another guy, a rigid, military-like man whose voice inflexions I recognized, with my trained ear working with the headphone, as being that of Eidinger, the person with whom the owner had important conversations. And, to reinforce my guess, I heard him saying that characteristic "Ja, wohl" which sounded like the sound produced by the slapping of military boots when saluting, and confirming something to the customs authorities, pointing toward the administrator.

I started to realize something that in the past would have troubled me a great deal, relative to my feelings toward the owner's persona, the man that I admired so much. But now it no longer troubled me; all that flood of contradictory sentiments was like happening alongside me, opaquely, and farther from the sparkle of these other things that were now closer to my heart which had that portrait carved on it, like a window opened to another world.

After having helped the administrator by dividing the papers and the processing windows among us, so that we may finish the formalities sooner - as those formalities were for customs, transportation, fiscal taxation and other seals that needed to be obtained - the administrator put the papers attesting to the ownership of the ten linotypes that had just arrived, in his sumptuous briefcase, a mark of the modern bureaucracy. The machines were so heavy that they were packed separately, one in each of those crates having inscriptions in German, and the crates put on those large platforms driven by traction horses; once we were ready to leave, I went with the administrator in the carriage in front of the convoy, finding it normal to go to Sarindari, where "Adevarul" had its typographies.

Even the next day, "Adevarul" no longer troubled me and no longer awoke in me those antagonistic feelings I had felt in the past, when, instead of the articles I was looking for, I found others, with big titles that were fuelling the obsession about the dead as being victims of the uprising. As if, untruly, someone sought to accredit the idea that Romania was now in the midst of a civil war: dead – the peasants shot by the army as a reprimand; dead – the soldiers that were fighting with the peasants; dead – even some among the administrators, land brokers and dead even landowners invaded by the peasants! Hundreds upon hundreds of dead, as if it were a long time since this all had started, rather the few days it really had: Hundreds!... In the beginning, in the news coming from different sources, they were talking about hundreds. Later, they were citing statistics that were showing thousands of dead nationwide, without accounting where these figures were coming from, how they were calculated, but merely citing them to demonstrate how spread the uprising was. To show that this was a massacre that could not be contained: a country with thousands and thousands of dead; as if the ghost of Death descended upon the earth and wrapped the feelings of the peasant driving them to revolt. A country in the middle of a disaster that needed foreign intervention!... That was the conclusion one would draw, reading the articles and especially the cover article which evaluated the statistics without specifying how they got the figures, sticking in there the enormous figure of eleven thousand victims.

Sticking in there that figure, yes; as if the pen was hesitating in the beginning but ultimately couldn't back up from who-knows-what commandment. It was the owner's own writing, the man I still admired, and, confused, I kept wondering, although I had seen with my own eyes the delivery of those linotypes. Other newspapers were now quoting his figures, saying: "According to Constantin Mille's statements, based on his correspondents' analysis…."

Or maybe I wasn't confused, maybe I just didn't want to think about it anymore, didn't want to nurture the suspicions arousing in me. Therefore, I was in a worse state of mind that when I had been thinking about the pistol and revenge. Confused, I was crying because I couldn't do anything; I would have shot anybody that they told me was behind this all!... I was confused and troubled! I don't know if was that troubled as to shoot the owner, but surely I would have shot those mysterious ugly faces that were parading through his office; but I surely was troubled!

So, when I picked up the copy of Pitaru's article, the one that I purposely asked the girl to copy for me, I no longer felt the need to comment it with my foreman, Axinte; instead, I only took him to the window, silently, and, showing him the article and looking him straight in the eyes, I asked him, like a final solution:

- The owner is obviously no longer publishing this kind of news, if he is writing about eleven thousand dead, which implies that the country is heading toward disaster. Shall we give Pitaru's article to the other guys?...

- What other guys, son, what other guys? – asked Axinte, as if reprimanding me for bothering him with such crazy ideas.

- At "Romania muncitoare"; didn't the doctor say that…

Axinte was silent for a little while, and then he looked me straight in the eyes, as he usually did; and, pulled me aside, although we were alone in the room, just to be able to speak in his vehement tone used when he was venting his frustrations:

- Well, didn't you notice that those guys are publishing the same kind of things?!...

- The same kind of things, master?

- Yes, son, damn the treason!... They too are using Mille's lie, about the eleven thousand dead.

- That means Pitaru is right when he says the revolt looks bigger in the newspapers that it is in the country… Master, I wouldn't have thought that our owner…

- Me neither, son – he repeated his favorite words, as if he wanted to spoil me – but at least he alerted the Government and the Palace; as a Romanian, he fulfilled his duty, in spite of the fact that he played a dirty game with his journal!... But I am wondering about the other guys; what benefit could they have?!...

Yes, I was confused and troubled; and I was crying; and I could have shot anybody that they told me was guilty!...

But, seeing my foreman so disconcerted, almost shouting his revolt, a desire to go away, anywhere, far away, nested in my haunted heart, making me want to not think of anything anymore.

There was only one thing now on my mind, the image that was carved in my heart, of those hazel eyes with tears in their corners, eyes that were beginning to mean the world to me; even if they slowly, slowly, irreversibly, went away, in the train's window frame.

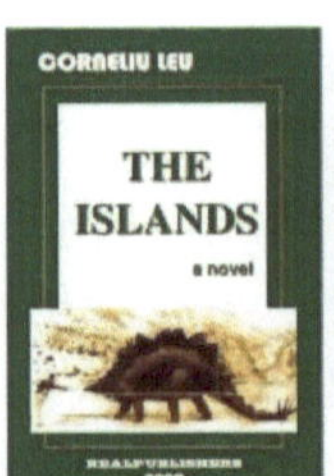

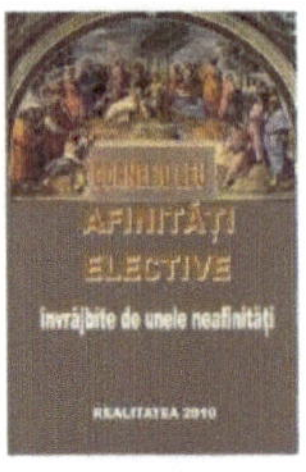

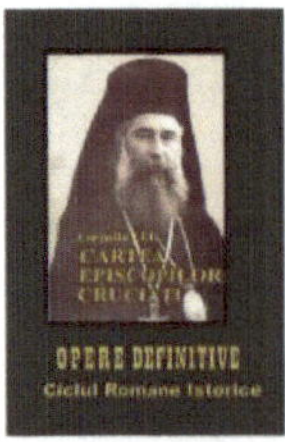

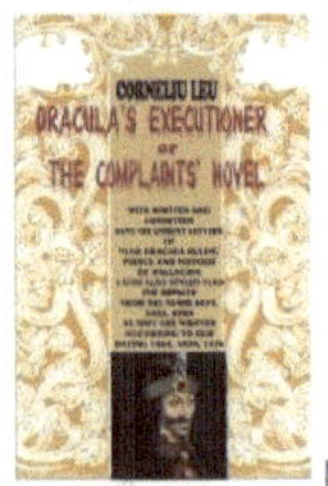

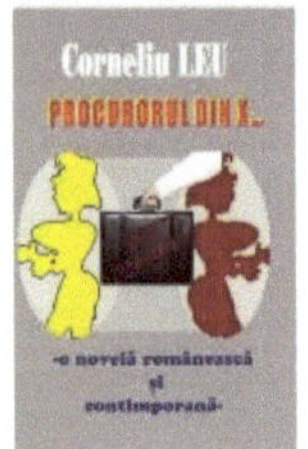

Covers of 24 of Corneliu Leu's books.